UNEQUAL PROFESSION

UNEQUAL PROFESSION

Race and Gender in Legal Academia

Meera E. Deo

Stanford University Press
Stanford, California

Stanford University Press

Stanford, California

Printed in the United States of America on acid-free, archival-quality paper

Library of Congress Cataloging-in-Publication Data

Names: Deo, Meera E., author.
Title: Unequal profession : race and gender in legal academia / Meera E. Deo.
Description: Stanford, California : Stanford University Press, 2019. |
    Includes bibliographical references and index.
Identifiers: LCCN 2018037167 (print) | LCCN 2018040490 (ebook) |
    ISBN 9781503607859 (e-book) | ISBN 9781503604308 (cloth : alk. paper) |
    ISBN 9781503607842 (pbk. : alk. paper)
Subjects: LCSH: Minority women law teachers—United States—Social conditions.
    | Discrimination in employment—United States. | Sex discrimination in
    employment—United States. | Sex discrimination against women—United States.
Classification: LCC KF272 (ebook) | LCC KF272 .D47 2018 (print) |
    DDC 340.071/173—dc23
LC record available at https://lccn.loc.gov/2018037167

Typeset by Newgen in 10/14 Minion Pro

Cover design by Rob Ehle

To the ninety-seven law professors who gave their trust
and shared their voices for the purpose
of improving legal education

Contents

Preface

M Y STORY IS EMBEDDED in the pages of this book. Perhaps yours is too. If you were (or are) ambivalent about entering law teaching, your concerns may be reflected here. If you have witnessed or endured racial discrimination, implicit bias, or gender privilege on your professional journey, you will find echoes of those struggles—as well as strategies to overcome them—in the following chapters.

A meandering path from public interest impact litigation and policy work through doctoral studies in sociology led me to legal academia. Although I was initially hesitant to return to legal education, given my previous experience as a woman of color law student, multiple mentors from graduate school pushed me to consider law teaching. They convinced me that it would be an altogether-different experience being in the front of the classroom.

Those mentors were right—and wrong. Though standing behind the podium affords faculty certain benefits as compared to students, the racial and gender inequity I remembered as a law student exists in parallel forms among the faculty. As such, I am not a neutral observer in this research. Qualitative interviews present the illusion of being conversations, although the interviewer drives the "conversation" and shares little of her own personal information. The research and interview questions for the project behind this book are steeped not only in the literature but also in my own experiences and those of my colleagues and friends in the academy.

When a first-year student submitted an anonymous letter to my dean complaining about my teaching early in my career, I was shocked, dismayed, ashamed, and told no one. A mentor might have assured me that complaints against young women of color faculty are so common as to be almost an initiation into law teaching. But I did not know. After formal positions at half a dozen institutions of higher education, I have encountered colleagues of all kinds. Many have become allies, confidants, friends, and mentors; others have asked puzzling or even insulting questions about race, ethnicity, gender, and other identity characteristics: Should faculty consider Middle Eastern job candidates to be white? (Of course not! Consider their racialized experience in America.) Should a professor apply for promotion while excused from teaching following childbirth? (Of course! Her tenure clock ticks on and the faculty handbook allows it.)

Throughout my journey in legal academia, I have collected anecdotes from fellow faculty about their professional experiences. Before starting the project behind this book on law faculty, I had been engaged for a decade in empirical research on legal education—with a focus on law students. As director of the Law School Survey of Student Engagement (LSSSE), I am now in a position to more fully contemplate the student experience. With the publication of this book, I have come to realize the parallel experiences of marginalized students and faculty. I also see that the slights, bias, and discrimination I have suffered pale in comparison to the indignities my research reveals occur daily for other underrepresented professors.

We all deserve better.

The following pages are filled with quotations from participants of my research. Their narratives might sound familiar to you. If you see your struggles in these pages, I hope you will see that you are not alone. And if you see your own privilege reflected in these pages, I hope you will recognize that you are a beneficiary of certain institutional structures that prefer some groups to others, and that you will carefully consider how you can assist in creating a more equal profession. Although I use pseudonyms to preserve anonymity among the research participants, you may guess at some of their true identities. More likely, though, you will remember that a similar or even identical event happened to someone you know who did not participate in my study. And the same thing has probably happened to a dozen others. These challenges, confrontations, and barriers are pervasive—they are not unique.

Law faculty encounter wonderful, horrible, strange, and confusing situations every day. Recognizing the power of preparation, I hope that being aware of the barriers will encourage aspiring law faculty to pursue their dreams fully aware and ready to meet common challenges. As a profession, we cannot blame these structural inequalities on a few bad actors or isolated events. Progress requires understanding across race, gender, and background. Individual strategies can help, but only a systematic analysis of diversity in legal academia can yield systematic change, with the entirety of those involved working to successfully correct these inequities.

The current crisis in legal education affords us an opportunity to rethink the entire structure and consider how we can do better. My impetus for the research behind the book was not only to shine a spotlight, in a rigorous and empirical way, on what for many in the legal profession can be an isolating experience but also to offer individual strategies and structural solutions for improvement. The primary and admittedly ambitious objective of this book is to improve legal education—for faculty of color, female faculty, women of color faculty, other marginalized faculty, even traditional faculty and students from all backgrounds. Without race- and gender-based classroom disruptions or challenges to their competency, all faculty will be free to focus on teaching, writing, and service, thereby improving the quality of each of these priorities. I hope this book helps faculty to see their struggles as surmountable and gives voice to the need for change so we can all benefit from a more equal profession.

Acknowledgments

THIS BOOK IS THE PRODUCT of steadfast support from numerous family members, friends, colleagues, students, and even strangers. My parents, Anuradha and Eknath Deo, encouraged my independent spirit, intellectual pursuits, and infinite curiosity from an early age. They were likely inspired, as I have always been, by the pioneering educational and professional achievements of their own mothers, Sulabha Moghe and Prabodhini Deo. I am fortunate to have acquired a second set of parents in adulthood; my in-laws, Sunila and Arvind Kulkarni, model a tenacious work ethic and profound commitment to family that I strive to emulate. My siblings, Meenaxi, Geetanjali, and Ravindra, were my earliest confidants and remain enthusiastic champions of my every endeavor. I draw frequently from lifelong friendships with Jennifer Westfall, Amita Shah, Ahilan Arulanantham, Chavella Pittman, and Priya Shah, while numerous baristas, librarians, flight attendants, and bartenders also contributed to the completion of this book. I thank these supporters along with extended family who inspire, motivate, and facilitate all of my accomplishments.

Many friends and colleagues in legal academia have been instrumental in guiding this project. Carmen Gonzalez, Angela Onwuachi-Willig, Catherine Albiston, Herma Hill Kay, Karla Erickson, and Linda Pololi provided critical input on the initial Diversity in Legal Academia study design, literature, and methodology. Exchanges with the following scholars also advanced the project: Bryant Garth, Elizabeth Mertz, Angela Harris, Camille Nelson, Kevin Johnson,

Lisa Ikemoto, Anupam Chander, Andrea Freeman, Gregory Parks, Carroll Seron, Michael Olivas, Sarah Deer, Jordan Woods, Bertrall Ross, Wendy Greene, Joan Williams, Mary Ann Mason, Paul Gowder, Mindie Lazarus-Black, Bill Hines, Rudy Hasl, Tom Guernsey, and Joan Bullock. Dozens of speaking engagements provided opportunities to think critically about the many topics included in this book; Gowri Ramachandran, Laura Gomez, Phoebe Haddon, Rachel Moran, Avi Soifer, Madhavi Sunder, Jennifer Chacon, Kimani Paul-Emile, Mario Barnes, Aaron Taylor, Anil Kalhan, Jonathan Glater, and Vinay Harpalani provided especially useful feedback during and after these presentations. My Thomas Jefferson School of Law colleagues have been universally supportive, as have my LSSSE partners Chad Christensen and Jakki Petzold. Outstanding research assistance was provided by former students Kale Sopoaga, Brittany Nobles, Jillian Kates, and Eva Kobi. The project also strengthened and improved through my time as a visiting scholar at Berkeley Law's Center for the Study of Law and Society (2013), visiting professor at UCLA School of Law (2014), visiting scholar at UC Irvine School of Law (2016–2017), and visiting professor at UC Davis School of Law (2018–2019).

Michelle Lipinski, editor extraordinaire at Stanford University Press, first solicited a book proposal on this topic in 2014; without her diligent persistence, valuable input, and prompt responses to my many emails, this book certainly would not have been published. Nora Spiegel from Stanford University Press stepped in as my fairy godmother—seemingly waving her wand to make obstacles disappear. Two anonymous reviewers also provided helpful suggestions.

Most of the ninety-seven law professors who participated in the Diversity in Legal Academia study were strangers when we first met. Over the course of a long interview, many shared intimate details of their personal lives, as well as professional challenges from the mundane to the horrific. Some cried, many laughed, and we parted as friends. I offer my endless thanks to these research participants, whose anonymous narratives are the heart of this book. You spoke out. I heard you. And I hope to honor you in these pages.

I also must share my deep appreciation for my children, Shreyas and Simrun, who put up with their Mama being away on many early mornings, some late nights, and frequently for days at a time for data collection, conference presentations, and visiting opportunities. In their own perfect ways, they have been devoted supporters lending perspective and even editing advice on this long journey. And finally, my deepest gratitude to Manoj Kulkarni, who always says yes, who pushes me to be my best, who leads by example, and makes everything better.

UNEQUAL PROFESSION

Introduction

Investigating raceXgender in Legal Academia

ALEXANDRA IS A SUPERSTAR. She earned undergraduate and law degrees from exclusive institutions, secured a prestigious federal judicial clerkship, and practiced law at an elite corporate firm. Even with these accomplishments, Alexandra had to overcome significant hurdles to become one of few Black female law professors. To start, she "honestly had not considered law teaching," thinking that career would "never be available to me"—since the majority of her own law professors had been white men. She applied for a teaching position only after a friend "who is a woman of color that was teaching" suggested it. Alexandra began as an adjunct, teaching a course or two while continuing her legal practice; other female professors encouraged her to apply for an academic fellowship. From there, she went on the teaching market and is now a tenure-track assistant professor. Alexandra's pathway—from elite education, prestigious practice, and adjunct teaching to a tenure-track position—is not unique among African American female law faculty or other women of color law professors. Her experience working as a legal academic is also representative. For one, students at her law school were "so excited" to finally have "involvement from a young woman of color professor"—since most of her colleagues are older, white, and male—that she was immediately inundated by requests "to be an advisor on several student notes," as well as "the faculty advisor for BLSA [the Black Law Student Association]," and the "coach [for] trial teams." While she contributes what she can, her sights are set on tenure, so "it's just been very difficult to give them that energy." Alexandra is the primary earner in her household, with a husband who works full-time but makes significantly less than she does and young children at home. Unsurprisingly, she says, "I never feel balanced by the day. [Instead,] I consistently feel like something had to give on that particular day," though she tries to take the long view to achieve balance over time.

Also searching for balance, an Asian American professor named Elaine "structured my [personal] life so that it was maximally conducive to a busy work life." When she started teaching two decades ago, Elaine chose to live close to campus, "so I could walk to work and get to work easily whenever I needed to." As the first pregnant faculty member at her institution, she did not feel she could take any time off; instead, "I had my baby one day, and I was back to work the next week." Like Alexandra, Elaine first taught as an adjunct while practicing corporate law, then went on the national market and secured a full-time tenure-track faculty position. While she "really tried hard to master the course material," teaching was an ordeal primarily because of disruptive students who questioned her authority; students challenged her in class, "particularly, it seemed young men, and it seemed young *white* men, [who would] throw out something to test my expertise." Her interactions with faculty colleagues have included similar "ups and downs," and while "there have always been people who I'm cordial with and friendly with, I don't have close friends on the faculty." This is in part because Elaine has been dismissed, overlooked, and silenced numerous times by her colleagues. She tried to contribute by "saying things at a faculty meeting, [but] no one paid attention to it; and then a man would say it and then everyone would pay attention to it." That same mansplaining and "hepeating" continue today.

A Latina law professor named Carla echoes Elaine and many other women of color in legal academia in asserting that "the most frustrating obstacle has been in the faculty groups where some faculty members are very comfortable dominating the conversation year, after year, after year." Some colleagues also take credit for the words of their female colleagues. As Carla notes, "I've counted over ten times on my faculty where I've said something and a male faculty has repeated it and another male colleague has said, 'Good idea!'" giving the man credit for Carla's original contribution. Over time, Carla has adapted to the norms and expectations of her institution, so different from the traditional Latino household in which she was raised. When Carla applied to college, she was "hoping to go east [but] my father did not allow me to do so," deeming it too far away from their home in the west. Instead, she attended an elite university in a neighboring state before pursuing law school. Within a decade of graduation, Carla had earned a PhD and landed an impressive fellowship. As a condition of the fellowship, she participated in the Association of American Law Schools (AALS) Faculty Appointment Register and accompanying recruiting conference in Washington, DC, the primary mechanism for securing a tenure-track position in legal academia. To Carla's "great surprise, I had many callbacks and I even had offers, at which point it becomes impossible to turn one down." That was over twenty years ago. At that time, her law school "didn't have written tenure standards and someone explained to me, 'You'll get tenure if people like you,' which was a terrifying concept" because it was so vague, completely outside of her control, and easily manipulated. She enjoyed teaching but dreaded reading student evaluations; in one particular set, "the numbers were fine but the comments were vicious and I felt like I had PTSD. I went home, I sat on the couch kind of comatose; my spouse said, 'This isn't like you.'" Nevertheless, she persisted. Today, Carla is a tenured professor of law. She has "been approached by a few institutions" to apply for deanships but is clear about her professional priorities, stating unequivocally, "I don't want to be a dean because I much prefer writing." Carla is superficially "friendly with everyone" on her faculty, although they keep their distance from one another: she has only "been invited into a colleague's home individually once in twenty-two years."

While each law professor's narrative is different, all are joined by the commonality of experiencing legal academia as outsiders, women of color in a landscape dominated by whites and men. Challenges associated with the intersection of race and gender are especially salient. From Alexandra's perspective:

> Everything—from teaching and the way that you go into the classroom, to the way that people filter things you say in faculty meetings, to the expectations put upon you, to your financial background—you can't disentangle it [from race and gender]. This is how you go through life and I think it comes largely into focus when you are in academia because privilege is so much in focus and different privileged vantage points are so much in focus. I can't identify anything that it doesn't touch and affect.

While women of color share commonalities with white women, men of color, and even white men, this book details the experiences of women of color in legal academia, revealing challenges and opportunities associated with race and gender that are unique to these underrepresented faculty. As Alexandra says, "My experience is completely different than it would be if I were not a person of color or not a woman."

Law Faculty Basics

Faculty of color and female faculty have been underrepresented in legal academia since law schools first opened their doors.[1] Women of color remain statistically underrepresented in legal academia today. AALS reports that women of color account for a mere 7.0% of the 10,965 law faculty members—including all levels of professors, deans, lecturers, and instructors.[2] Of the 771 women of color law faculty identified in AALS data, 408 are Black/African American, 138 are Hispanic/Latino, 112 are Asian or Pacific Islander, 58 are "more than one race," 34 identify as some "other race," and only 21 are American Indian or Alaskan Native. In contrast, a full 5,090 are white men (a whopping 46% of existing law faculty), 2,741 are white women (25%), and 860 are men of color (7.8%). Put differently, almost three-quarters (71%) of all law faculty are white. The American Bar Association (ABA), which publishes annual data on law faculty, reports similar figures.[3] ABA statistics for all full-time teaching faculty, deans, and associate or vice deans include 935 women of color law professors, out of 9,759 law faculty total (9.6%); this includes 511 African Americans, 186 Asian Americans, 191 Hispanics, and 29 American Indians, compared to 4,683 white men (close to half, at 48%), 3,093 white women (32%), and 918 men of color (9.4%).

In spite of these significant disparities and increasing interest in diversity generally, few scholars have investigated how race and gender affect the law faculty experience. Student diversity, even in law school, has been an area of interest for courts, the public, and academics, with a large volume of scholarship to match.[4] Faculty diversity has only recently become a hot topic, although many of the same laws apply, and many of the legal and social issues overlap with student challenges. Three particular studies of faculty help construct a foundation for this book. In 1989, legal scholars Derrick Bell and Richard Delgado published findings from an informal study of law faculty. Noting that faculty faced "discrimination in hiring and promotion, alienation among their colleagues, hostility from students, and a lack of support,"[5] they predicted little improvement in the near future.

Two recent works confirm ongoing challenges facing underrepresented faculty now thirty years later. *Presumed Incompetent* is a 2012 anthology exploring the experiences of female faculty of color across disciplines, including law.[6] Reflections on the law faculty experience by women of color note challenges in navigating a hostile campus climate and suggest mechanisms for coping with ongoing institutional bias.[7] In response, individuals and institutions have become eager to learn strategies and solutions for combatting these challenges, though there has been little empirical guidance for how to do so.[8] Also in 2012, Katherine Barnes and Elizabeth Mertz published an article examining tenure satisfaction among law faculty, revealing that a higher percentage of female professors of color (35%) than white males (12%) see the tenure process as unfair.[9] A negative campus climate, challenging law school culture, and implicit bias contribute to the overall "negative themes" characterizing the experience for many people of color in legal academia.[10]

This is a critical time to invest in faculty diversity as legal education as a whole is in flux. Declining student applications and rising law school costs threaten to deplete faculty diversity even further, as schools become more conservative in their hiring.[11] With declining enrollment, fewer opportunities exist in legal academia altogether, and current law professors may be even more likely to hire only those who meet traditional—albeit unproven—criteria for success.[12]

Given the current "unprecedented crisis in legal education and the legal profession," it is even more imperative that institutions understand the value of diversity.[13] This is the time to focus more, not less, attention on faculty diversity. Law schools are changing to adapt to coming times, becoming more student centered, focused on skills-based learning, and creating incentives for both student recruitment and retention.[14] The ABA recently asserted both that "the basic purpose of law schools is to train lawyers," and that "law schools are in the business of delivering legal education services."[15] These characterizations of legal education highlight the business of law school, where students are akin to consumers gaining the product of legal education and training. The revised Standard 301 of the ABA requires that law schools "establish and publish learning outcomes" related to the curriculum to demonstrate their graduates' capacity for "effective, ethical, and responsible participation as members of the legal profession."[16] Small wonder that accreditors, law firms, and students themselves expect a "more cost-effective legal education that [will] produce better-trained and accomplished lawyers."[17]

Recent empirical scholarship suggests that diverse faculty can contribute to the success of legal education, in part by improving these outcome measures. Traditionally underrepresented law faculty are more likely than white male professors to include relevant context in classroom discussions of substantive law.[18] Students from all backgrounds appreciate these opportunities to engage in *diversity discussions*, which enliven otherwise abstract legal material.[19] Recently, the Law School Survey of Student Engagement (LSSSE) conducted "a large-scale, multi-year study of the effects of diversity in legal education," concluding:

> When students perceive that their law school encourages diversity and fosters diverse interactions, students report having both a better understanding of people from other racial and ethnic backgrounds and better training in solving complex problems.[20]

Prospective students may be especially drawn to law schools with diverse faculty, knowing that the likelihood of their own retention and success improve when they are engaged in learning, mastering practical material, and connected with their institution—all indicators that increase with faculty diversity.[21] Furthermore, diversity promotes "gains in critical thinking skills, greater levels of satisfaction with the educational experience, positive perceptions of the campus environment, and enhanced leadership skills."[22] Because students "both learn how to think and acquire professional training by forging *personal* psychological connections with individual faculty," hiring and retaining diverse faculty who personally engage with students is critical to the success of legal education.[23]

Despite deep investment in students, women are more likely to be presumed incompetent in the classroom, enduring challenges to their authority and direct confrontations; these disruptions create a taxing classroom climate that may detract from the learning process for everyone. Understanding common challenges and sharing best practices in ameliorating confrontations can help improve both teaching and learning in law school, at the individual and institutional levels. Women of color faculty are similarly thwarted by colleagues, from the hiring stage through tenure, and even when pursuing leadership opportunities. Extra service burdens at work and expectations of household management further stymie their progress.

Though abysmal, the numerical lack of diversity in legal academia tells only part of the story; to grasp the full context, and improve it, institutions must also evaluate the qualitative faculty experience and make a committed effort to support all faculty on their path to tenure, administrative leadership, and other professional success. Law schools are successful only "through individual teachers. Law school faculty are not fungible."[24] The unique strengths that individual faculty bring to their school thus contribute to the school and the success of its students. Law professors who are not criticized by colleagues or confronted by students can place their full attention on scholarship, service, and teaching. Additionally, students can concentrate on learning and better engage in class when their classmates stop disrupting and challenging particular professors.

The Effects of Intersectionality, Gender Privilege, and Implicit Bias

The once-disparate areas of critical race theory (CRT) and empirical methods merge to provide a framework for this book. CRT originated with a narrative style, drawing on novel parables to reveal the experiences of the vulnerable and giving voice to the downtrodden.[25] Qualitative empirical research similarly centers those from marginalized communities by analyzing their experience using their own words in the form of quotes drawn from the data.

Within CRT, this book draws from an *intersectionality* framework that acknowledges the challenges facing particular individuals whose background combines multiple devalued identity characteristics. The experiences of women are not universal, as they are also "shaped by other dimensions of their identities, such as race and class," which intersect and meld together to affect outcomes.[26] Those with an "intersection of recognized sites of oppression" have experiences that differ from not only the norm but even from the norms attributed to particular minority groups.[27] The experiences of women of color differ from individuals who are racial minorities (e.g., Black) but in the majority with regard to gender (e.g., men), or vice versa (e.g., white women). In the traditionally white male establishment of legal academia, one would expect that people of color have unique experiences as compared to whites, that women have different experiences from men, and that women of color—doubly marginalized by race and gender—have different experiences still.[28] This book draws out intersectional distinctions while also making meaningful comparisons between intersectional groups.[29]

Women of color may suffer oppression based on what is referred to in this book as *raceXgender*. This term highlights the compound effects often caused by holding multiple devalued identity characteristics, namely the intersection of race and gender. Rather than thinking of a woman of color as Black "plus" female, or female "plus" Black, utilizing the raceXgender nomenclature emphasizes the multifactorial effects of race "times" gender for women of color.

Structural racism, and the related concept of *institutional discrimination*,[30] refer to a "complex, dynamic system of conferring social benefits on some groups and imposing burdens on others" based on race.[31] Sexism, homophobia, and other social ills also fit within this broad framework, where we assume that those in the dominant group (e.g., males) structure aspects of society within their control to further the interests of their own group at the expense of those with less power (e.g., women).[32] Intersectionality is a natural lens through which to consider discrimination in legal academia, where opportunities to exercise complex bias abound; we can think of those who exercise their power over doubly marginalized individuals as operationalizing *intersectional discrimination*.[33]

Racism and other *isms* refer to internally held biases about individuals from particular groups that are based on that identity characteristic, whereas *discrimination* refers to the exercise of power over others based on the relevant "ism."[34] Thus, "racial discrimination refers to unequal treatment of persons or groups on the basis of their race or ethnicity."[35] When a person holding racist views exercises power over a person of color to deny her a job or refuse to sell her a car, this is racial discrimination. *Microaggressions* and other subtle forms of bias may be just as harmful as overt discrimination. These "subtle verbal and non-verbal insults" that are "based on one's race, gender, class, sexuality, language, immigration status, phenotype, accent, or surname," specifically anticipate intersectional discrimination.[36] *Intersectional discrimination* refers to the ways in which institutional policies and practices, as well as institutional leaders and even coworkers (e.g., colleagues) and consumers (e.g., students), exercise not only white privilege to discriminate against people of color, or male privilege to discriminate against women, but also a combination of their multiprivileged status to discriminate against women of color.[37]

A lens of *privilege* is thus critical to understanding the mechanics of legal academia.[38] Stephanie Wildman defines privilege as a "systemic conferral of benefit and advantage [based on] affiliation, conscious or not and chosen or not, to the dominant side of a power system."[39] Because privilege is often perceived as a "normal" part of everyday life, its benefits may be largely invisible to those who reap its benefits, nevertheless structuring the lives of those without privilege.[40] As elite institutions and escalators to power, law schools reflect and even amplify broader structural inequality in society as a whole, including inequality based on privilege.

Implicit bias shapes the experiences of legal academics as well, especially as thoughts and behaviors that "affect social judgments but operate without conscious awareness or conscious control."[41] Implicit bias is especially dangerous because it infects even those who believe themselves to be egalitarian.[42] Because it is not based on deliberate thought but operates "wholly outside of conscious, rational awareness,"[43] implicit bias "leak[s] into everyday behaviors such as whom we befriend, whose work we value, and whom we favor—notwithstanding our obliviousness to any such influence."[44] Implicit bias exists in our everyday lives, our workplaces, our justice system, and other institutions—including legal academia.[45] When faculty members connect with those "like them" and prefer those candidates in the hiring process to those who may seem "different," that is implicit bias at work. It also colors outcomes and experiences for promotion, tenure, leadership, and even everyday interactions among faculty.

Empirical Methods: The Diversity in Legal Academia Project

Although many challenges facing women of color faculty are well known personally and anecdotally, they have never been fully investigated as the focus of a formal empirical national study. The Diversity in Legal Academia (DLA) project is the first systematic multimethod analysis of the law faculty experience to utilize an intersectional lens in investigating the personal and professional lives of law faculty from assistant professor through dean emeritus. The core sample of the study includes 63 women of color law professors, with data collected from 30 white men, white women, and men of color providing for comparison and contrast (Table 1). All research subjects completed an online survey before discussing questions in an in-depth interview. Together, these methods covered the personal and professional experiences of diverse faculty in legal academia. The Appendix provides additional details on the methodological approach for the DLA study.

TABLE 1 DLA Participants, by Race and Gender, DLA 2013

	n	*%*
African American women	21	22.6
Asian American women	15	16.1
Latinas	13	14.0
Native American women	5	5.4
Middle Eastern women	2	2.2
Multiracial women	7	7.5
Men of color	11	11.8
White women	11	11.8
White men	8	8.6
Total	93	100.0

Looking Ahead

This book is divided into six chapters, each one highlighting a particular pressure point for law faculty. In each chapter, the relevant topic is framed with quantitative data from the DLA survey, providing a broad overview of the relevant raceXgender effects. The qualitative data—actual quotes from DLA participants—are the heart of each chapter, delving into how and why race and gender intersect in the experiences of law faculty. Each chapter ends with comparison and contrasts with the white men, white women, and men of color whose own intersectionality influences their experiences.

The chapters progress chronologically through the career of a law professor, beginning in Chapter 1 with barriers to entering legal academia, based largely on a formalistic hiring process and the requirement of elite but unreliable credentials. Subsequent chapters explore interactions between women of color law faculty and their colleagues (Chapter 2) and students (Chapter 3), revealing how a presumption of incompetence yields silencing, mansplaining, and hepeating in faculty meetings and biased confrontations in the classroom and on evaluations. Chapter 4 discusses intersectional (raceXgender) obstacles to promotion and tenure involving scholarship, service, and teaching—resulting in resignation from some but inspiring many others to fight. The current crisis in legal education provides increasing opportunities for leadership, which are examined in Chapter 5; yet the few female faculty of color who believe they could succeed in these roles find their authority undermined while the roles themselves shift from powerful to clerical. In Chapter 6, the book tackles work/life balance, including challenges navigating raceXgender-based personal responsibilities along with added professional obligations. The Conclusion offers broad implications of this research, drawing first from sources of support to bolster underrepresented faculty in trying times; it also proposes individual strategies for faculty as well as structural solutions that policy makers and institutional leaders should adopt to create and sustain meaningful diversity in legal academia and improve legal education overall.

1   Barriers to Entry

A DECADE AGO, WHEN JENNIFER was practicing law and "didn't have an interest in teaching," an acquaintance who was a woman of color law professor invited her to present at an academic conference. Before that, Jennifer says, "it had never occurred to me that I could do such a thing." As a Native American woman, she had neither role models nor mentors with a shared background whose path she could follow—not surprising, given that there are only twenty-one Native American female law professors in the United States. Even after Jennifer published a law review article based on her remarks, she still "certainly didn't plan on teaching." Friends "who were teaching were saying things like, 'Oh, you should go into academia,'" but Jennifer "just didn't think I would be good at it; but I did continue to write periodically." When a visiting position became available at a local law school, she applied, "just to sort of try it on and see how it would fit." She loved it from day one, deciding soon thereafter to pursue a tenure-track position. She did not join the formal Association of American Law Schools (AALS) job process to consider teaching options nationally, mainly because at the institution where she was visiting "I actually had two tenured professors come in and say, 'We will be hiring you and we don't want you to go on the market because somebody else will get you and *we* want you, so don't go.'" Looking back, she realizes that "wasn't necessarily the most strategic choice," but "at that time, I . . . was just so grateful to be where I was and I didn't think very critically about it." Now, Jennifer recognizes, "I wasn't getting a lot of other kinds of advice," with few mentors to guide her through the hiring process. Plus, she and her husband were already settled in their town, where he had a stable job that he enjoyed. So, "we thought it would be awesome if I was to stay here because we [mainly] thought how convenient would that be." Her decision to enter legal academia was not "this big strategic [thing]," where Jennifer realized she could get a "big job and start this really amazing career as an academic." Instead, she says, "It was just luck and comfort more than anything." Reflecting on her entry into legal academia, she realizes, "I just accidentally fell into it."

Jennifer's pathway to legal academia is characteristic of the journey of many women of color who join the law faculty ranks. This chapter explores the first step toward legal academia, which is also where women of color encounter the first intersectional raceXgender barriers in law teaching: securing a tenure-track position. DLA data reveal multiple obstacles in the path of women of color who pursue the unequal profession of legal academia. The chapter begins with a brief introduction to the formal process organized by AALS and the elite credentials that most law schools require of candidates vying for a tenure-track position. Quantitative DLA data on credentials frame the detailed qualitative findings—actual quotes from law faculty participants in the DLA study—detailing how an interest in law teaching, access to mentors, various forms of bias, and gender privilege influence hiring from start to finish. The chapter concludes with data from men of color, white women, and white men offering comparative and contrasting experiences to further understand the position of women of color faculty.

The Problematic AALS Hiring Process

Recent scholarship indicates that racial and gender disparities in legal academia cannot be blamed solely on a lack of qualified potential candidates, as the pool of possible law professors contains higher percentages of both women and people of color than are in law teaching today.[1] A reliance on credentials may account for part of the disparity, especially as it is almost a prerequisite that potential hires graduate from elite law schools, work as judicial clerks, and collect other accolades before applying for a tenure-track position.[2] A survey of hiring completed at the top eighteen schools found both that more new hires hold JDs from Yale, Harvard, or Stanford than all other law schools combined and that a full one-third of new law faculty hires hold doctoral degrees in addition to the JD.[3] One posting, "What Makes a Good Teaching Job

Candidate?," lists the "the most important factors" as "getting excellent grades at a distinguished law school, being a law review member or (preferably) officer, and having a prestigious clerkship after graduation"; it does not mention scholarly execution, teaching effectiveness, or commitment to service—the actual criteria most law schools use to determine tenure, the primary marker of academic achievement.[4] None of the listed requirements or preferences has been correlated to success in academia.[5]

Table 2 shows that many women of color faculty work their way up from less prestigious adjunct or lecturing positions to tenure-track employment while others secure prestigious fellowships and scarce visiting assistant professor (VAP) positions to signal their future academic success to potential employers. These other markers of success indicate that hiring nontraditional women of color faculty is not risky, but rather a safe bet on their future success.

Imani, a Black law professor, blames a lack of diversity on the fact that "in recent years the criteria for becoming a law professor just keeps getting [higher]." Brianna, a Black professor and administrator, combines escalating credentials with a current climate "where everybody is concerned about [declining] law school applications, and everybody is concerned about skills-based education, [and I worry that] what's going to be cut from budgets are [faculty] diversity initiatives." Nowadays, she notes, the expectation is that candidates not only have "the Harvard or Yale or Stanford [box] checked" but also "the law review check, they have the judicial clerkship box checked, and they have the VAP and the fellowship checked." While increasingly impressive credentials may seem race and gender neutral, Imani notes:

> A lot of women and a lot of people of color cannot afford to spend a year [in the relatively low-paying position of] a judicial clerk, then spending a year or two years being a VAP where they have time and space to write and produce articles [but are paid little], then go out on a full market knowing they're going to have to move again for their full-time [permanent] position. A lot of [women of color] do not have the financial capability or the support system to allow for them to do that.

Intersectionality is therefore at play even at the prehiring stage, with women of color less likely to accumulate the expected accolades for purely non-merit-based reasons, because they lack both class privilege and gender privilege. Nevertheless, Imani knows that hiring committees compare "Candidate A,

TABLE 2 Employment Before Tenure-Track Position, by Race and Gender, DLA 2013

		Visiting assistant professor	Adjunct	Lecturer	Fellow	Legal writing instructor	Other legal academic	Other nonlegal academic	Nonacademic
African American women	n	0	5	2	5	1	1	3	7
	%	0.0	20.8	8.3	20.8	4.2	4.2	12.5	29.2
Asian American women	n	1	2	0	4	1	0	0	2
	%	10.0	20.0	0.0	40.0	10.0	0.0	0.0	20.0
Latinas	n	1	1	1	5	1	0	1	3
	%	7.7	7.7	7.7	38.5	7.7	0.0	7.7	23.1
Native American women	n	2	0	1	1	0	0	2	0
	%	33.3	0.0	16.7	16.7	0.0	0.0	33.3	0.0
Middle Eastern women	n	0	1	1	0	0	0	0	1
	%	0.0	33.3	33.3	0.0	0.0	0.0	0.0	33.3
Multiracial women	n	1	1	1	1	0	0	1	2
	%	14.3	14.3	14.3	14.3	0.0	0.0	14.3	28.6
Men of color	n	0	2	0	3	0	0	1	4
	%	0.0	20.0	0.0	30.0	0.0	0.0	10.0	40.0
White women	n	4	1	0	2	1	2	1	1
	%	33.3	8.3	0.0	16.7	8.3	16.7	8.3	8.3
White men	n	0	2	0	3	1	2	0	0
	%	0.0	25.0	0.0	37.5	12.5	25.0	0.0	0.0
Total	n	9	15	6	24	5	5	9	20
	%	9.7	16.1	6.5	25.8	5.4	5.4	9.7	21.5

Note: Multiple responses permitted

who does have the resources because they have a stay-at-home wife that can take care of the kids while you go out and do a VAP and clerkship" that allows Candidate A to publish "two or three articles," against "Candidate B, who's been working full-time, still has the passion and drive, and will be a great professor, but yet did not have those structures to help them produce and turn out these articles." She sees how this structure results in "a true detriment and true hindrance for female faculty as well as faculty of color getting these positions," since Candidate A is frequently a white male, whereas Candidate B is often a woman of color. In addition to the structure being unfair to candidates of color, Imani emphasizes that law schools also "lose out on a lot of great prospective professors because we have increased the criteria so much that we want all these boxes checked." Perpetuating inequality harms law schools, too.

The formalistic and inflexible hiring process itself contributes to an unequal profession. The traditional route to tenure-track law teaching is through the AALS Faculty Appointments Register (FAR) and accompanying conference in Washington, DC.[6] Successfully navigating this intricate pathway requires fortitude, stamina, money, and mentorship.

First, aspiring law faculty should begin preparing "more than a year before the start dates,"[7] completing a FAR form that includes basic demographic information, teaching and scholarly interests, geographic limitations, and a list of references.[8] Although the form appears self-explanatory, there is an art to strategically responding—one that is hard to master without the guidance of a mentor. For instance, under "teaching interests," applicants should "identify one basic first-year course . . . in addition to a more specialized area of interest," rather than simply listing those courses that the applicant would most enjoy teaching.[9] As gender norms and personal responsibilities often limit geographic options for women of color law faculty, this also creates an early intersectional raceXgender disadvantage. Mentors stress the importance of submitting FAR materials "as early as possible,"[10] as "many schools . . . don't look at candidates whose material comes in later."[11] There is also an art to the initial interviews in Washington, DC, including the need for the applicants to "do some homework about the schools [and] the professors" they will meet, so they are sufficiently "prepared to ask questions."[12] Ideally, candidates ask the right questions and stay away from those that are taboo, though differentiating between the two can be tricky without mentor assistance.[13]

Candidates will have paid hundreds of dollars to participate in the FAR distribution before they pay their own way to DC, including all costs for transportation, lodging, and meals.[14] Those who need a new suit to successfully portray the role of aspiring law professor will incur additional expenses, as will women of color who need to invest in makeup, jewelry, and hair products deemed appropriately professional. Most also take time away from work to attend, which can lead to other financial and emotional costs ranging from childcare expenses to additional pressures when back in the office.

If the DC interview goes well, the applicant will be invited to a full day of meetings with each institution's faculty, dean, and students on campus, where applicants give a *job talk*, a formal academic presentation. Mentors might advise candidates to "practice and time your job talk, [ideally] in front of an audience that can ask probing questions."[15] While some elite schools arrange mock job talks for favored alumni on the market, many candidates of color have no available audience.[16] Though mentorship is key to landing a tenure-track position, women of color candidates rarely have engaged mentors throughout the faculty hiring process. Which material to present as part of the job talk (safe but boring, or controversial?), what to wear to dinner (suit? slacks? dress?), how to act when colleagues openly bicker (engage or ignore it?)—many applicants ponder these questions, but women of color have few mentors to provide answers.

Faculty hiring is stressful not only for the individuals seeking employment but also for existing faculty of color and female faculty. When DLA participants were asked about the statement "I would prefer that there were more faculty diversity at my school," 100% of Black, Native American, multiracial, and white women signaled that they agreed, along with a majority of every other racial and gender group (see Table 3). Even supporters may express a preference for outcomes they believe to be socially desirable (i.e., diversity) without commensurate support for the means of achieving those outcomes (i.e., affirmative action).[17] Implicit bias also prevents even those who tout their own support for diversity from acting on those beliefs by hiring diverse candidates, as most people tend to implicitly prefer people like themselves.[18] The qualitative data bear out these hypotheses.

A multiracial professor named Grace is a recent lateral hire at her institution. She currently has a pleasant relationship with her full faculty likely because they have not yet engaged in the heated diversity debates that characterize

TABLE 3 Preference for More Faculty Diversity, by Race and Gender, DLA 2013

		Strongly agree	Agree	Neither agree nor disagree	Disagree	Strongly disagree	Total
African American women	n	10	11	0	0	0	21
	%	47.62	52.38	0.00	0.00	0.00	100.00
Asian American women	n	5	7	0	3	0	15
	%	33.33	46.67	0.00	20.00	0.00	100.00
Latinas	n	7	3	0	2	0	12
	%	58.33	25.00	0.00	16.67	0.00	100.00
Native American women	n	3	2	0	0	0	5
	%	60.00	40.00	0.00	0.00	0.00	100.00
Middle Eastern women	n	2	0	0	0	0	2
	%	100.00	0.00	0.00	0.00	0.00	100.00
Multiracial women	n	3	4	0	0	0	7
	%	42.86	57.14	0.00	0.00	0.00	100.00
Men of color	n	5	2	4	0	0	11
	%	45.45	18.18	36.36	0.00	0.00	100.00
White women	n	8	3	0	0	0	11
	%	72.73	27.27	0.00	0.00	0.00	100.00
White men	n	4	3	1	0	0	8
	%	50.00	37.50	12.50	0.00	0.00	100.00
Total	n	47	35	5	5	0	92
	%	51.09	38.04	5.43	5.43	0.00	100.00

faculty hiring, usually with faculty of color pitted on one side and white faculty on the other. Grace says: "I have no issues that I personally have with anyone. To be frank it's probably because we haven't gone through a recruiting season yet. I find that going through a recruiting season can often change your views of some of your colleagues." The hiring process is often characterized by an emphasis on elite educational and professional credentials that have never been shown to relate to success in legal academia, as well as overt and subtle discrimination in the hiring process itself. In contrast, as discussed at the end of this chapter, white men enjoy the support of mentors who propel them into legal academia, with gender privilege providing an extra boost.

The Road Not Taken

Law faculty hiring begins with the tendency to focus on elite credentials, none of which have been shown to correlate with future success in the profession.

More than 40% of current law professors attended either Harvard or Yale Law School and the vast majority (over 85%) of current law professors attended one of twelve elite law schools, regardless of where they themselves currently teach.[19] Recent AALS statistics show that 62% of law professors are men and at least 71% are white; though faculty diversity is low now, it was even lower in past decades.[20] Thus, most current law professors were educated predominantly by white men.[21]

Women of color law students have so few faculty role models who share their race and gender background that few consider law teaching as a viable option. Even women of color who are currently legal academics rarely saw themselves in the role until they entered the academy themselves.[22] Karen, a Black professor, states, "I am not one of those people who planned at all to go into teaching." Although "I knew that I wanted to be a lawyer from a very young age, probably since I was about 10 years old," Karen saw herself as a public interest lawyer and worked as a civil rights attorney before adjunct teaching. Similarly, a multiracial professor named Jane accrued many of the resume standards that are virtual prerequisites to law teaching—such as law review service and a clerkship; still, "it never occurred to me to be a law professor. I thought, 'Oh, well, I have my private practice lined up.'"

Even women of color with exposure to academia through family or friends are unlikely to choose law teaching. Hannah, a multiracial law professor, "grew up in an academic environment, but I had always imagined that I would never follow in [my parent's] footsteps. And I did just about everything I could to not follow in [those] footsteps because I wanted to be a litigator." Laila, a Middle Eastern law professor, had a similar trajectory—including early exposure to an academic lifestyle through a parent; yet she says, "I didn't go to law school knowing I would be a law professor. I actually went to law school because I wanted to be a civil rights advocate." The vast majority of faculty of color participants from the DLA study stepped into legal academia at least somewhat by happenstance. Cindy, an Asian American professor, echoes many others who marvel about their pathway to legal academia, stating, "It was a real freaky kind of divine intervention. I just really lucked out." Or, as a Native American woman named Erin states, "I think that I've been very fortunate in that I have kind of stumbled my way into this great position."

Many women of color were not on a clear path to the profession from law school or earlier but moved from practicing adjuncts to visitors or fellows to tenure-track faculty. Some female faculty of color who begin as adjuncts never make the switch to more permanent positions. Melanie, a Latina professor, "would like to see more faculty diversity" but also has "qualms about the fact that it seems like the easiest route to diversity often seems to be through the least secure positions within the institution." Given recent threats of faculty layoffs and little tenure-track hiring, Melanie's concerns that faculty diversity will be relegated to the least secure positions are especially timely. A Black professor named Danielle believes she became a law professor simply "by luck." She had been practicing, then had a baby, and moved to a new town; when she "got a job teaching" at a local university, but not in their law school, she caught "the teaching bug." After that, "I started learning how one becomes a law professor," eventually participating in what she calls "the 'cattle call'" (i.e., the AALS faculty recruitment conference) to secure a tenure-track position.[23] Because most students of color see few professors who look like them, becoming a professor rarely seems like an attainable goal. As an Asian American professor named Leanne notes of her law school days, "I had no idea that teaching was even an option. I guess I knew it was a career, but it was never something I would even consider doing." When law students consider who has the privilege of becoming a law professor, most think of their own professors, most of whom were and are white men.[24]

Because law teaching seems beyond their *habitus*—an unfamiliar position that seems somewhat out of reach or beyond their own sense of what is normal, attainable, or seemingly acceptable for people like them—mentors must help women of color overcome this impediment.[25] Sonia, a Latina law professor and administrator, credits a high school mentor with early encouragement. Her mentor "took my parents aside" to highlight her abilities and convince them to let her leave home to attend an elite college in a neighboring state. Until then, "my goal had been to go to college, but not necessarily to an elite college." As she sees it, "that changed everything. I might not be [a law school leader] today if that didn't happen." Karen, who started as a public interest attorney and is now a tenured law professor, believes that mentors "have just been really critical" to her career. When she first was hired in a non-tenure-track position to teach legal research and writing, her supervisor was "a fantastic African American woman" who was "just really great to be around" and managed to be "an incredible role model" who balances mentoring and activism while she "also does a really amazing job of being a scholar." Karen had seriously contemplated "whether going back into nonprofit work or continuing on the teaching path . . . was the direction I wanted to go in." Yet "being around [this mentor] really made me feel like I could be a law professor." Karen "went on the tenure-track teaching market, got a couple of jobs, and picked the one [that] was the closest to where [my partner and I] were already."

Some female law faculty applied for positions in legal academia only after being encouraged to do so multiple times. A Latina named Armida repeatedly refused to apply for a research fellowship that she had been invited to pursue, though these jobs are traditional entrees into legal academia. Armida says, "The first time around I said no; still, I knew I wanted to do it, but the practical side to me where I was at a major law firm, where I achieved this and the income that comes with it [made it hard to switch]." The financial disincentives of giving up a lucrative law firm practice for law teaching are especially pronounced for the many women of color who come from lower socioeconomic backgrounds and have greater financial obligations to extended family.[26] Initially, Armida "told the person no, and he was really upset. [But] maybe a year later, he contacted me again" and convinced her to apply. Armida has been a law professor ever since.[27]

Mentors provide advice and guidance, not only at the outset but also along the entire path to securing a job. Though she had no formal mentorship from external sources, Jennifer "had a lot of encouragement" throughout the faculty hiring process and felt relieved that she could "check in with folks, just about dumb questions, like, 'What's a job talk?' [laughing]." Although she felt "really out of my league," she is grateful that "fortunately, I had people I could go to and ask those questions."[28]

Without the level of mentorship that Armida and Karen received, many potential law professors never consider the role, or unwittingly squander opportunities. Hannah, who is now the recipient of numerous teaching awards, had no one to guide her early on. She notes: "I really wasn't looking for an academic position when I was in law school. [I had no mentors] while I was in law school and for most of practice." Elaine initially received a tenure-track offer at a top-twenty law school close to the private law firm where she had just begun her first legal job; she turned down the academic position "because I was committed to practicing at least for one year," accepting instead an adjunct position at the same school. Quickly, she realized, "'Oh, I really kind of like this,' and so I went back to them [to inquire about the tenure-track job] and they said, 'I'm sorry.' They [had] filled the position." She went on the formal AALS teaching market and ultimately joined a less prestigious institution in another state where she still teaches today. She acknowledges that "thinking [back to my first offer], I didn't understand what I was giving up." A senior Black scholar named June graduated from an elite law school in the early 1980s, then practiced corporate law at a prestigious big-city firm before starting a tenure-track position. Her path follows a traditional trajectory, so "looks very clear cut, but of course there is a bigger story behind it." June was "not at all . . . mentored by anybody to become a professor. No one I knew of color was mentored in that way, but I had in the back of my mind [the idea that] perhaps at some point I would become a professor." A white male professor she had met at a networking event invited her to give a talk at his law school. Although she "had ignored his letter for many months," she finally agreed to go because her husband was considering working in the same city; once there, she realized she would love to stay to teach. The school had just concluded a failed search when "here I am walking in the door in February, where I had the right credentials from the right kind of school. I had published a law review article." After a return visit for a full-day interview, she was hired. "Nobody mentored me into that process, [but by sheer luck,] it turned out very well."[29]

Overt Discrimination and Implicit Bias

In addition to the initial hesitancy of some women of color to consider law teaching, and a lack of mentorship to guide them, some face structural constraints based on outright discrimination as well as intersectional bias and gender-based expectations. Recent scholarship suggests that women and people of color are frequently overlooked for employment positions, even when they become finalists. If only one woman is included in the finalist pool, the statistical probability of her landing the job is zero.[30]

The most blatant acts of discrimination evident in the DLA data are against Muslim and Arab American faculty candidates. A professor of color recounts how her white male colleague blocked the candidacy of a Muslim candidate dressed in hijab who performed well at her initial interview and was invited to campus for a full-day visit. Afterward, at a faculty meeting discussing the candidate's qualifications, a white male faculty member publicly voiced his objection to hiring her, without complaining about her credentials, teaching, or scholarship. As recounted by a colleague, this white male faculty member objected simply because, "'I just wouldn't feel comfortable having her in the office next to me.'" This is a clear example of implicit bias, where faculty prefer people like them to those whom they see as different. Another DLA participant reflecting on recent potential hires admitted that particular candidates might have cause to sue for employment discrimination if they knew the full story behind their rejections: "We've had visiting faculty who are Arab or Muslim who've been run out of town on a rail. I think it's offensive and actionable."

Existing faculty face their own challenges during the hiring process.[31] Zahra, a Middle Eastern law professor, recalls a colleague who was on the school's Appointments Committee but was rude to candidates, "made them feel uncomfortable," and "wasn't making the school look good." She and a group of other junior scholars suggested the administration replace him, but "nothing happened." This simply added to the "sense, broadly, from the junior faculty that we are hitting our heads against a brick wall and it's not changing and it won't change, so that was frustrating." The fact that colleagues ignored their concerns was especially trying.

Even after they secure a tenure-track position, nontraditional faculty face challenges associated with their hiring. Some faculty attribute the hiring of faculty of color to affirmative action, presuming these candidates are unqualified but hired solely to satisfy diversity goals.[32] Being viewed as an "affirmative action hire" can negatively influence the landscape for faculty of color whose colleagues see them as less deserving of their positions, adding pressure on them to overperform.[33] Sonia's colleagues were seemingly uninterested in diversity before she started in a tenure-track position many years ago, as she was "the first entry-level person of color they ever hired." She believes that in those situations, "people tend to you think you were a political—not an academic—appointment." On her campus, as on many others more recently, "there had been a lot of pressure from the students to diversify the faculty," perhaps resulting in the faculty being more aware of diverse candidates, and perhaps creating the impression that Sonia was hired at least in part to placate them. Unfortunately, "you have to overcome some presumptions when you're the first one," when colleagues believe that "'maybe she's not on par with everybody else because she was brought in to diversify, not to [intellectually] enrich the school.'" While the presumption of incompetence by students against women of color faculty has been studied in increasing detail, some faculty are also guilty of making incorrect assumptions about candidates or colleagues. Sonia also faced internal pressure to succeed; she knew that "if I failed, that would have been a setback in terms of hiring [other diverse candidates, because the faculty] would not have done it as quickly and as broadly." Because of her accomplishments, her colleagues "realized that maybe . . . we should seize more opportunities" to hire diverse qualified candidates. Her success "was really valuable. It was personally difficult, but it was good at the end of the day that I had the fortitude to go on" since many other diverse hires followed.

When Cindy was hired, she recognized deep-seated institutional issues at her school, especially "a lot of stuff based on race and gender." A white male was hired when she was "and there was a major difference in how he was treated and how I was treated." Though their professional obligations were the same, Cindy "was treated like the 'dumb one,' sort of an affirmative action hire in the worst sense of the word [meaning that I was unqualified, but hired because of my race and gender,] and he was the 'real one.'" Because Cindy witnessed "a lot of favoritism towards him from particular faculty members," she internalized her colleagues' intersectional discrimination until she too "felt like he was the real deal, and I'm not." Ironically, "as it turned out, it was kind of opposite," with Cindy outperforming her colleagues' expectations and the white male hire falling flat.

In addition to overt and actionable discrimination, microaggressions in the form of subtle bias and discrimination also color the experience of potential hires. Discrimination in the hiring context often occurs through implicit bias, as subconscious determinations that draw from race and gender stereotypes, negatively affecting those with less privilege, especially those with intersectionally devalued identity characteristics (i.e., women of color).[34] Because it is based on subconscious thought, "implicit bias coexists with egalitarian beliefs and the denial of personal prejudice."[35] Thus, biased "attitudes or thoughts [are ones] that people hold but might not explicitly endorse" in theory.[36] A woman wearing hijab will make some faculty members unfamiliar with this dress uncomfortable, not necessarily because they have conscious prejudices against Muslims, and even in spite of a sincere belief that they are egalitarian, simply because their subconscious reacts negatively to the image and association of a woman in hijab, given media and other common American portrayals of Muslims.[37] Regardless of whether the discrimination is overt or implicit, the outcome is the same: the woman of color faculty candidate is not hired. When Ellen's faculty recently considered a faculty of color candidate, they entertained "a series of questions [about] whether critical race theory was 'real' scholarship, [which included] a lot of pretty harsh judgment that it was not." When people in power devalue the theoretical framework that shapes the work of many scholars of color it is no wonder that they are not hired.

Efforts to improve faculty diversity can be especially daunting. Given the large body of scholarship in various fields on the topic, it is "well known that people have a bias in favor of preserving the status quo; change is uncomfortable."[38] A white professor named Joe is unapologetic about the lack of diversity on his faculty, seeing it as a regular outcome of how most institutions operate; he notes, "As institutions tend to do, they've hired people who look like themselves." A white law professor named Scarlett sees this as more problematic, worrying that diversifying the faculty is "an uphill battle because the white people, especially the men, are really holding on to their positions of power. They're trying to bring in people like them." Whether conscious or not, her faculty and many others reproduce themselves, instead of recognizing that other routes to success may also be viable. Sofia, a multiracial faculty member, explains that "the typical thing that happens" is that there is a "subtext that the white male candidates are more qualified." Her colleagues may agree "to interview every diverse candidate on the AALS market, but many of the faculty members don't really think of them as qualified," so they ultimately will not be hired. Institutions with a core commitment to diversity are those that "incorporate the knowledge and perspectives of its diverse members to eliminate embedded bias and enhance organizational efficacy."[39] Without a core commitment to diversity and inclusion, institutions will remain as white and male as ever.

A purely superficial commitment to diversity plays out in different ways. At Sofia's law school recently, "there was one candidate who was slated as an IP [intellectual property] candidate; I looked at her resume and was like, 'Oh, she's really a law and democracy person,' and she was a person of color." Sofia's colleagues were interested in interviewing her in part because she is a person of color "and she was super qualified, that was not a question." Nevertheless, Sofia "anticipated how the conversation was going to go," with her IP faculty colleagues rejecting the candidate since IP was not her primary focus, "and the fact that this woman could teach Intellectual Property because she had written one piece on it wasn't going to satisfy them." With "too much lip service to diversity without thinking about the fact that we should find candidates who the faculty will really think fit the need," her institution rarely hires diverse candidates. The strategy to "just sort of bring in everybody [without] a lot of thought of why we are bringing them in other than that they are diverse" yields the unsurprising result of primarily white male hires.

As former Yale Law School dean Robert Post acknowledges, deans have great power to "influence hiring decisions," though they could do so either to preserve the status quo or increase faculty diversity.[40] Brianna, a professor and administrator, clarifies: "Let's be real. If you don't want people and women of color to be hired, you just stack the [hiring] committee a certain way, right?" Confusion also abounds about race and ethnicity. Noriko, an Asian American professor, recalls a colleague who wondered aloud how to categorize a South Asian candidate for a tenure-track position, asking, "'Is he really a person of color?'"[41]

Gender norms, especially those involving family constraints, also shape opportunities for women who aspire to legal academia. When Karen received multiple offers through the AALS faculty appointment process, she selected her institution in part because she and her partner already lived nearby; Jennifer did not even look beyond the city where she and her husband already lived. Many women are unwilling or unable to relocate for work—a significant difference from many men, who pursue positions nationally with a legitimate interest and availability to take the position that best fits their professional goals. Scholars have published widely on the *two-body problem*: when hiring one woman, schools actually need to concern themselves with "two bodies" (the woman and her partner), whereas when hiring men, institutions often know that if the man gets the job, his partner will follow regardless of available employment opportunities.[42]

A Latina named Mariana has "a significant other" who is an academic in a different discipline. For years, she laments, "we couldn't find tenure in the same institution, [which] was really hard for us and I had to travel" back and forth between their home in one state and her job elsewhere. Laura, a Native American professor, worked at a law school in a small town thousands of miles from where her partner worked and lived. After being in a committed relationship for many years, while living apart, they "actually got married giving up trying to be in the same town." Emma, a multiracial professor, and her partner strategized "to find two academic jobs in the same place" in different disciplines. She went on the national market first, scheduling twenty initial interviews and eight callbacks. She "got seven offers and then my husband subsequently worked with those seven schools and got offers at five."

Each school's willingness to facilitate her husband securing a suitable position "greatly influenced my decision of where I accepted a job."

Like so many other Black female professors, Destiny concedes, "I don't think I ever considered being a law professor" while in law school. She got married and earned an LLM at an elite institution to better leverage herself professionally. She later applied for a PhD program, "but I never even enrolled because [my husband] at the same time was applying for teaching positions" and received an offer. "So we came here and so I've trailed him," she admits. While the institution was "pretty good with spousal accommodations," they looked primarily for "some sort of appropriate administrative position" for Destiny; not surprisingly, as she had been a practicing attorney and held both a JD and LLM, "I wasn't interested [laughing]." Instead, Destiny "started going around to conferences" with a Black female colleague of her husband's— who became a friend and mentor and "put it in my mind that I was going to write some articles and go on the market at some point." This mentor is "the one who I want to say really took me by the hand" and began "helping me kind of clarify my thoughts and helping me to develop a series of courses that I've continued to teach and build off of." Within a year, Destiny was working as an adjunct at a local law school and teaching university-level courses in another discipline. When her husband received an offer to visit out of state, Destiny "decided, 'Well, if he's moving, then I'm going on the market right now [laughing]—and I did!" She received offers from multiple schools across the country and "eventually got an offer from [my husband's institution]. So that was the easiest for us, so we stayed." Destiny is grateful for the advice of a mentor who suggested that to get an offer at her husband's institution, first, "you have to get an offer better than [here] for them to really consider you. And even when you've done that, we still probably will consider how important it is even to keep [your husband]." Gender norms and expectations limited Destiny at every turn. She moved to the city where her husband had a job, went on the market only when he received an offer to visit elsewhere, and was told directly that she would need to turn down a better offer if she wanted to stay and teach at her husband's school.[43]

Susan is one of those rare Black female law professors who knew as a student that she wanted to be an academic. Though a mentor advised her that an LLM would better position her on the law teaching market, Susan grew up in "extreme poverty; I was homeless my first few weeks of law school, and I could not afford to continue to go to get an LLM." Gender norms and family complications added to the class limitations that were early barriers to her success, compounding intersectional bias. Susan remembers, "I told my husband that I wanted to leave the practice of law to go get an LLM, so I can enter law teaching because that's really what I wanted to do." It also seemed a more manageable "family lifestyle [than] both of us at large law firms." Her husband's "response was, 'So let me get this straight: you want to leave, give up your law firm income to go spend money on a degree, to get a job to make less money?' and I said, 'Exactly!' [laughing]." Her husband "was not supportive of it at all, and so it didn't happen." When a law firm colleague encouraged her to pursue legal academia even without the LLM, Susan "thought, 'There's really not a chance that I'm gonna get a job in law teaching,' but I decided to try it nonetheless." After successful initial interviews, multiple schools invited her to full-day interviews, but "they were all across the country so I knew I had another issue because my husband really wasn't portable." Yet "thankfully one [school] was in [my state] and they made me an offer and I accepted it." If not for that local offer, Susan would likely not be the law professor and administrator she is today.

Stacey's husband was always supportive of her professional ambitions, but as an academic himself they also faced the two-body problem. Stacey was on law review at her elite institution, clerked for a judge after law school, and practiced at a corporate law firm. During those years, Stacey was "just waiting for a time when we both could go on the market [together]." She "got a ton of interviews" at AALS, though she suspects some met her primarily for surface diversity purposes—schools that clearly "were not serious" about hiring her but included her simply "so they [could] say they interviewed a Black person."[44] The school she selected was one where "everyone was so nice," and her being there "just felt right," in part because "a lot of the junior people I met at that time were [also] people of color." Ironically, Stacey had almost canceled that visit "because my husband and I got a match [elsewhere]. And we thought, 'We're going to get one match and that's where we're gonna go.'" While her husband did not initially "have any prospects" at Stacey's first-choice institution, they found a way to make it work and started there together soon after. Class issues also complicated the hiring process for Stacey, as she had "to front the money" for airfare and hotels, with limited expendable income. In this and other ways, socioeconomic status merges with race and gender disadvantage to further limit prospects for women of color. Stacey recalls:

"I mean I had friends who've gone on the market and didn't have the money on their credit cards to put their ticket on there. So there's a lot of class-based assumptions in academia."[45]

Once they are tenure-track faculty, many women of color actively participate in appointments decisions, including heated debates of diverse candidates.[46] Carla set a goal "to bring one diverse candidate onto our faculty; and the candidate I was able to bring on was a female JD/PhD who had stepped out to raise her children." Ultimately, this candidate "was a wonderful hire, everyone loves her, she got a teaching award, I mean she's really terrific." Yet Carla "was surprised at how difficult it was to get the hire through," given her impressive qualifications. Carla's colleagues expressed many gender-related concerns, including asking "a lot of questions about the 'gap,'" in her CV, wondering whether a decision to take time away from work signaled that a candidate is "not as good as the person with no gaps." Men rarely take off years to raise children, again bringing gender privilege in hiring to the forefront. Carla "had to keep saying, 'Well, she stopped [working briefly] to have children.'" Even a senior female administrator (without children) saw this as a risky hire, worrying that the candidate would take the position and later "'just blow us off.'" Carla voiced her confidence that "clearly if somebody has a JD, PhD, has clerked for a federal court and [then] stopped to raise children, that's not [really a risky]" hire.

Overall, women candidates must navigate numerous manifestations of gender bias and combat entrenched gender norms on the path to legal academia. Many give significant consideration to larger family constraints and priorities. Laila felt "fortunate to find [a tenure-track job] in the city that I wanted because one of the biggest drawbacks of entering legal academia is having very little control over where you are going to land geographically, and for me geography was very important," both because she is "very sensitive to racial issues" and wanted to raise her kids in a diverse environment and because she knew that she would have family support in the city where she ultimately accepted a job. A Black professor named Patrice "found out I was pregnant like the month before" she went on the market. Unsurprisingly, she remembers, "I was tired and nauseous and it [was] awful." April, a Black professor, "started on the tenure-track with an eight-month-old." The hiring process was both a blur and a nightmare: "Yes, I had to go and buy [a suit] while I was on maternity leave [from my firm job]. Me and the Baby Bjorn [infant carrier], out trying to find a suit." Her husband could not take time off from work, and April was nursing their newborn, so "I had to take the baby to each of these call[backs]," along with her mother, who watched the baby while April was interviewing. Adding to her complications, "midway through my day in the interviewing [process], I would have to go in somebody's bathroom and pump, because no one had a pumping room." She can still envision herself taking "breaks" from interviews, "sitting on top of a toilet, trying to double pump to get the milk, my liquid gold for my baby." Even then, she recognized, "It was crazy. But it worked out. It worked out. I got the job."

Comparison and Contrast

While men of color and white women share some similar hiring trajectories and challenges, including a lack of mentors and little initial interest, the experiences of white men are quite different from those of everyone else. An Asian American named Vijay worked for the government and clerked before he considered legal academia. He started as an adjunct at a local law school as "a trial run because I wanted to see how that environment was, to see what it would be like to be a law professor." His first time through the formal AALS process, he "went in without sufficient preparation and understanding of what the process was like." Without mentorship, he was unprepared for "what to expect, what questions may be asked of me, . . . and as a result the first time around was not successful." On the market again the following year, "my core interest in law teaching and teaching interests, scholarly agenda, were all the same; everything was identical—except for the fact that I had a lot more guidance." After failing to find a job the first time, he "called several folks and prepared myself in a manner that I hadn't prepared myself beforehand." With mentorship, he scheduled over a dozen interviews in DC and received half a dozen callbacks. Unsurprisingly, his "experience was much better having been adequately prepared." When a Native American named Stuart was a student, he "never considered [law teaching]—seriously, any more than I would have considered becoming president [of the United States]," until a guest speaker encouraged him and other students of color to pursue it. He practiced for a few years while also "publishing law review articles." Soon, "friends of friends began telling me that there's a market for [Native American] law professors and encouraged me to apply." Eventually he did, but without formal mentors to support him. Though most people advise including the FAR form in the first distribution, Stuart "didn't send my FAR form in until the third distribution." Nevertheless, he "got some interviews in DC" and ultimately received an offer. Thinking back, Stuart realizes, "I was a nontraditional law professor candidate as far as I can tell," much like many of the women of color who start with little or no guidance but are ultimately successful once they enter the profession. Whereas most candidates boast of "federal or state court clerk-ships, federal government jobs, or big-time law firm jobs," Stuart himself "had none of that stuff." He believes, "I tossed my hat in the ring and kind of got lucky." His trajectory mirrors that of many women of color, from a lack of mentorship to a nontraditional pathway to the feeling that he stumbled into law teaching by luck.

Ryan had a much different experience as a Black man. While a third-year law student, he started tutoring; eventually, his "tutoring session be-came popular, [turning from just one student] to seven or eight of his friends, [and then] grew a little more to twelve students." He quickly "realized I really liked what I was doing and that's what opened my eyes" to a law teaching ca-reer. He practiced law, earned a PhD, held multiple fellowships, and endured a "nerve-wracking" AALS hiring process to secure a tenure-track position. Jack's experience also has useful comparisons and contrasts. Like other Asian Americans, Jack had no "concrete plan" to pursue academia, though he served on law review and later clerked. His entry into law teaching occurred through "happenstance": after "applying for jobs and academic fellowships," he "didn't get the jobs, and got the fellowships," so assumed academia was his path. His wife is also an academic, but gender privilege helped him avoid the two-body problem. Years after he was hired at his law school, his wife "got a position at my school as well, in [another] department." While they did "consider going on the market" together to look at jobs nationally, a position opened up at the university where Jack was already teaching, and his wife "got the job; it [just] worked out that way," with Jack and his wife not even considering other op-tions.

White women enjoy the benefits of white privilege but face gender-related challenges during the hiring process. After a "horrible" AALS job-market process, during which Marybeth "got callbacks, but no job," she secured a tenure-track position "through connections." The law school professor who first "suggested to me that I could become a law professor" initially took her "under his wing and mentored me and helped me with the whole process of preparing myself and going on the market." When she still did not secure a position, that professor "got me this job by calling around." She understates,

"Mentoring was a big part of it," one rarely available to people of color seeking tenure-track employment. Isabella's mentors "helped groom me" for law teaching, telling her "what was necessary: getting a judicial clerkship, going to a big law firm, and getting an LLM." Giving credit to mentors, she notes, "I would say the reason I am where I am right now has more to do with the people along my path than my own skill set." Lisa, a nationally renowned senior scholar and former dean, also believes mentors "helped along every step of the way. You don't do these things by yourself." She had assumed she would attend a local law school; yet a mentor suggested she take advantage of a new scholarship, which placed her at a much more prestigious institution away from home. Then, a "law professor [mentor] sent me to [work for a judge, and that judge] sent me to [my first tenure-track position]." Lisa feels deeply indebted to that first mentor, who convinced her to leave home. He "assured me that [the faraway school] was a much better law school and, of course, he was right." Just as Sonia notes about the importance of early mentors, Lisa also firmly believes, "If I had gone to [my local] law school, you would have never heard of me because I would have never gotten a [faculty] job offer."

Family issues can also affect white female candidates. Jordan was "going through a divorce" while on the market. Ultimately, her ex-husband remained in their former city, while Jordan and their children moved for her tenure-track position. She recognizes that it "certainly helped in the job market to not be geographically confined," because she received no offers in the city where she had lived. Chloe was recruited from her clerkship in the mid-1970s by a local institution that "came to me and said, 'We're looking to add women to our faculty. Can we talk to you?' and I said, 'No. I don't want to be a law professor.'" Ultimately, they convinced her to try it temporarily, after which she practiced, met, and married her husband. Her return to law teaching was a decision made jointly with her husband as "it's a good job to have with children because [of] the way you can juggle working at 2 a.m.," after spending the evening on child-care duties.[47] She thinks of herself nonpejoratively and gratefully as "an affirmative action professor"—but for the school's interest in diversity, she would not have entered law teaching.

A white woman named Ellen, like Laura, Destiny, and other women of color, encountered the two-body problem firsthand. She boasted a traditionally impressive résumé, cultivating law faculty mentors even as an undergraduate student, graduating from an elite law school, and clerking for a federal appellate judge; she even taught undergraduate- and graduate-level courses while clerking to confirm her interest in academia. After a few years of law firm practice, "one day out of the blue I got a phone call from a member of [my undergraduate institution's] law faculty asking me to apply for a position there." As with June, this institution turned to a nontraditional prospective professor, who was not even a formal candidate, to fill an immediate hiring need after a failed search. Ellen notes that, at the time, "I knew nothing about going on the academic job market. I had not applied for anything formally, or informally actually." She stresses, "I cannot tell you how little I knew about going on the job market," but she cobbled together a talk "based on my law review note" and got the job. Later, she applied nationally for a permanent position through AALS and believes "my résumé got pulled out of the pile . . . because I knew someone on the faculty here. I had met him at a conference and he was a proponent of my candidacy and my work so I'm sure that was very helpful." Networks were a benefit to Ellen. Yet Ellen had another "massive" obstacle, what she calls the "two academic career problem," as her partner is also an academic. Over many years of dating and marriage, "trying to get two good jobs in the same location [has] been our biggest challenge." They alternated strategies, first "trying to get him on the faculty here," then "trying to get me on the faculty there," all the while accepting that "neither of us had to have our best possible outcome." Because their priority was being together, "we were also looking for a lot of jobs in third locations that were possible for both of us." Since "our professional identities are very much a part of who we are," Ellen believes it "would have been toxic for the relationship" if "one of us had a great job" while the other one simply tagged along. She is relieved, noting, "Thank heavens it worked out."

In contrast, many white men raced directly toward legal academia early on, with mentors and sponsors to guide them. Adam says, "I only went to law school to be a law professor." Most white men in the DLA study began cultivating the idea of joining academia when they were law students, often inspired and encouraged by their own law professors—usually also white men. Matt's interest in legal academia "probably started just by admiring law professors that I had" and believing he could be like them. Ken did not seek out faculty, but he "did meet a faculty member . . . who became a kind of mentor of mine." Ken is "quite sure if it wasn't for his mentorship I also would've never become a legal academic." Similarly, a senior scholar named Christopher "attribute[s] my being in the profession largely to a teacher I had in law school for whom I was a research assistant and who encouraged me to think about teaching law as a career." These mentors, like Matt, Ken, and Christopher themselves, were all white men. Race and gender privilege provide a significant boost to white men at the earliest stages, contributing to the unequal profession of legal academia. Law faculty role models give white male law students an image they strive to emulate, a dream they hope to live up to—in contrast to women of color law students, who rarely see someone with a similar name, face, or background at the front of the classroom to inspire and guide them.[48]

Sometimes, mentors go above and beyond, exploiting white male privilege to contribute to ongoing homogeneity in legal academia. Decades ago, because Christopher's mentor "recognized that having [a] clerkship was something that enhances your status as a law teacher," he arranged a clerkship for Christopher with a judge he knew. Christopher's mentor also "arranged with [a top-five] law school to grant me a teaching fellowship," a stepping-stone to secure academic employment. Although most mentors have less power over the trajectories of their mentees, many outline a strategy geared toward legal academia, including clerkships, publishing, and other particularly useful credentials for entering legal academia. Joe "got out of law school and had no idea what I wanted to do," but he had applied for and accepted a clerkship because his mentors all said, "'Clerk! It's such a wonderful experience.'"

Many white law professors recognize that they benefitted from privilege, whether family connections or social capital helped propel them along their trajectory.[49] Joe received both a tenure-track and a non-tenure-track offer simultaneously. While many women of color candidates would have had to make that choice alone, Joe solicited advice not only from mentors but also from immediate family: "My mom was a lawyer so I had people to talk to. Everyone said, 'You don't need to go any further. You take the one that is tenure-track.'" Christopher, whose mentor secured his clerkship, has paid that forward, arranging a clerkship with a judge who "was a close friend of mine" for a white family member who is now a legal academic. Neither Christopher nor any other participant in the DLA study discussed making similar arrangements for women of color aspiring academics. None of the women of color in the DLA sample mentioned family members making similar arrangements for them, likely because there have been so few law faculty of color over the years who could make those sorts of grand gestures and provide that level of sponsorship. In these many ways, intersectional (raceXgender) discrimination clouds the hiring process, preventing women of color from entering legal academia and perpetuating the existing disparate status quo.

2 Ugly Truths Behind the Mask of Collegiality

ZAHRA, A MIDDLE EASTERN LAW PROFESSOR, pursed legal academia by reaching out "to a bunch of schools" in cities where her husband was applying to work. She interviewed "at a handful of schools in places where we were willing to live, and then ended up [here] because that's where he wanted to go too." Initially, she was enthusiastic about her tenure-track position; but after a few years of race-and gender-related challenges, she says, "I feel frustrated that I don't have any voice in faculty decisions, especially appointments and important things. . . . I wonder if that is even possible for a woman of color." She and "a lot of junior colleagues of mine . . . have felt judged" by colleagues, perhaps because she is viewed as "a younger woman who looks a little different, acts a little different [than] what a law professor [traditionally] looks like or how [they think one] should behave." A few "older white men" have provided guidance, although some senior white female colleagues are "more antagonistic than helpful." Zahra characterizes her overall experience as "pretty positive," including "strong relationships with the junior colleagues," especially women. Ideally, though, she would "change the dynamic" by increasing "the proportion of women and minority faculty." After years of microaggressions on campus and with colleagues, she now welcomes opportunities to move laterally to a new law school, especially because "I don't feel that I am really that appreciated here or wanted and I don't really have much of a voice."

Many law faculty members report cordial relationships with colleagues and frequent interactions with faculty of different racial backgrounds. However, there is marked racial variation with regard to the quality of these interactions and inclusion in close-knit groups. The qualitative data show that a mask of collegiality often covers underlying hostility. Invisibility and silencing—especially through mansplaining, hepeating, and whitesplaining—are frequent occurrences especially during faculty meetings, leading to negative health effects for the women of color who endure them. The faculty interactions of white men, white women, and men of color highlight the prevalence of gender privilege even beyond intersectional discrimination in legal academia.

Quantitative data from DLA confirm high levels of interaction among faculty members. More than 75% of faculty from all racial/ethnic backgrounds report "a lot" of interaction with white faculty, indicating significant interracial interaction.[1] Yet when considering the quality of these interactions, white professors have the best relationships with other whites, with a full 73%

TABLE 4 Quality of Interactions with White Faculty, by Race and Gender, DLA 2013

		Very friendly	Sociable	Distant	Hostile	Total
African American women	n	11	5	5	0	21
	%	52.38	23.81	23.81	0.00	100.00
Asian American women	n	9	5	1	0	15
	%	60.00	33.33	6.67	0.00	100.00
Latinas	n	5	6	1	0	12
	%	41.67	50.00	8.33	0.00	100.00
Native American women	n	3	1	0	1	5
	%	60.00	20.00	0.00	20.00	100.00
Middle Eastern women	n	0	2	0	0	2
	%	0.00	100.00	0.00	0.00	100.00
Multiracial women	n	4	3	0	0	7
	%	57.14	42.86	0.00	0.00	100.00
Men of color	n	6	4	1	0	11
	%	54.55	36.36	9.09	0.00	100.00
White women	n	8	3	0	0	11
	%	72.73	27.27	0.00	0.00	100.00
White men	n	6	2	0	0	8
	%	75.00	25.00	0.00	0.00	100.00
Total	n	52	31	8	1	92
	%	56.52	33.70	8.70	1.09	100.00

of white women and 75% of white men reporting "very friendly" interactions with fellow white faculty, compared to only 42%–60% of women of color and 55% of men of color (see Table 4). Interestingly, white faculty members believe their relationships with faculty of color are much better than faculty of color view those same relationships.[2] Despite one-quarter (24%) of Black female faculty characterizing their relationships with white faculty as "distant," (Table 4) no white men and only one white woman characterize their relationships with African American colleagues this way (Table 5).[3]

Perceptions of tolerance or inclusion also differ by race and gender. Participants were asked for their level of agreement with the following statement: "Most of my colleagues are open-minded and respect opinions that are different from their own" (Table 6). A full 100% of white men agree with the statement, seeing their colleagues as particularly understanding; similarly, 91% of men of color and 82% of white women agree. This reveals a strong gender contrast, with the male participants overwhelmingly reporting their colleagues as

TABLE 5 Quality of Interactions with African American Faculty, by Race and Gender, DLA 2013

		Very friendly	Sociable	Distant	Hostile	Not applicable	Total
African American women	n	14	6	1	0	0	21
	%	66.67	28.57	4.76	0.00	0.00	100.00
Asian American women	n	12	3	0	0	0	15
	%	80.00	20.00	0.00	0.00	0.00	100.00
Latinas	n	7	5	0	0	0	12
	%	58.33	41.67	0.00	0.00	0.00	100.00
Native American women	n	2	1	2	0	0	5
	%	40.00	20.00	40.00	0.00	0.00	100.00
Middle Eastern women	n	1	0	0	0	1	2
	%	50.00	0.00	0.00	0.00	50.00	100.00
Multiracial women	n	6	0	1	0	0	7
	%	85.71	0.00	14.29	0.00	0.00	100.00
Men of color	n	9	2	0	0	0	11
	%	81.82	18.18	0.00	0.00	0.00	100.00
White women	n	7	3	1	0	0	11
	%	63.64	27.27	9.09	0.00	0.00	100.00
White men	n	4	3	0	0	0	7
	%	57.14	42.86	0.00	0.00	0.00	100.00
Total	n	62	23	5	0	1	91
	%	68.13	25.27	5.49	0.00	1.10	100.00

TABLE 6 Believe Most Colleagues Are Open Minded and Respect Differing Opinions, by Race and Gender, DLA 2013

		Strongly agree	Agree	Neither agree nor disagree	Disagree	Strongly disagree	Total
African American women	n	3	7	0	9	2	21
	%	14.29	33.33	0.00	42.86	9.52	100.00
Asian American women	n	4	6	0	5	0	15
	%	26.67	40.00	0.00	33.33	0.00	100.00
Latinas	n	1	4	0	7	0	12
	%	8.33	33.33	0.00	58.33	0.00	100.00
Native American women	n	0	3	0	2	0	5
	%	0.00	60.00	0.00	40.00	0.00	100.00
Middle Eastern women	n	0	0	0	0	2	2
	%	0.00	0.00	0.00	0.00	100.00	100.00
Multiracial women	n	2	2	0	3	0	7
	%	28.57	28.57	0.00	42.86	0.00	100.00
Men of color	n	3	7	0	1	0	11
	%	27.27	63.64	0.00	9.09	0.00	100.00
White women	n	3	3	3	1	1	11
	%	27.27	27.27	27.27	9.09	9.09	100.00
White men	n	4	4	0	0	0	8
	%	50.00	50.00	0.00	0.00	0.00	100.00
Total	n	20	36	3	28	5	92
	%	21.74	39.13	3.26	30.43	5.43	100.00

open minded and respectful. It also shows unity among white law school professors, with the vast majority of whites (men and women) believing faculty to be tolerant. Likely, this reflects their own personal experience of being respected and accepted. Yet women of color feel strongly that many of their colleagues are not accepting of difference, with 33% of Asian Americans, 40% of Native Americans, 52% of African Americans, and 58% of Latinas disagreeing or strongly disagreeing with the statement.

Existing literature indicates that women of color often lack a sense of belonging when hired to teach at predominantly white and male-normative law school campuses.[4] This chapter explains why they feel unwelcome in elite spaces that have traditionally excluded them, especially if no meaningful efforts are made to include them.[5] Diversity and inclusion must go hand-in-hand to create lasting improvement.[6] Although pleasant interactions usually outnumber hostile for women of color faculty, the negative encounters tend to color the environment overall. The most positive relationships are generally among women of color faculty or a cohort of junior scholars. Unfortunately, gender discrimination is especially pronounced, with regard to both the invisibility and silencing of women and through blatant sexual harassment.[7]

The Mask of Collegiality

Faculty from all backgrounds enjoy some friendly interactions with colleagues. A Black professor named Corinne sees her law school as "a very civil place [where] we can really disagree [one day], but then we can go out to lunch and hang out in someone's office the next day." Hannah expresses a common refrain, noting, "For the most part, we are a collegial faculty." She adds: "I know a lot of people say that, but I mean it. Everyone gets along [and] is just very nice and very kind." She admits there are "one or two folks that it's a little more challenging to get along with," but "with a third of the faculty, easily [I could] call them if my car got stuck," and another five are "my friends for life." Corinne and Hannah are lucky to be so comfortable on campus. More commonly, women of color faculty agree with Aisha, an Asian American professor: "The faculty at the law school is very polarized." Valeria, a Latina professor, similarly notes, "I think with every law school there are different factions."[8]

Guests and Intruders

Most female faculty of color are reticent at best in their interactions with colleagues. Michelle, a Black professor, is "cordial with everybody" at her law school, though she "purposely, consciously" maintains only "very professional relationship[s]" with colleagues. She has strategically disengaged socially from her professional environment. This hesitancy at being close to fellow faculty comes from a general distrust that many female faculty of color have toward white colleagues after recognizing that some are focused on their own self-interest and advancement, and threatened when women of color succeed. Others have witnessed white male faculty actively working against the interests of women of color. This duplicity goes against the sense of community that many female faculty of color seek, which they often find with others who share similar backgrounds.[9]

A common injustice invoking intersectional raceXgender bias involves the negative treatment of junior women of color faculty compared to positive affirmations given to junior white men. Cindy made a lateral move to her current institution at the same time as a white male but was treated as a less-deserving "affirmative action hire." Though that open display of favoritism affected her confidence initially, she ultimately became one of the most widely respected members of her faculty. Nevertheless, her colleagues' initial uninviting reception continued to color Cindy's interactions with them.

Martha, a Latina professor, also maintains arm's-length relationships with faculty colleagues, trying "to keep things cordial and superficial," because "I have a hard time really trusting other faculty." Martha has seen white faculty members utilize a mask of collegiality to hide the true negativity they feel toward faculty of color. In Martha's many years of experience, her colleagues will not "tell you to your face that they don't agree with what you said at the faculty meeting, or [say,] 'I think your perspective on this is wrong.'" Instead of engaging in open conversation, "they go around your back and say that to each other. And then label you as mean [or] unkind." This labeling and the "gossip and bad talk behind your back undermines your voice in a very significant way." Past attempts at "just saying what I think is the truth or what needs to be said" has led to her being "undercut [by] people who talk about you behind your back." Now, Martha decides strategically when to "corral the right people at the table, get them to say the right things, get them to agree" in advance, and pledge to back her up.

Laila's distrust of her colleagues stems from the troubling shift in climate soon after she started her position:

> The first semester everyone was very welcoming it was just kind of like I was their guest [in their] home. I was new and exotic and different and I was, you know, energetic and they thought, "That's so neat!" "This new person!" Sort of fresh blood. Then second semester I think jealousy sort of set in and I really sensed it. I got to the point [that] I didn't even want anyone to know what I had accomplished because . . . instead of being complimented it was like you would get these very negative looks.

Neither Laila's initial reception as a "guest" as a woman of color faculty member on a predominantly white campus nor her colleagues' jealousy is unusual. Some have felt their presence was more akin to an "intruder" than a guest.[10]

After many years in legal academia, Carla has concluded that while women of color may be hired, "our presence . . . is not really welcomed." Thus, "we are allowed to be here, but no one is expecting us to actually thrive." Like Laila, when she nevertheless flourishes, "people sometimes feel threatened by me. I'm shocked." Though she thinks she is "a really nice and friendly person," she gets the sense that to "my colleagues . . . whatever I accomplish somehow feels like it diminishes [them]." As a senior scholar, "competition for merit increases, or chair, or whatever gets a little more fierce." Combined with competition is "gossip about my personal life, which is odd because honestly I don't really have a huge personal life [laughing]!" April identifies similar race-based rationales for her treatment by colleagues. She attributes it to them feeling she does not truly belong; even if she keeps to herself, "there's never enough distance for them because I show up and I'm still Black. That's going to be forever a sore spot for them. They're never going to get over that." She further believes that certain colleagues expect her to grin and bear the intersectional raceXgender obstacles she faces, and even show appreciation for her position and deference to her colleagues for allowing her to join their space. Instead, "they're never going to get over the utter audacity that [when I see] a problem, I t[ake] it upon myself to tell them how to fix it." Because of her initiative, she has been labeled "a bossy bitch," and "nobody likes a bossy bitch." Instead of welcoming and appreciating April, her colleagues ignore and reject her.[11]

Alicia, a Latina professor, also has dealt with difficult colleagues.[12] In her first semester teaching, a white male student was "very hostile" toward her.

When the student complained to a "white male faculty member," her colleague promptly "assumed that of course the student was correct in his complaints" and approached Alicia as an advocate for the student. For Alicia, the "unfortunate circumstance of this faculty member taking the student's side is that [it] empowered the student to act out even more" in class, which in turn prompted other students to challenge her. Ultimately, she had "a little cabal of problematic students that I then had to manage" all semester, disrupting her teaching and ruining the learning environment for everyone. Alicia's challenging situation could have been nipped in the bud with the proper support; instead, her colleague made the situation worse.[13]

Birds of a Feather

Women of color do seek out close relationships with colleagues who come from similar backgrounds, endure common professional experiences, and otherwise share worldviews.[14] Valeria is not close to her colleagues, but she and other junior faculty "do things outside the office every now and again, so it's very collegial." Junior faculty stick together, perhaps recognizing their unity through a shared lack of job security, marginalization from faculty governance, and other ways in which their professional position bonds them.

Vivian, an Asian American professor, has "very strong relationships with particular colleagues." Erin also has "some good friends" and believes her law school has "a really wonderful environment."[15] She is "particularly close to my African American male colleague and my [white] lesbian colleague, because sometimes I just think that they get things better than colleagues who are not necessarily from [underrepresented] backgrounds," as they share the experience of being marginalized in legal academia and society generally. Similarly, Imani's "closest relationships are with the female faculty, particularly the three or four female faculty of color that we have."

Many female faculty of color agree with Annalisa, an Asian American academic, about the importance of support from those with similar backgrounds or experiences: "I was able to survive because I had a core group of professors who were my friends, and we challenged each other's work and also provided moral support." When Grace's dean offered faculty summer funding for innovative projects, another administrator tried to block Grace's funding by arguing to the dean that Grace would do the work even without the funds. While she was committed to the work, her colleague's interference made Grace "crazy with that whole assumption [of thinking] that was an appropriate way to [act]." Instead of directly confronting the white administrators involved, Grace called two colleagues "who are both people of color, both women, to talk through [it,]" and they both "totally [were able to] understand" her disappointment. Her first calls after troubling incidents are to colleagues of color whom she trusts, both "to make sure that the way I'm reacting is appropriate" and also "to figure out strategies for how to respond and what to do." Because she ultimately got summer funding that year, she decided to not pursue the matter further, though she says, "It still pisses me off" that administrators would take advantage.[16] While many faculty are cordial with one another, their civility masks underlying distrust and distance. Of notable exception are the close relationships female faculty of color enjoy with one another and other underrepresented and often marginalized faculty members.

Invisibility, Silencing, and Sexual Harassment

Research on teaching and learning has highlighted the raced and gendered law school environment for students, where "white males are the primary focus of classroom attention," often at the expense of women of color, men of color, and white women.[17] Women students tend to be "called on less frequently than men," and their comments are often ignored or met with skepticism.[18]

Silencing of female law faculty is strikingly similar. Women professors rarely "enjoy the status, authority, and opportunity equal to that of white men working in the legal academy."[19] There are ongoing "disparities in terms of pay, tenure denials, and employment [as well as] double standards in assessing identical credentials."[20] Likely because of this bias, women of color—who are viewed by others and often consider themselves to be "outsiders" in the white male culture of legal academia—have lower retention rates than white men.[21] DLA data confirm and elaborate on these past studies, specifically documenting ongoing gender concerns relating to invisibility, silencing, and outright sexual harassment.[22] In fact, intersectionality is almost completely obscured by gender privilege, which rampantly affects women regardless of their other identity characteristics and contributes to an ongoing unequal profession.

Mansplaining, Hepeating, and Whitesplaining

As an example of the male-centered workplace, Imani notes the numerous "times where I felt like some of the male colleagues look at themselves as above others and [are] not always respectful of others' contributions." Trisha, a Black professor, blames these tensions for her current "extremely marginalized" position on the faculty. This echoes a contributor to *Presumed Incompetent*, who notes of her first appointment as a legal academic, "I can recall being almost invisible. . . . I seemed not to exist" to the other faculty.[23] Zahra and her other "junior female colleagues" have been "shown over and over" that "our voice doesn't matter when we express opinions." When they do nevertheless speak out, "it's not heard, we're not understood." Jennifer embodies this invisibility, despite her good-humored response:

> [In] the four-and-a-half years I've been here there's a couple of people I haven't even had a conversation with. And they don't look at me. They don't acknowledge me. They don't seem to know who I am [laughing]. [They] just treat me like a non-entity.

Even Jennifer's identity is invisible: "I spoke up at a faculty meeting last week and said, 'As the only woman of color on the faculty I think this,' and I think some people actually looked at me like, 'Oh yeah! That's right, you are Native American! I forgot.'"[24] Elaine has one faculty colleague "who really has never acknowledged my presence." Similarly, April recalls a one-way interaction with a white male faculty colleague: "I was walking down the hall and I said, 'Hi.' He didn't say a word. I was mortified." Yet she is just one of many women of color professors who is ignored.

Male privilege is most prominent during faculty meetings, where invisibility and silencing are especially pronounced. For a Native American professor named Melissa, the "silencing that goes on in our faculty meetings" is part of a larger pattern of entrenched intersectional raceXgender bias, where "junior white males . . . get coddled, get laughed at, get remarks made, get floor time, get affirmations, and the women don't ever." This reproduces the male-dominant culture of law school.

Mansplaining and hepeating are other mechanisms of asserting and deepening white male privilege. Both inside and outside the workplace, a woman's ideas, suggestions, or observations may be ignored until a man unnecessarily explains her thoughts, asserting himself as the expert and claiming the ideas as his own. This common occurrence, outside of legal academia as well as within, falls into the "archipelago of arrogance" of mansplaining.[25] *Mansplaining* is an occurrence that many women readily recognize from their own experience of "having their expertise instantly dismissed because of the lady-shaped package it came in."[26] Mansplaining occurs at "the intersection between overconfidence and cluelessness."[27] When men take it upon themselves to interpret for women or explain to women, they assume that a woman is simply "an empty vessel to be filled with their wisdom and knowledge," forgetting that women may even know more than the man himself on particular topics.[28] Relatedly, *hepeating* occurs when a man simply repeats what a woman has already said, claiming and accepting credit for her original thoughts and words.[29] Before women can even provide arguments to support their ideas, they must first fight "simply for the right to speak, to have ideas, to be acknowledged to be in possession of facts and truth, to have value, to be a human being."[30] The challenge of being credited with their own words, regardless of what is expressed, "keeps women from speaking up and from being heard when they dare [or] crushes young women into silence by indicating . . . that this is not their world."[31] Both are common in legal academia.

Mansplaining and hepeating signal that women do not belong, should know their place, and remain silent.[32] As an example, Carla has "counted over ten times on my faculty where I've said something and [nobody has responded; then] a male faculty has repeated it and another male colleague has said, 'Good idea!'" Hepeating thereby provides weight, acknowledgment, and appreciation for men while devaluing women.[33] When Elaine started her first teaching position more than thirty years ago, she expected her voice would be heard and her perspective would be welcome. Yet she quickly realized that she was largely ignored as one of few women of color faculty at her institution. Her biggest complaint involves hepeating, as she would make valid points at faculty meetings that were ignored—until "a man would say it, and then everyone would pay attention to it," giving him credit for Elaine's original remarks.

Combining the intersectional framework with the concept of mansplaining and hepeating, *whitesplaining* is also prevalent in legal academia. Smita, an Asian American professor, knows that what she says "would carry more weight with the faculty if it were being said by white people." This is true whether she talks "about the importance of diversity or whatever else. We don't hear it enough from my white colleagues, even those who consider themselves progressive. So there is a sense of your voice being discounted in a lot of respects," specifically because she is a woman of color. White validation of Smita's suggestions or observations would give them more weight, highlighting ongoing white privilege. For women of color, the invisibility, silencing, and discrimination is cumulatively challenging—mansplaining and hepeating multiplied by whitesplaining—because it is based on both race and gender.[34]

Surprisingly, gender disparities in legal academia are stark even when compared to those in corporate law.[35] Many women did not experience as pronounced gender discrimination in previous legal practice, even in elite law firms.[36] Camila, a Latina scholar, says her "biggest challenge" in law teaching was navigating the cultural transition from being respected by colleagues and clients in legal practice to being virtually ignored by fellow faculty in legal academia; this involved "going from a place where I felt that my opinion was valued, work was valued, partners listened to me with respect," to being at an institution where her colleagues "don't want to hear what you say, people talk over you in faculty meetings, . . . or make faces while you're talking." She notes that "this kind of incredibly immature behavior" is gender based, targeted specifically at women by men.

Especially when considering the earnings difference between practice and academia, some women of color wonder whether the trade-off is worth it.[37] Erin sees academia as comparatively "hard[er]. It's downright hard." Although private practice was challenging, the intersectional discrimination she faces as a law professor is much more intense and personal: "We encounter racism. We encounter sexism. It's kind of like we get both '-isms' as women of color. We get both the sexism and the racism and it happens. It happens regularly [in academia]." In addition to implicit bias, Erin knows that "some people are just blatantly racist or sexist. I definitely encountered [both in legal academia]. And that makes it very, very hard [to stay]." Some days, she thinks "it would be easier to just go back to private practice [and] not deal with that, and not be judged constantly." She asks herself:

> When you're encountering sexism and racism in your professional life on almost a daily basis and you're making [so comparatively little]—I mean right now I'm making less than what I made my first year in private practice, you know? Why stay with it? [I could] just go back to private practice. I think it's easier.

Zahra recalls a meeting where women voiced gender concerns that others pretended to care about, but ultimately ignored:

> Several of us junior colleagues were concerned about how a new [potential] hire was going to interact with women, and specifically we had heard com-

plaints that he doesn't work well with women. There were, you know, four of us [women] that expressed things in the appointments committee meeting, saying, "Look, we are concerned about this," and some of the male colleagues acted like they cared; they said, "Well, you know, that sounds disappointing and we wouldn't want that," but everyone voted for him anyway [aside from the four of us women and two male junior colleagues].

That candidate was ultimately hired and will be starting at Zahra's law school shortly. While she is approaching him with an open mind, "it was just surprising that . . . we made our worries known, but [were] ignored. No one cared." This speaks not only to gender bias but also to the prevalence of expressing a "surface" interest in diversity without making it a "core" priority, and thereby failing to act in a manner representing a true commitment to diversity.[38] When female faculty of color find better opportunities elsewhere, they leave their schools—either teaching in a more inclusive environment or leaving legal academia altogether. Laura's law school suffered "a huge drain of women from our faculty" after enduring for many years "an environment of women not being involved in decision making, there were no Chairs [that were women], there was no involvement [by women], they were really closed out of every process in the law school." Not surprisingly, most of the female faculty left for greener pastures.

Causes of the Clyde Ferguson Syndrome

Silencing and harassment draw directly from gender privilege, though marginalization based on both race and gender create unique intersectional challenges for women of color. Susan acknowledges that "the problems we encounter in legal academia as women of color, we share some of those things with our white female colleagues." Most women in the DLA sample, regardless of racial/ethnic background, have endured silencing, harassment, mansplaining, hepeating, and gender bias. Yet Susan notes that there is "an added layer when you're a woman of color" that relates specifically to "male colleagues [who] question whether we should [even] be in the role that we're in," because of race. The emotional challenges facing traditional outsiders in legal academia have been tied to ill health and even untimely death. In response, women of color must suppress their emotions at work to succeed in legal academia. This *emotional labor* includes "the management of feeling to create a publicly observable facial and bodily display," where women of color faculty regulate their true "emotions to comply with [workplace] norms."[39] The toll of daily performance of emotional labor has been linked not only to broad "negative psychological outcomes," but also to depression and low job satisfaction, self-esteem, and overall health.[40] These resulting negative health effects for academics of color have been termed the *Clyde Ferguson syndrome*, after the revered Harvard Law School professor, a Black man who faced numerous professional challenges before his premature passing.[41]

At Patrice's institution, junior faculty give regular talks to the full faculty—which generally benefit the presenter because "the critiques are [supposed to be] constructive to help you get to the next point [in your research]." Yet because Patrice's scholarship focuses on race and ethnicity, some white male colleagues have been hostile rather than supportive, with the purpose of their "critiques [being] to shut it down and steer you in a different direction" rather than develop the ideas further. Patrice quickly decided never to present her work to her faculty, purposefully disengaging. She lost the benefit of potentially constructive feedback but kept her sanity by not subjecting herself to open hostility. As "an effort to be true to myself and just to sleep at night I felt like I had to [avoid presenting my work,] stay in my head with it, which is also just very difficult and not particularly as fulfilling." Coupled with other ongoing challenges with colleagues, she confides, "I have post-traumatic stress disorder."[42] Patrice's intellectual disengagement from campus and resulting health consequences are not only individually problematic but also setbacks for the institution as a whole, as active engagement from all faculty would be ideal.

Patrice is just one of many women of color suffering with serious health effects resulting from a career as a law professor. Melissa notes, "I find myself missing more days from illness and being a lot more stressed with no breaks." Existing scholarship indicates that many women of color faculty believe that remaining silent is "the key to [their] survival in academia."[43] Some make the calculated decision not to speak out and to find coping mechanisms that allow them to function professionally.[44] This self-censorship, the tendency to "bite your tongue and make no sound when you want to speak," also exerts a psychological toll.[45]

As the first woman of color hired at her institution decades ago, Sonia "tried to do the best I could" in the hopes that "someone else will want me" so she could move laterally, away from unsupportive colleagues. She considered quitting during her first year of law teaching, when she had neither support nor basic resources, because "I just thought it was humiliating." In the end, "I felt like I had to do a lot myself" to combat "the presumption . . . that I didn't have it and that I would never write." She remembers how cruel her colleagues were, both gossiping behind her back and telling her to her face that they did not believe in her. She recalls:

> Even after I was in the midst of writing, I remember someone coming up and saying, "There's a rumor that you're paralyzed and can't write." "Well," I said, "I don't know why, because I have several pieces, and they're coming out."

Though she survived, and even thrived at that institution and elsewhere, these first colleagues created a "difficult transition" for her into legal academia. Sonia did ultimately earn their respect. She remembers "one of the most conservative people on the faculty coming to me later saying, 'You know what we have in common, Sonia? You and I are both fighters.'" In Sonia's case, however, she was fighting for survival.

Carla also has endured the effects of the Clyde Ferguson syndrome. Although she is a senior scholar, Carla still does not feel she has the power to say no to demands from administration—even when their requests are unreasonable. At times it has been "really shocking," what she has been asked to do, but "I deal with it with my ordinary strategy, which [i]s to say, 'Okay.'" The fact that Carla immediately acquiesces to even unreasonable requests sheds some light on the Clyde Ferguson syndrome, the negative health effects of being stunned, disappointed, knowing you are the victim of injustice, and yet remaining silent and doing as you are told in order to survive on the job. Carla is always accommodating at work: "If someone said, 'Do this,' I did that. If someone said, 'Teach that,' I taught that. If someone said, 'You'll teach [at] 8 a.m.,' I taught at 8 a.m. If someone said, 'You teach summer school,' I taught summer school." Carla never felt she could say no, explaining, "I didn't feel that I had [a choice] or wanted to risk saying no because then the gossip would start up: 'She's difficult,' 'She's not a team player.'" This drama had played out with the only other woman of color on her faculty, who was "very, very well-credentialed," but "said no early on[,] got pegged as not a team player," and was subsequently voted down for tenure. Carla's experience personifies sociological research indicating that female faculty face "grave consequences if they are not perceived as team players," although expectations of male faculty are more relaxed.[46] Carla interprets this as "the price of saying no," and therefore feels "that I had to [always say yes to] survive. I had to take in these requests and produce quality work." Her strategy has paid off professionally: Carla is well respected both on campus and nationally. Yet the personal emotional costs have been high: "I felt like I had PTSD."

Erin recalls other more egregious gender-based violations at her former law school workplace, also resulting in PTSD. She recounts an instance of senior male colleagues "coming into the office and petting my hair, and telling me what beautiful hair I have, telling me I have large luscious breasts." There was a clear power imbalance—based on race, gender, and job status, among other things. Erin's intersectional experience of embodying so many devalued characteristics clearly worked against her as a young, untenured woman of color. Because the perpetrators were white male "senior tenured members" and she was a woman of color and a "junior faculty member, you just don't want to rock the boat, so you don't say anything—at least I didn't say anything. And you regret it later and you carry that guilt" that comes from not speaking out. The emotional toll of coping with that hostile workplace haunts Erin even today; she notes, "I actually have PTSD syndrome because of the amount of stress. I still have nightmares on a regular basis even though I'm very happy at my current institution." Overt intersectional—raceXgender—discrimination is a recurring theme in the experiences of women of color.[47]

Comparison and Contrast

White women share in the experiences of women of color, facing obstacles that stem from gender privilege. Abigail remembers that in the early days of her long career in legal academia, women were meant to take on subservient, silent roles. She recalls, "If we had a meeting and we needed a notetaker there would be the turning of all eyes to whichever female was in the room and she would become the notetaker." Decades later, the situation has improved, her faculty "isn't full of cliques," and her colleagues "genuinely like each other and get together and are happy to see each other." Yet at Ava's school, "some of the senior [male] colleagues in the building . . . treat me as a 'gal' and not as an intellectual equal," perhaps being unfamiliar with professional women—or taking cues from the administration. When Ava was a junior scholar, the dean "hit on me." The dean (who had recently divorced) invited Ava to what she thought was a professional lunch at which he clumsily professed his feelings for her:

He asked if I was dating anybody. He made this big point of saying, "I hope you know it wouldn't be appropriate to date because I'm your boss, but I find you really attractive and awesome. And if I could I would really be interested in dating you."

Ava's response at the time was characteristic of young professional women in her situation: "It made me really uncomfortable and I was shocked, because he was my boss, that he would make it clear he was interested in me romantically." Yet, like Erin, she did not feel she could speak up. Coupled with other gender-based employment concerns, both women became depressed, sought therapy, and fought their way back to succeed.

The gender bias inherent in harassment, mansplaining, hepeating, silencing, and a presumption of incompetence traverses racial lines—again highlighting some limits of intersectionality. Soon after Isabella joined legal academia a decade ago, "one of my first faculty meetings there I spoke out on an issue and didn't realize women were meant to be seen and not heard." One of her white male colleagues approached her afterward to say, "'Wow! You're really articulate!' And that stunned me because I thought all of us on the law faculty would be articulate, but it really took this faculty member aback" that a woman had spoken up and spoken so well. Reflecting on the experience today, while working at a different institution, Isabella acknowledges, "There were some real serious gender issues while I was there."

In contrast, men of color have a relatively straightforward relationship with work colleagues. Vijay is especially close with fellow junior faculty; together, they "talk a lot about issues: faculty governance issues, difficult votes, how things are going in the classroom. We socialize together. We are just a good group." Jorge, a Latino professor, has "strong relationships with the junior faculty" and feels "completely supported by senior faculty too." As a group, they "have lunches, poker night, [an] open door policy." In general, "the vibe is really cooperative and collegial." Michael, a Black professor, says his faculty relationships are "fine," but adds, "I probably need to do more schmoozing [though I'm usually too busy] in the office, class prepping and doing stuff for [students,] and I publish a lot." Still, he and the junior scholars "hang out" occasionally for dinner, and he prioritizes time to "get together" with fellow Black colleagues. There are "one or two [problem faculty]. . . . We don't deal with each other. But those are outliers, they don't deal with anybody."

An Asian American professor named Andrew says, "The vast majority of the faculty are really supportive, helpful, very collegial," though, he adds, "of course there's certainly a faction that is not." Andrew has "a few core people that I go to again and again for help," but there are "a couple that I barely ever talk to [anymore]; though I've tried to interact with them, based on history I know it's not worthwhile." Jack characterizes his overall faculty relationships as "very good," especially spending time "socially [with] the junior faculty" and forging "strong relationships with . . . some of the senior faculty" who, like him, are prolific scholars. He does note "a factional battle among some senior faculty members" that has created "kind of a mess," though "for the most part, I try not to get involved in that." Ryan also has "a very good" relationship with colleagues and believes he has a "unique faculty in the sense that we are very much like one big family." For the most part, "we all get along," with the most challenging moments occurring "during the hiring process, where we experience some disagreement," usually involving diversity issues—again highlighting racial tension in the earliest stages of legal academia. Stuart enjoys working with people who share the "same political views and passion for social justice" while also being "amazing scholars with national reputations." Yet there are "issues with collegiality and civility about race on the faculty that are very, very challenging." Faculty governance has been another "highly contentious" topic on campus, especially involving "whether non–tenure stream faculty can vote and what can they vote on." Stuart sees "the undercurrent of race" in these debates too, since "many of the faculty that have been disenfranchised by these rules . . . are women and people of color," while most of those debating and voting on the policies are white men. He characterizes the past few years as "a rough time on faculty morale." The challenges men of color face when interacting with colleagues revolve around racial diversity.

Senior male scholars of color have endured more contentious relationships, whether this signals recent progress or because issues develop over time. Dwayne is a nationally recognized Black academic whose colleagues "are respectful of me because of my scholarship." Yet even after decades of teaching, a relationship with the faculty "doesn't really exist. I don't associate with them privately. I see them at faculty meetings." A Latino named Fermin joined academia with impeccable credentials but has amassed "formidable friends and formidable enemies over the years—though time took care of most of the enemies." Recounting a conversation with a white male colleague,

Fermin says, "He told me I was only hired because I was Mexican," asserting the perception that Fermin was an "affirmative action" hire who did not belong and was not deserving.[48] At the time, Fermin "was just furious he would say something, even though I secretly knew he felt that way." Yet because an outburst would not serve him well, he flippantly countered, "'When has that ever been a positive here?!'"

The experiences of white men provide a significant contrast to those of their female and faculty of color colleagues. Matt's response when asked about fellow faculty is representative: "I really enjoy my colleagues. There's a lot of collegiality among young faculty, older faculty. It's a nice place to be." Although Matt dislikes the inefficiency of large meetings, his "overwhelming thought when I go [into faculty meetings] is, 'I really like these people.'" None of the women or men of color in the DLA sample responded similarly. Matt and the other white men in the sample mention no stress based on sexual harassment or experiences of silencing from colleagues, as their female colleagues do. Christopher is also "very close" to his colleagues, especially with people who were hired around the same time, including "five couples who socialized together and vacationed together and sort of did everything together" for many years. Ian recognizes that there is a "broad diversity of views" on his faculty but believes there is "a feeling of mutual respect." While he has "good relationships with everyone," he is especially close with "several of my colleagues," meeting socially for "dinner parties [and other events] outside the law school." An even larger group meets frequently for "drinks or having picnics or other events together."

Very few white male faculty members note confrontational or complicated relationships, instead highlighting close interpersonal relationships. Where female faculty and men of color perceive the white male climate pervading the culture of the law school as one that excludes them, white male faculty feel at home.[49] John notes, "I don't have any particular challenges in terms of getting along"—although his female faculty colleagues might see their interactions differently. While white faculty report positive relationships with one another and with colleagues from different racial backgrounds, those feelings are not equally reciprocated—faculty of color characterize these same relationships as less friendly (Tables 4 and 5). A white male named Joe asserts that he has "good relationships with everybody," and though he is especially close to those who research and teach in his field, nobody "would describe us as a clique" because "there aren't any factions" at his school. He insists both that all faculty members "respect and are nice to each other," and that he is comfortable openly expressing his views, whatever they may be, since there is no institutional norm of self-regulation even when saying something that "wouldn't be politically correct or [might] offend somebody." Joe's female faculty of color colleagues may see his comments as politically incorrect or offensive, but he nevertheless feels comfortable speaking his mind. Joe's own comfort speaking out, regardless of the audience or the effects of his words, is a stark contrast to the silencing and emotional labor that characterizes the law faculty experience for women of color. This highlights how raceXgender privilege pervades faculty interactions, again providing qualitative support for the quantitative data presented in Table 6 showing that whites see their colleagues as open-minded even though many faculty of color do not.

3 Connections and Confrontations with Students

HANNAH IS PART OF "A COLLEGIAL FACULTY," where she teaches large sections of a core first-year subject. She feels "very fortunate" to have students who are "kind" and "feel very comfortable with me." In private meetings, students seek clarification on substantive course material but also "ask for advice" on everything from "what to do with their lives, or if they have difficulty in a particular *other* class how to prepare for that, or what courses I might recommend." It also is not unusual for students to "cry in my office because of personal issues." Hannah's first few years of teaching were "so hard," in part because she "was working [the equivalent of] large law firm hours" not only to master the subjects but also to "make the material engaging" and be "as good as I can be for my students." Two white male mentors encouraged her early on to "stop them in the hallway" or "regularly just shoot them questions" over email. In less a decade of law teaching, she has won two teaching honors, one from faculty colleagues and an Outstanding Professor of the Year award from students. Nevertheless, particular students—they "tend to be white men"—regularly challenge her in class and have even badgered her with inappropriate personal questions outside of class. Hannah, a multiracial law professor, has "to do more to prove that I [know what I'm] talking about than I would if I were a white male. I firmly believe that." Her "lighthearted personality" coupled with her "race, gender, and age" make her an easy target for white male students who think, "'She doesn't know what she's talking about'"—and assert their race and gender privilege to test her, even though she is the professor. Some have brought up tangential questions, just "to see if I knew the answer," or asked about "things that were a few pages ahead in the text beyond what the reading assignment was for that given day" to try to trip her up. In the many times she "got challenged," the student would use a "tone of voice that demonstrated it was a challenge rather than a legitimate question," and with a "look on the face [signifying], 'Let's see if . . . she can handle it.'" In response, she "infus[es class with] references to things that demonstrate the depth of my knowledge," relying on prior legal practice to signal her expertise. DLA data confirm that Hannah's experience is representative when she notes, "I feel strongly that it was more confrontational than it would have been if I was a white male."

As Hannah's experience demonstrates, faculty interactions with students can be simultaneously wonderful and trying. DLA data show that women of color faculty members enjoy nurturing relationships with some students but have fraught relationships with others. The vast majority of faculty, regardless of their own background, report "a lot" of interaction with white students, likely because white students are the majority at most schools.[1] While 88% of white men report "a lot" of interaction with white students, faculty from other race and gender groups also report high levels of interaction with white students, including 67% of Latinas, 71% of Black women, 80% of Native American women, 91% of white women, 91% of men of color, and 93% of Asian American women; these statistics bolster existing empirical findings that women of color, white women, and men of color faculty provide significant service not only to female students and students of color but to white male students as well.[2] The Law School Survey of Student Engagement (LSSSE) similarly reports that 76% of law students characterize faculty as "available, helpful, and sympathetic," while a whopping 93% believe their instructors "care about my learning and success in law school."[3]

Although faculty from all backgrounds report frequent interactions with white students, the quality of those interactions differs depending on the background of the faculty member (see Table 7). While the vast majority of faculty enjoy positive relationships with students, less than one-third (29%) of Black women faculty characterize their interactions with white students as "very friendly," compared with almost two-thirds (63%) of white male faculty, and almost three-quarters (73%) of faculty who are white women or men of color.

Qualitative data presented in this chapter highlight many positive faculty-student interactions involving individuals from various racial and

TABLE 7 Quality of Interactions with White Students, by Race and Gender, DLA 2013

		Very friendly	Sociable	Distant	Hostile	Not applicable	Total
African American women	n	6	12	2	1	0	21
	%	28.57	57.14	9.52	4.76	0.00	100.00
Asian American women	n	11	4	0	0	0	15
	%	73.33	26.67	0.00	0.00	0.00	100.00
Latinas	n	6	5	1	0	0	12
	%	50.00	41.67	8.33	0.00	0.00	100.00
Native American women	n	2	2	1	0	0	5
	%	40.00	40.00	20.00	0.00	0.00	100.00
Middle Eastern women	n	0	2	0	0	0	2
	%	0.00	100.00	0.00	0.00	0.00	100.00
Multiracial women	n	3	3	1	0	0	7
	%	42.86	42.86	14.29	0.00	0.00	100.00
Men of color	n	8	1	1	0	1	11
	%	72.73	9.09	9.09	0.00	9.09	100.00
White women	n	8	3	0	0	0	11
	%	72.73	27.27	0.00	0.00	0.00	100.00
White men	n	5	3	0	0	0	8
	%	62.50	37.50	0.00	0.00	0.00	100.00
Total	n	49	35	6	1	1	92
	%	53.26	38.04	6.52	1.09	1.09	100.00

gender backgrounds. Female faculty of color are so in demand that service to students displaces their other obligations. Despite many pleasant student interactions, most women of color faculty also suffer students who challenge their authority both in the classroom and during private meetings. Students also unleash their biases in evaluations, which tend to focus more on the woman of color professor's personal appearance than on her pedagogical approach. This chapter ends with a discussion of gender bias, drawing from data showing that white women have similar gender-based interactions with students, though those of white men and men of color are both less frequent and less fraught.

Positive Personal Interactions

Most women of color faculty enjoy positive interactions with students from all racial/ethnic backgrounds. Many are so accessible that they are overburdened by service.

Role Modeling

Many women of color faculty members are positively glowing about their students. Martha's students are "the best part of the job, really." Laura agrees, stating, "Oh well, of course, your relationship with students is one of the best parts about the job." Similarly, Zahra says that "the best thing about the school is the students. The students are really smart, and I enjoy interacting with them." Grace gushes: "I love my students as a general matter. I always have."

Female faculty of color are especially receptive to students of color and other marginalized students who seek them out. Aisha has "a following. . . . I have my groupies and they follow me from class to class." Imani is also "very close to the students." Because the first institution where she taught had a majority of students of color, "I could earn my stripes as a new teacher in a room full of students that generally looked like me."[4] Perhaps because of their shared identity, Imani's former students accorded her respect from the outset; she therefore "did not have to deal with a lot of the challenges" facing faculty of color at predominantly white institutions "in regards to white male students challenging them and this presumption of incompetence."[5]

Many students at predominantly white institutions are grateful for the few faculty of color employed there.[6] Erin's students "are very hardworking" and "dedicated." The deference they give her may be due, in part, to their being "thankful" to finally have a Native American woman on faculty.[7] Alexandra was inundated "as soon as I got here," with requests to advise student notes, coach trial teams, and "be the faculty advisor for BLSA [Black Law Student Association]." The students "are so excited that I'm here [and] they need involvement from a young woman of color professor." Yet given her additional personal and professional obligations, she struggles to enforce boundaries with needy students.

Overburdened by Service

Most female faculty of color, like Alexandra, are overwhelmed by student requests. Female faculty play a central role in "taking care of the academic family," where they "perform more service than male faculty," especially student mentoring and committee work.[8] Research also indicates that *proportionality* creates more of a burden for underrepresented women of color faculty, who "are called on to do more service when there are fewer of them [on campus]."[9] Because most law schools have at most a handful of female faculty of color, proportionality likely affects each one. Empirical scholarship using law student research subjects has shown that "students of color and white students alike report that faculty of color are often more accessible than whites and that female faculty tend to engage students more than male faculty."[10] By engaging students, underrepresented faculty improve learning outcomes, as

> students who are most frequently engaged in educationally effective practices—studying, participating in class, discussing materials with peers, and receiving feedback from faculty, for example—learn more and are more satisfied than those who [do not].[11]

This accessibility comes through in the DLA data. A Latina law professor named Bianca has "a number of students who frequently stop by my office," some of whom are not even in her classes, but "that just simply know about me or hear about me and want to come get advice about this or that." Haley, a multiracial faculty member, has "a lot of women coming into my office complaining about sexual harassment, stalking, or domestic violence they are experiencing." Likely, "they feel comfortable and they seek my help" because Haley covers these issues in her Criminal Law course, whereas "a couple of the men who teach Crim Law [here] don't cover rape, sexual assault, or domestic violence."[12] Previous literature makes clear that white women, women of color, and men of color are more likely than white men not only to discuss real-life legal implications of the law but also to include relevant context in classroom conversations of substantive law through diversity discussions; empirical scholarship has shown that students from all backgrounds appreciate these opportunities to engage with what is often abstract legal material on a practical level.[13] Not surprisingly, students seek out faculty members who raise these realities in class.[14]

Though rewarding, frequent activities and emotional meetings with students also burden female faculty, creating a gender imbalance in workload. Their "ethic of caring" also leads to the mistaken perception that women of color faculty are *other-mothers*.[15] Treating women of color professors as other-mothers relegates them to the familiar role of "Mammy," where they are "categorized as a service worker, here to provide instead of guide."[16] Students and faculty alike also associate other-mother faculty not "as leaders with positions of power, but instead as caretakers" who should cater to the needs of others.[17] Extra student service obligations facing women of color faculty are but one of "a myriad of demands [that] are placed upon their professional lives," without equal distribution to white male colleagues.[18] Kayla, a Black law professor, notes, "I definitely feel I bear the disproportionate impact—the brunt—of service [especially] to students of color." Students turn to her in times of need in part because of proportionality, as she is one of the few female faculty of color on campus.[19]

A Black law professor named Gabrielle appreciates "the opportunity here to mentor African American students. I spend a lot of time. I do the [Frederick Douglass] Moot Court and all those things with them and all those things are personally rewarding for me." Though rewarding, these experiences take up time that could otherwise be spent on scholarship, class preparation, or even personal endeavors. Research has consistently shown both that women of color faculty take on enormous service responsibilities and that these undertakings are rarely rewarded or even acknowledged when considering their tenure or promotion, course reductions, or yearly bonuses.[20] Jane used to schedule "particular, private meetings" with students even for routine clarification of course material, but she now expects students to make an effort to attend her set office hours. When Jane worked around her students' schedules, her own family life and other work obligations (i.e., research) suffered. Still, she remains accommodating and approachable, admitting, "Even now if someone has a personal issue that they need to talk about, I would always set a private meeting for that purpose."

Classroom Challenges: Dissatisfaction Leads to Confrontation

Despite strong relationships with many students, female faculty endure confrontations from others. Scholarship has begun documenting the ways in which female faculty, particularly female faculty of color, endure a disproportionate share of student challenges.[21] These are especially rampant in the classroom, where "both minorities and women are presumed to be incompetent as soon as they walk in the door."[22] As individuals belonging to two devalued groups, women of color law professors are seen as particularly incompetent and suffer accompanying ordeals. Mariana's first semester in the classroom "was rough." Her students expected an older, white, male professor—virtually the opposite of the young woman of color hired to teach them. As a Black professor named Patricia says, "Their image is the white male professor who scares them, and that's just not a model that I can follow. Not being a white male, and not really being privileged enough to be able to scare them." Grace agrees, noting, "I'm certain that they feel differently when I'm teaching than when the older white male professors [at my school do]." Decades ago, female faculty of color

> were "shouted down in the classroom by white males, shunned by colleagues, had their teaching credentials openly challenged in the classroom, received anonymous and detailed hate notes critical of their teaching style, syntax and appearance and discovered colleagues had encouraged students to act disrespectfully."[23]

Sadly, little has changed. Although there have been numeric increases in faculty diversity, these alone are not sufficient to maximize the benefits of diversity.[24] *Structural diversity*—diversity in numbers—does not automatically translate into meaningful cross-racial interaction, either in the classroom or elsewhere on campus.[25] *Critical mass*, creating sufficient diversity in numbers, is a necessary but insufficient condition for ensuring the benefits we expect from diversity. For actual benefits of diversity to accrue, individuals from various backgrounds must be in mutually respectful environments where they have an opportunity to listen and learn from one another.[26] This environment is not the standard in law schools today, either for faculty or for students. Classrooms would foster more open and honest conversations if there were fewer student disruptions based on bias toward particular faculty. Expectations of an older white male law professor lead students to engage in intersectional discrimination when confronted with a woman of color authority figure at the podium, negatively affecting both teaching and learning.

Presumed Incompetent
Women of color faculty expend significant energy responding to disrespectful students in a way that seeks to maintain control of the class without alienating other students. Erin "was heavily criticized my first year of teaching," both inside and outside the classroom. As part of an end-of-term skit performed on campus in front of faculty, students mocked her publicly by making "a lot of jokes about me having a chip on my shoulder or me having a stick up my ass, just being perceived as being very cold." Clearly, the students felt comfortable publicly airing their crude and critical thoughts about Erin, regardless of her status as their professor and in a way that was not replicated with white male faculty. Aisha has "felt the presumption of incompetence" from students, attributing it to those who have never before encountered a woman of color authority figure. Gabrielle recalls that "for my first couple of years, [students]

were openly disrespectful in the classroom." Emma attributes the pushback to their disappointed expectations:

> They don't necessarily appreciate somebody in my position, as a new professor, as a woman, and as a person of color, having power over them. So I got a lot of push back particularly from male students about, "Do you know your stuff?" "Are you a credible source of authority?" "Why should I listen to this stuff from you?"

Proportionality merges with *tokenism* to further complicate matters. When women of color are admitted into the academy in such small numbers and without meaningful inclusion, they are perceived and made to feel as if they are mere tokens rather than full participants.[27] "Tokenism masks racism and sexism by admitting a small number of previously excluded individuals to institutions" while also limiting their "role options" and maintaining "barriers to entry for others."[28] Because there are very small numbers of female faculty of color at most institutions, each one stands out as starkly different from the white male professors in the majority whom students expect. Coupled with outright racism and implicit bias, this difference translates into doubting the competence of women of color law professors.[29]

Because of this presumption, Emma notes, "I have a harder barrier to prove myself to students, [which includes] proving that I'm qualified to teach them, that I know my material." Gabrielle acknowledges that "being young and looking very young" combines with her race and gender to count against her; the "looks on their faces on the first day of class when it comes to first year students [suggest their confusion and disappointment], 'You can't possibly be my professor!'" Similarly, a tenured professor named Annalisa still feels that "as a small Asian American woman I feel that I have to establish authority in the classroom. I feel that my tall white male colleagues . . . have an easier job of establishing a sense of authority." Annalisa's stature works against her with students who correlate her small size to a lack of authority, especially coupled with responses to her raceXgender identity. Susan noted the disappointed looks on her students' faces on her first teaching day, attributing it to them thinking "they had the dud professor," and comparing their misfortune to the "lucky" other section of law students: "'Oh my god, we got the Black lady teaching us and they got the white guy?!'" Their sense of entitlement to have a white male law professor and the injustice they felt at finding their law professor was a woman of color was palpable.

Aisha sees the students' disappointment at having her as their professor as coming from her position as "a woman of color in front of students that don't see women of color in those positions of power oftentimes and don't know what to do." Mariana got the sense "early on [that] they resented me because I was a woman of color. I didn't look like the other guys [teaching]." Of course, she is correct; with only 771 women of color out of almost 11,000 total faculty nationally, women of color look like neither the traditional law teacher nor most of their faculty colleagues.[30] Increased faculty diversity could help avoid this tokenism. Gabrielle believes that "it might make it seem more normal for me to be at the head of the classroom if there were more people [of color faculty]" in law teaching. Sonia agrees that "there will be presumptions because you're anomalous." Stacey teaches "in a really white place with people who are really white. I don't know how else to describe it!" She notes that for many of her students, "I'm the first Black professor they ever had, maybe even their first professor of color." Accordingly, she witnesses "a lot of ignorance," especially racial insensitivity. Proportionality—the very small numbers of women of color on most faculties—thereby highlights the intersectional raceXgender hostility students display in class.

Confronting the Unexpected Authority Figure

Examples of student confrontations run the gamut—from microaggressions to physical intimidation. Emma uses "the Socratic method" in class, calling on students to answer specific questions. Yet "I've had students who refuse to answer the question and then put me in a spot where I have to enforce my authority that they need to answer." The way that Destiny's students respond to her—even more than what they say—signals their disappointment in having her as a professor; they exhibit a "tone and attitude that they just don't have with some of my male colleagues."[31] She attributes it to "a disbelief" that she is their professor, "just saying things that they would not normally say. My students still get kind of [confrontational, with an attitude like] how dare you try to teach them." Zahra has had faculty observers in class "say to me, 'Wow, I can't believe that so-and-so guy said this to you in class. Like, they would have never done that to X male colleague." The confrontations are always attempts at "challenging me, kind of [saying], 'That doesn't seem right,' [or], 'You're wrong.'" Confrontational students are not only "challenging my knowledge, my ability," but also disrupting her teaching, ruining the learning environment for everyone. Before she started teaching, Zahra had "heard this from other female colleagues: the first couple weeks you watch out because they're going to test your limits, see if you're smart enough, and if you 'win' then they'll stop, but if you don't then they'll continue to do it."

While verbal confrontations are insulting, some female faculty of color also endure open hostility and even gender-based physical intimidation at the hands of white male students. When Grace was a new law professor teaching rape as part of the first-year Criminal Law course curriculum, she encountered a particularly appalling example of white male privilege in class:

> [A] group of white, kind of "frat boy" types . . . were sitting [together] in the classroom. One kid brought in a noose and in response to a question—so he must have planned this—he pulls a noose out from under his desk, holds it up, and says, because he's "well hung." I am certain that would have not have happened to a [white male] professor. It was so shocking.

Lola, a Latina law professor, endured another common first-year incident for female faculty of color: a student who submitted a letter of complaint about Lola to the administration. She recalls:

> I had someone go out of her way to write a very disgusting letter. [Though it was unsigned,] I know who wrote it. This is someone who came to my office four days after I started teaching and told me that I wasn't from around here. And I needed to basically learn how things are done in [this state].

Lola knows she is defying stereotypes, noting, "I shake their sense of reality just by being here, being a female, being a Latina, and teaching what I do [meaning not the] typical 'female' subjects or what a minority 'should' teach." Even without "opening my mouth, I think I disrupt some people's reality" and they act out in response.

Ignorance sometimes spills into open hostility. Gabrielle's first semester teaching "started off very bad, very hostile" because of "some students who were unhappy to have the young Black professor . . . and [they] referred to me outside of the classroom as 'that Black professor.'" After her very first class meeting, "a big group" of students were so "up in arms" about her being their professor that they complained to the assistant dean.[32] Gabrielle recalls that "the basis of their complaint was, 'She's the new professor. We don't want her. We want the other Con Law professor'—who had been teaching for all of two years." While the students built a façade of preferring the other professor because Gabrielle was new, the white male professor's own minimal experience reveals that their deeper (perhaps implicit) rationale for preferring him was likely based on raceXgender bias. Laila also received more than hostile looks on her first day as a law professor:

> I had this young white male come to me and right in my face, right before we start, I hadn't even started teaching yet, I'd just come to the podium and he looked at me and he goes, "Have you ever taught before?" And I looked at him and I said, "Yes." And he goes [angrily], "Yeah, but have you ever taught Torts before?" Literally in that [aggressive] tone and I said, "No, but you'll be okay." He just scowled at me and he walked away.

Sofia recalls that "the very first class that I taught was a disaster." There was "sort of a mutiny" early on not only because her students saw her as a young woman of color but also because she banned laptops, which few others had done at her school. The rest of the semester was "truly dreadful," with a variety of confrontations in each class meeting: "People being very obnoxious and defiant and texting—like having their iPhones out and texting right in front of me." In addition, "three students ran a campaign about how I should lose my job," petitioning the administration.[33] Sadly, once "race was brought up in all of this hostility," she decided to never teach the course again. Similarly a Black professor named Keisha remembers that "one student basically told me that they had other things to do than to do my written assignments." Although failure to complete required coursework would eventually count against the student, his brazen disrespect made for a challenging classroom environment for Keisha and emboldened other students to act out. Women of color can rarely push back against these defiant students, especially without administrative support. Martha notes that "the toughest part of the job is to pretend to be neutral about stuff you don't feel very neutral about." She invests considerable emotional labor keeping her feelings in check, knowing that "if I voice the outrage that I feel even in a mild way, I will be punished for it. So I have to really keep it under control."[34] Otherwise, students will punish her by acting out more and colleagues will punish her by enabling those students. Silencing herself and managing her emotions is a daily struggle, which comes at a cost to her emotional health.

When asked directly about whether there was a racial or gender pattern to the confrontational students, most faculty identify white men as the primary culprits. To be clear, the vast majority of white students, male and female, enjoy positive interactions with faculty from all backgrounds. Yet the few students who do cause disruptions are usually white men. When Patrice thinks of the students who initiate confrontations in the classroom and disrupt learning for fellow students, she says, "They're primarily white men." Armida recognizes that the students who are constantly challenging her "tend to sit together" and are "white, male, [and] arrogant." This is especially true for Armida's second-semester students who "know they've done really well" in their first semester of law school, which gives them "this confidence that they know more than I do," leading to "a lot of challenging within the classroom." Again, their disrespect stems from intersectional raceXgender bias: the students' belief that the woman of color in front of the room is unqualified to teach them. In Armida's experience, the confrontational students are "always white males," whereas her white female students "tend to appreciate what I'm doing," and students of color "relate to me" and act accordingly. Natalie, a multiracial woman, recalls how race and gender contributed in a "huge" way to her early years in the legal academy, when she "was tortured by those standards. Oh, the males, everything you can imagine how women are treated by men students, disrespected and everything like that. In the classroom, out of the classroom, you name it." Once, a white male student "came in forty-five minutes late to a fifty-five minute class and I told him to get out and he had me up against the wall with his finger [in my face] like, how dare I kick him out of the class." Though blatant physical intimidation may be rare, it is still a threat facing female faculty of color.

Patrice, who taught upper-level classes before being assigned a first-year course, was similarly "unprepared for the level of . . . racism and sexism that people have told me about forever but [that] I'd never experienced" in previous upper-level courses. She remembers most vividly "the [white] guys with their baseball caps on backwards that are challenging just everything you are saying." She tried to maintain the upper hand, to not "follow them down that road and try and maintain control of the class and just teach the class, [but] they are like the gnat just driving you crazy!" Despite being a seasoned law teacher, she learned how much of a challenge it is to make first-year students take her seriously when they simply "see young, Black, and female. And I'm not young but I don't think they know how old I am!" Because of these ongoing challenges, Patrice feels "like I just have to work a lot harder to prove my authority and mastery." Patrice does have to work harder than most of her colleagues since she is one of few Black women law professors and therefore battles the presumption of incompetence that accompanies women of color into the classroom.[35]

Private meetings frequently invoke the other-mother perception of women of color faculty, creating additional obstacles. Bianca recalls "my very first semester a student coming in[to my office], and I think he thought he was maybe doing me a favor, and saying, 'I'm just not used to someone who teaches like you,'" suggesting she change her teaching style and pedagogical approach. Bianca was likely this student's first Latina law professor, given the paltry numbers of female faculty of color in legal academia.[36] Yet he either failed to register as disrespectful his request that his law professor change her style to accommodate his preferences or was unabashedly rude. Either way, he expected Bianca to respond as an other-mother, changing her teaching to cater to his needs. Even more dramatically, Trisha recalls, "I had one student tell me once—and he thought he was being a friend—he said, 'I never had a Black woman tell me anything who wasn't dressed in white.'" Initially confused about what this meant, she says, "It took me a minute. I had to think about that. What do you mean, 'Dressed in white'? [Then I realized that] the roles he was assigning me were maid, nurse, [and so on]." Again, the student had relegated his Black female professor to a caretaking role, in line with being an other-mother. As Aisha, Mariana, and others note, they are often the students' first woman of color authority figure; Trisha's student went further by making explicit the service roles he expected Black women should play in his life and his confusion at finding one in a position of authority. Instead, Trisha's student expressed this sentiment to her directly, drawing on his own white male privilege to attempt to put her in her place. Jennifer had a private meeting with a white student who felt she deserved a better grade than the one she earned. Jennifer recalls:

> [The student] was very disrespectful. And when I explained to her why she received the grade she had, she rolled her eyes and crossed her arms and [responded], "Well you didn't explain this right." At one point I just stopped her and said, "I don't think we're communicating in a positive way right now," and so I said, "Maybe we should take a break and check in after we've both had some time to cool down a little bit." And she got up and stormed out of my office. She left and I said, "I think we should talk again." And she said, "No, don't bother."

Even when female faculty of color reach out to be inclusive and understanding, their efforts are rebuffed by students who are unable or unwilling to recognize the authority of women of color faculty, treating them more as service workers than professors.

Biased Student Evaluations

In addition to personal confrontations, course evaluations give students a risk-free opportunity to convey biases anonymously. Many women of color receive comments focused on personal appearance, laced with both subtle and direct racism and sexism.[37] Helen, an Asian American professor, uses the same word to describe both her early teaching evaluations and her emotional response to them: "terrible."

Channeling Sofia Vergara
Brianna notes that teaching evaluations give students an opportunity to be "hypercritical," forgoing comments about their woman of color professor's teaching in favor of critiquing how she looks, dresses, talks, and even moves through the classroom. Trisha's evaluations include many "inappropriate personal comments about my appearance." June had students who seemed focused on style over substance even in class, including a student who "said, 'I came to class [because] I wanted to see what you were going to wear.'" Annie, an Asian American senior scholar, remembers that early in her career "there were a lot of comments about my appearance. I think women tend to get that more than guys." One that stands out is: "'She flips her hair over her shoulder too much.' And actually I'm not a coquettish person; I really don't know how to flirt, and I think this student was interpreting me as being flirtatious." Some students see and respond to female professors of color as sex objects rather than legal experts, envisioning a different type of service work. This betrays both the unprivileged status of being a woman law professor and the biased perception of these professors as women on display for the consumption of the students rather than the intellectual superstars they are.[38]

Because student evaluation comments often focus on race, ethnicity, personal style, sexual orientation, gender, or other topics irrelevant to learning, some faculty members eventually avoid reading them. Danielle is unapologetic, saying: "I don't even read my evaluations anymore. I don't read my evaluations because I know I'm being evaluated based upon things that do not have to do with my teaching ability." She once "got an evaluation that [read],

'She's Black, enough said.' So I'm being evaluated based upon things that have nothing to do with my teaching, like my skin color." Carla is concerned about the students' emphasis on her appearance but tries to approach this fraught reality with humor:

> As a woman, there is a constant kind of student concern with my looks. I know my hotness factor is low [laughing]. Why? Why? I'm not supposed to be Christie Brinkley in the front of the room and yet, am I? Answer: No, I'm not! [B]ut that's another element on which I get graded [on student evaluations]: am I "attractive."

Research indicates a correlation between positive teaching evaluations and (supposedly) "objective" measures of beauty,[39] with professors who are judged to be better looking receiving better evaluations from students, and a significant penalty facing faculty of color deemed unattractive.[40] As a result, women of color must devote time and attention to their personal appearance before walking into the classroom, in a way that few other faculty members do. Women of color must also manage how their own cultural and ethnic perceptions of appropriate attire, style, and beauty will be evaluated.[41] When a Muslim woman uses a hijab to cover her head, students complain. Whether their Black professor's hair is natural, in locks, or in braids, they will write about it in evaluations. While Carla laughingly acknowledges that she does not look like a famous female celebrity, much to the disappointment of her students, her evaluations would likely go up if she channeled Sofia Vergara. Yet that would perpetuate the pattern of students perceiving and responding to her as a sex object—commenting on her hair, style, dress, and other aspects of her appearance rather than on her legal expertise and teaching efficacy. When women are on display, even as law professors, they are still subjected to gender bias, even from their students.

Microaggressions and Biased Comments

Intertwined with volumes of research on raceXgender bias in teaching evaluations,[42] scholars have documented how student evaluations punish traditional "outsiders" for how they look, dress, and speak—regardless of how well they teach.[43] Faculty expressiveness trumps content, especially when students lack motivation.[44] In a recent study, a "charming" actor hired "to spout gibberish" scored higher on evaluations than "a more forthright expert [teaching] actual substance."[45] Distributing chocolate is also "directly correlated with an increase in objective measures of teaching effectiveness."[46]

DLA data highlight the extent to which comments on evaluations are blatantly discriminatory in an intersectional raceXgender way.[47] In one particular semester, Carla's evaluations included allegations that "I let students ask [too many] questions, [as well as that] I don't let students ask questions—very illogical. The numbers were fine but the comments were vicious." The inconsistency of the comments also calls into question their veracity. After Lola's first year of teaching, her evaluations included a number of "very personal comments just unrelated to my teaching. That I was a disgrace. I remember that was one of them. That I was a disgrace to the school, with no basis [given]." Again, if students suggested that Lola were not well versed in a particular area of the law, or that her pedagogical approach were too theoretical or abstract, she could consider varying her technique; simply calling her "a disgrace" attacked her personally without providing an opportunity to improve.

Even women of color with excellent numeric evaluation scores receive comments with racist and sexist undertones. Grace's evaluations "have been fabulous" at every institution where she has taught; yet on occasion she does "get the random comment from students, like, 'Professor Grace doesn't like white people,'" without explanation. June had especially vicious evaluation comments "early in my career," including "this statement: 'I know we have to have affirmative action, but do we have to have this woman?' That was pretenure," so could be used against her later.[48] These comments neither explain student difficulty mastering the material nor provide suggestions for an alternative pedagogical approach; they simply exploit stereotypes about women of color, attempting to stigmatize the professor by labeling her as undeserving of her position. Similarly, Aisha gives the following examples from past evaluations, when she exactly tracked material from her casebook: "'Don't know why she's teaching.' 'She's terrible.' 'You should have hired somebody else.' 'There was not enough law.' 'There was not enough [state] law.' 'Too much social science.'" Natalie's comments frequently have subtle racial and sexual overtones, including evaluations that "run the gamut from 'Why doesn't she wear her wedding ring? Is she trying to tease us?' to 'She thinks she's so smart [though actually she isn't].'"

Lola's evaluations have "more microaggressions than blatant racist comments,"[49] though plenty of student detractors have been overtly nasty:

"She's not very smart." "She's not prepared." "She's hostile." The "hostile" comment seems to come up at least once a semester on the evaluations. And it's consistent with the comments that the Black professors [here] are getting.

Lola is not facing an individual problem—in which students identify concerns about her teaching that she can address through careful response—but is on the receiving end of a larger structural problem where course evaluations are used as an avenue to denigrate female faculty of color by drawing from intersectional raceXgender bias, sometimes causing dire and long-lasting professional consequences.[50] Stacey has reached "a point where I'm really kind of bitter and I'm just sick of it." Because she is "the only person, or one of very few" at her current institution who encourages diversity discussions in the classroom,[51] her doing so "stands out" and students accuse her of "hav[ing] an agenda, even if they like me. Oh, they like me, but they're still unfair to me. You know, I can read it in their comments, and I see it in their numbers" on the evaluations. But because "my white colleagues don't think about" how evaluations may be biased against women of color, Stacey worries that they see her as less accomplished when her "numbers" (i.e., scores from evaluations) are lower than she merits. This only drives her to work harder. Although doubling down professionally may be an effective "strategy as resistance to a negative campus racial climate," it comes at an exhausting cost of constant work coupled with the fear that no amount of success will overcome the intersectional discrimination, gender disadvantage, and implicit bias working against them.[52] This contributes to the Clyde Ferguson syndrome, worsening the mental and physical health of women of color faculty.

Of course, some students write glowing remarks on evaluations of female faculty of color—especially those students who specifically seek out these faculty for private meetings and have other shared experiences with them.[53] When students reveal their background in evaluation comments, their appreciation in private meetings often tracks their enjoyment of the course and the professor. Vivian recalls that she was "shocked" after her first teaching experience as she "was reading these evaluations saying, 'Oh, she's a terrible teacher,' and 'I didn't learn anything.'" She then read another evaluation in the same batch "from a student saying, 'I am a woman of color. This is the first class that I've taken at this law school that has made me feel like a human being.'" Although the negative evaluations did not specify the race or gender of the writer, most were likely from the white students who constituted the majority of students in her class, including those who presumed her incompetent and openly challenged her.

Comparison and Contrast

Classroom teaching raises challenges for almost all new faculty. White men in the DLA study admit that the material and workload are difficult—though none face student confrontations, manage a presumption of incompetence, or endure vicious comments about their appearance. Men of color hew to a middle ground, devoting less time to students overall but facing some race-based issues. White women, in contrast, have experiences that parallel those of women of color—investing in students to the point of overload, navigating complicated classroom dynamics, and enduring gender-based slights in evaluations. This section, separated into comparisons by interactions and in evaluations, highlights how gender bias may even overshadow intersectional discrimination when dealing with students.

Contrasting Student Interactions

Some men of color make a concerted effort to connect with students. Vijay's "relationship with students is very positive," perhaps because he "believe[s] faculty members are there to serve the students." He is never considered an other-mother, and easily maintains boundaries along with his caring attitude. A small percentage of men of color share the experience of their female counterparts of being inundated by student requests—leaving less time for research and other responsibilities. Stuart knows he carries this burden because of proportionality, as "the diversity of the students is much [higher] than the diversity of the faculty in terms of mere numbers, [which means that] faculty of color are inundated with all this extra work." Stuart is "constantly asked to advise on papers and for groups and to go to events," especially by students of color. Although he "want[s] to do as much as [I] can," he has "little kids at home and it makes it difficult." The literature supports his perception that students disproportionately seek out faculty of color, concluding that students of color "simply feel that there is no one else on the faculty who can understand their problems or who really cares about resolving them."[54] A Black professor named Michael "handpick[s] mentees from the 1L class" and is so devoted to them that he "stay[s] up at night thinking about them and how to get them the next opportunity." While Michael—like Vijay and Stuart—puts "a lot of time and a lot of investment" into his mentees, most men in the DLA sample do not.

Men of color also face race-based challenges from students. Michael uses a pedagogical approach that differs from the norm at his institution, including cold-calling on students using the Socratic method; the students "don't like it, so they complain about it." He makes clear to the students that their "grade isn't dependent" on their answers; "I even tell my students, 'I'm not here to terrify you,'" and suggests relaxation techniques they can employ to stay calm. Still, some resist his authority. Michael "had a student who would routinely show up five or ten minutes late, and he would have to walk behind me [at the podium] to get to his chair." Michael eventually took the student aside to "say, 'Look, that's disrespectful. You can't do that.'" He also has endured "students who answer their cell phones in class," and otherwise push back. He is not surprised, rationalizing, "When you're the young Black guy who . . . doesn't teach like others, students probably are unhappy," especially if they expected the older white male professors that teach their other classes. Dwayne remembers it was "very difficult" when he first started teaching decades ago, in part because he "spent eighteen-hour days preparing" for class. He "had a good rapport with the students" so "enjoyed it" overall. Yet one white male student specified that he "did not want to take instruction from a Black person." Dwayne believes that because the student "hadn't been around Black people and everything he had heard about Black people was negative," the student "without even really experiencing my class, as a preemptive, went to the associate dean [to say] that he wanted out of my [course]"—drawing on his own white male privilege to request a move out of a Black professor's class.

The experiences of most white men and some men of color in the DLA study differ considerably from those of female faculty of color. Ed, a multiracial man, and Ian, a white man, offer interesting and representative contrasts. While Ed's relationship with students overall is "pretty good," even the students of color "really don't lean on me." He admits, "I've never been a professor who students approach when they have issues." Similarly, Ian notes, "I probably don't have as deep a relationship with students where I'm their first call for situations or issues." Students' first call is likely to the female faculty and especially the female faculty of color they sense as the most receptive to addressing their needs.

While many women of color fight against those challenging their authority in the classroom, students respect white men and men of color alike.

Adam, a white man, says, "I really like our students," and recalls no issues with authority or confrontations. Joe, like almost all faculty in the DLA sample, found his first days of teaching "very stressful," in part because he was new to the material and "wasn't as in command of the subject matter" as he would have liked. Nevertheless, within "a month or two, I got the hang of it and everything felt fine." His only difficulty was mastering the material, not fighting to earn respect. When Joe reflects on the large first-year classes he taught, he remembers that he "enjoyed that" in part because the students were "intimidated by me." Joe's students were so respectful of their white male professor that they rarely interacted with him at all—the opposite of the confrontations facing female faculty of color in the classroom and expanded service duties to students outside the classroom.

Similarly, when asked to reflect on his first year teaching, an Asian American named Andrew recalls, "It was overwhelming how much work it was," even in comparison to earlier full-time positions as a judicial law clerk and law firm associate. Yet Andrew had no confrontations from students or challenges to his authority. Instead, "even my first year, everyone was supportive." Now, "looking back, I feel that the quality of my teaching wasn't great." Yet Andrew nevertheless "consistently got amazing reviews and feedback from the students."[55] Andrew's male privilege in the classroom afforded him a measure of respect absent from the classrooms of his female colleagues, enabling him to focus on mastering the material, with his students encouraging and supporting him as he improved.

Susan, a Black professor, once went to great efforts to answer a complicated student question in class; discussing it later with her white colleague Tim, she realized he had an easy out that was unavailable to her:

> Tim was like, "You know, gosh, I would definitely have said, 'I don't know, I'm going to have to get back to you on that,'" which is the privilege of being a white man; you can say, "I don't know," and it's not going to damn you to being the ignorant law professor. But I don't have that privilege.

If Susan were to admit ignorance, she would confirm existing intersectional raceXgender stereotypes: that she is incompetent, that she is an unqualified "affirmative action hire," that she is not fit to teach law.

The experiences of white women are similar to those of women of color, regarding their enjoyment of student interactions, the overwhelming amount of service to students, and the confrontations that occur in the classroom and beyond. Chloe says, "To me the students are the best part of any law school." Yet her first year teaching involved numerous student issues involving "who's in control of the class." These challenges to Chloe's classroom authority parallel what many of the Black, Latina, Asian American, Middle Eastern, Native American, and multiracial women faculty face. Ava recalls that when she first started teaching more than a decade previously, "I was one of the few women in the building and certainly the only young one." That may be why she "got surrounded by students all the time [who] wanted my attention." Because her colleagues contributed less to students, Ava personified research revealing that women are "weigh[ed] down . . . with university service and mentoring responsibilities," taking on disproportionately more than men.[56] Although Ava "wanted to be the professor that [was always] available for them," when she gave her students full access, "they would just suck up every ounce of time I ever had." A pre-tenured professor named Madison finds it "easy" to interact with her students, especially as most "are not hesitant to come into the office or to send an email and ask a question." Yet she recognizes that "there is a challenge being a younger-looking female professor," especially because there are always some "male students" who end up "challenging your authority." When white male students draw on their racial and gender privilege, even white female faculty pay a price.

Comparing Evaluations

White male law faculty, representing at least 43% of all legal academics nationally, enjoy generally positive student evaluations. When recalling his success in the classroom, Joe notes that "my teaching evaluations have always, consistently been very strong." This is true of virtually every white male professor in the DLA sample. Justin's teaching evaluations are "on the whole very positive," despite his coming "to class a little scatterbrained." His first semester as a law professor, he taught a large Criminal Law section to students who "cut me a lot of slack, so it was nice and a lot of fun." The generous students and his clear enjoyment of the first-year teaching experience are at odds with how most women of color view the early years. Ian's students see him as "one of the most challenging professors," but instead of complaining about the workload, "they appreciate that, in terms of the subject and expectations I set." John's evaluations from students are also "really strong, [above] the college average [on numerical scoring. Plus the] written comments are almost always very positive." Again, the experience of these white men is in stark contrast to those of their women of color colleagues, most of whom endure negative as well as inappropriate raceXgender-based comments.

Male faculty of color also enjoy positive evaluations, with occasional comments tinged with intersectional bias. Dwayne is proud that, over the years, "my teaching was good. I got very good teaching evaluations." Asim, a Middle Eastern professor, says his evaluations "have been good. In the small courses they are very strong; in the required classes they started out middle-of-the-road but have gotten very strong too." Vijay laments that he had a rocky start to teaching, although even then his evaluations were more positive than he expected. He thinks the students were "overly generous" with him and "were not as hard on me as they should have been." He "talked to the dean about it, and he said, 'That's common.'" Perhaps it is, for men. For women of color faculty, it is much more common for students to be unreasonably demanding and complain about style while ignoring substance. Over time, Vijay's evaluations have gotten even stronger: "I routinely get perfect [scores] from a majority of the students. Some students have said I'm the best professor there, or best professor they've had." He is especially grateful that the glowing reviews "give me a lot of confidence going into the promotions process" ahead of him, in stark contrast to the ways in which evaluations stymie the process altogether for some women of color.[57]

Not all comments written about men of color are positive. Comments from Michael's student evaluations include numerous complaints: "'He doesn't answer our questions.' 'He's teaching Black history in class.' 'Maybe he doesn't know this material particularly well, after all it's not his research. And he's a new professor.'" They voice a suspicion based in racial animus—whether implicit or overt—that Michael may not be qualified to teach them. In five years of teaching at his current institution, Ryan "won [teacher of the year] twice." Students do not directly confront him or challenge his authority in the classroom or in private meetings. Ryan regularly receives excellent scores on teaching evaluations, which are "anywhere between 98% [and] 100% in just about every category." Nevertheless, anonymous comments have accused him of "picking on the police," and called him both "a racist and a sexist." One student mentioned that she was a woman and said Ryan "made her afraid in the classroom," drawing from intersectional raceXgender stereotypes to construct a criminal persona of her Black male professor.

Many white women have consistently strong evaluations. Scarlett is new to her tenure-track position, although she previously taught as a fellow and visiting assistant professor. Over the years, she says, "I always have good classes [and usually earn] the best reviews you could ever get, like the students have loved every class I've taught." Similarly, when asked about her evaluations, Jordan responded, "They are excellent."

Yet gender bias clouds many evaluations. Isabella has "always had extremely good teaching evaluations" and has "been professor of the year" multiple times. Nevertheless, she says, "I hate teaching evaluations," in part because "when I was a younger faculty, they would always talk about what I wore and things that are so irrelevant." A white lesbian professor named Sydney has "really good" teaching evaluations and recently won a university-wide teaching award, though negative and irrelevant comments stand out to her as well. She notes, "My evaluations included mean things about why it's 'offensive' the way that I dress, [such as,] 'She makes herself gender neutral and that's offensive.'" There is no accompanying explanation of how Sydney's choice of dress and personal style are relevant to teaching effectiveness, let alone how presenting oneself as gender neutral could be offensive. Sydney knows that the comments are "due to my gender and [sexual] orientation and the way that [students] responded to those things." For Sydney, "the experience of reading [evaluations is] so bad and that's why I haven't read my evaluations since [early on]. Which isn't to say I don't want to improve my teaching, I care a lot about that. But I don't think evaluations are the way," especially when they are focused on style, ignore substance, and invoke intersectional (gender×sexual orientation) bias.

Despite the challenges facing white women, and ongoing gender bias, the intersectional race×gender bias plaguing women of color is even more pronounced. When Ellen taught Property at a previous institution, a colleague "was also teaching Property, [using the] same book. Our syllabi were identical and our coverage and approach was the same." The main difference is that Ellen is a white woman, while her colleague was "an African American woman with natural hair." In spite of their identical coverage, their evaluations were starkly different:

> [My colleague] got comments all about her "crazy civil rights agenda" on her student evals. I didn't, not one. Did we both cover the Civil Rights Act? Yes. Did we both touch on issues of race and issues of privilege in a whole lot of different ways? Yes.

Ellen believes it is "easier for me" as a white woman to bring up issues of race with students than it is for women of color. She is "familiar with all the literature essentially saying that when you do this it's not part of your own agenda because these are not 'your own people' or 'your own concerns.'" Ellen's experience that semester, especially in comparison to her colleague's challenges, "really reinforced my commitment to [incorporating diversity discussions in the classroom]," in part to normalize it so that female faculty of color are not penalized for doing so. Intersectional discrimination—drawing from stereotypes involving race, gender, sexual orientation, and other devalued identity characteristics—continues to plague faculty in legal academia, especially in student interactions and on evaluations.

4 Tenure and Promotion Challenges

L OLA HAS RECEIVED "a lot of really inappropriate comments" on student evaluations over four years of law teaching. She initially dismissed them as "mean" and "racist," expecting her colleagues would also see them as a product of intersectional (raceXgender) bias, as she is the first Latina on the faculty. But she was in for a rude awakening. Lola "went up for promotion last year," the "first minority" to apply for advancement from assistant to associate professor at her school. After the faculty vote, she was summoned to a "tense discussion" where "the dean tells me, 'You've met all of the criteria, but we're not giving you promotion.'" Lola stands by her teaching, service, and scholarship, believing she was denied based on "informal criteria," namely "who likes you and who doesn't." Though the dean asserted that Lola's "teaching evaluations were a bit polarized," Lola notes, "I don't know how much more I can improve. I'm almost at the 100% mark for everything" numerically, despite receiving some "[biased] comments." Her colleagues "couldn't get me on scholarship because I published more than they require," and her service efforts "to mentor and really guide" students helps propel them "into successful attorneys." Teaching effectiveness as measured by student evaluations was the "only thing they could knock." A year after the denial, she notes, "Ironically, I got awarded professor of the year yesterday, so everything came full circle." Her colleagues have also "come to learn that [the whole ordeal] was a huge screwup and [they made] a complete huge mistake." Lola now knows that "at this school, they ride a fine line between doing things that are professional and doing things that might trigger a lawsuit." She also has learned that "white men and white women have gotten *tenure* on less criteria than I had [for] promotion." Armed with this new knowledge, when she applies for advancement next year, "if I don't get tenure, I'm suing the school."

Tenure, "that important gateway to professional success and stability" that leads to "virtually unrivalled job security," is also "the crucial institutional process through which the legal academy could block or open the doors to gender and racial integration."[1] Those doors remain partially obstructed, with women of color obtaining tenure at lower rates than white men and enduring intersectional challenges along the way.[2] Elaine notes of tenure, "I don't think it changes your life on a day-to-day basis, but it certainly changes the fact that you don't feel quite as vulnerable." June shares, "I felt tenure freed me to really do whatever I felt like doing or writing. [Once I had it,] I felt I had freedom, and so I just kept cranking [out publications]."

Each requirement of tenure serves as an intersectional barrier preventing women of color from maximizing success in legal academia, contributing to the unequal profession. Tenure basics include examples of tenure done right as well as common problems facing women of color faculty. Overwhelming service burdens leave little time for scholarship, while particular methods and topics of scholarship are devalued or even denigrated. The intersectional discrimination and implicit bias that characterize the hiring process, faculty relationships, and student interactions are even more pronounced at the tenure and promotion phase, affecting women of color faculty disproportionately. The chapter concludes with data on white and male faculty perceptions of tenure, revealing the culprit of intersectional bias.

Intersectional raceXgender barriers explain in part why women of color have historically earned tenure at lower rates than white men. In 2005, the AALS Committee for the Recruitment and Retention of Minority Law Faculty released a report comparing rates of tenure among faculty by race and gender.[3] Table 8 presents data from that report revealing wide disparities in tenure and promotion percentages seven years after initial hiring as a tenure-track assistant or associate professor.[4] Almost two-thirds (63%) of women of color who are expected to attain tenure have not done so after seven years, compared to under one-third (29%) of white women and white men.

A recent publication similarly reports that "despite significant progress toward more diversity, women and scholars of color face continued difficulties," especially with tenure.[5] Those empirical findings reveal that 35% of

TABLE 8 Attainment of Tenure by Tenure-Track Professors, by Race and Gender, AALS Committee for the Recruitment and Retention of Minority Law Faculty 2005

		Total	TENURED		UNTENURED	
		n	*n*	*%*	*n*	*%*
People of color	Women	19	7	36.8	12	63.2
	Men	22	10	45.5	12	54.5
	All	**41**	**17**	**41.5**	**24**	**58.5**
Whites	Women	45	32	71.1	13	28.9
	Men	83	59	71.1	24	28.9
	All	**128**	**91**	**71.1**	**37**	**28.9**
Total		169	108	63.9	61	36.1

female professors of color report the tenure process as unfair, compared to only 12% of white men; similarly, 61% of female faculty of color "disagreed with the statement that the tenure process was easy," compared to only 33% white male professors, indicating the relative ease with which most white men achieve tenure.[6]

Tenure Basics

Most law schools require successful applicants for tenure to demonstrate excellence in teaching, scholarship, and service. For Emma, "the process is to have a review by my law school faculty that includes getting external review of my scholarship by outside scholars in my field, as well as teaching evaluations, and service evaluations. So teaching, research, and service are the three categories by which tenure is evaluated." At Danielle's school, the applicant will first "submit a letter of application/letter of intent describing your scholarship, teaching, and service." Then, colleagues "come to view your class, they look over your scholarship, and they ask you about your service." Smita's law school follows "a fast process" in which faculty members "go up for tenure for most people in your fourth or fifth year of teaching." Formally, the policy states that applicants should have "two full-length articles written," plus "quite a bit in terms of committee work and other activities like coaching a moot court team." However, demonstrating effective teaching "is the most onerous part of our tenure requirements" because it includes a "classroom visitation process, which is over two semesters and requires every member of your tenure sub-committee—so, five people—to visit each of your classes twice," resulting in an "exhausting" "total of forty hours of class visitation."

Though exhausting, Smita's policy is relatively transparent. Aarti, an Asian American professor, is also grateful for clarity: "I mean, it's definitely a stressful process, but I can imagine it being much more stressful if it was less transparent." In contrast, April laments, "The tenure process at my school is vague and not exactly laid out." Applicants know that they "have to publish a certain amount of articles, but nobody really knows what the amount is." They are "judged on scholarship" in addition to service and teaching effectiveness—assessed primarily by student evaluations. Yet the expectations are unclear, facilitating differential application and abuse.[7] Bianca suffered through an unsuccessful bid for tenure that "was absolutely mysterious, confusing, and just filled with deceit." Looking back, she partially blames herself for the tenure denial, recognizing that "I was naïve about it all, so I didn't understand it" and expected "the whole system [to be] much more fair than it turned out to be."

Even when policies are clearly laid out, the way that various requirements are applied to women of color and other underrepresented faculty affects both the process and the outcome. As Alicia notes, "The criteria are maybe a little bit less opaque than other institutions, but then of course how they are applied is still a different story." At Zahra's school, the "formal policy is you have to publish about three or four articles [within five years] and your teaching evaluations have to be pretty good, not amazing. And then you have to do citizenship—so serve on your committees; citizenship also includes service outside of the school." Yet applicants are actually assessed by additional unwritten standards: "I think informally what [is required is] like five articles, at least one a year is recommended, and teaching evaluations should be really good. Citizenship doesn't really count outside of the law school [just] mostly committee work that's really important to the school." The unwritten policies can easily trip up nontraditional faculty who are unaware of additional requirements.

Recent research suggests that a negative campus climate, challenging law school culture, and implicit bias contribute to the overall "negative themes" characterizing the experience of many women of color in legal academia.[8] Although the qualitative DLA data confirm this, the survey data alone indicate general satisfaction with the tenure process, despite intersectional (raceXgender) differences. When asked about their level of agreement with the statement "I am satisfied with the tenure process at my law school," a full 100% of white men and white women agree, along with smaller percentages of men of color (91%) and women of color (57% of multiracial women, 60% of Native American women, 75% of Latinas, 87% of Asian American women, and 91% of Black women).[9]

Tenure Done Right

Although the majority of male and female faculty members from all racial/ethnic backgrounds are satisfied with the tenure process, many women of color substantiate earlier research indicating intersectional (raceXgender) bias.[10] Some female faculty of color find the tenure process at their law school relatively straightforward. Imani appreciates that at her institution "there's really not a lot of unwritten rules that I hear about at other institutions." She notes the transparency of the process and clarity of the standards as central to her own positive experience: "We have a very clear standard. When faculty are voting they make their votes based on that standard, so for me it was very positive."

Many faculty of color ensure that they far exceed the required standards for promotion, safeguarding their application with a "buffer" of extras. Emma has a general rule of thumb for professional success as a multiracial woman: "whatever the marker of success is, that I meet and exceed it." Laura "did twice as much as I probably needed to do for tenure," including "a record number of publications and a book, which was kind of unprecedented. Nobody [before me] had that many publications." Tenure "was a good process for me" specifically because she "had way over the top of what was expected." After spending years working diligently toward tenure, the actual process was similarly "very easy" for Melissa. Because she had planned "to exceed all tenure requirements," her application included "four times the [number of] articles [required]; I built a program; I'd been the diversity person the entire time I've been here; [and] I received two teaching awards." For Keisha, the process was "a little bit stressful" though she felt "pretty good about it because I felt that I had done everything that I needed to do" as well as "everything that I could do." She "exceeded all service requirements," demonstrated that her "teaching was effective" (including mastering "several . . . different courses in a short period of time"), and "exceeded the scholarship requirement by four articles, technically, but two articles by practice." This last acknowledgment demonstrates that Keisha had also investigated the informal requirements of tenure, understanding that the written policy required three articles, the expectation was five—and producing seven to be safe.

After being denied tenure, Bianca moved to a new institution where she "basically just walked right into tenure. It was really very easy," with clear guidelines and a supportive faculty. Vivian also had a positive experience with tenure, saying, "I felt very empowered. Nobody ever questioned the content of what I wrote. I remember somebody saying to me, 'You know, it seems as if you're tenured [already].' I never really felt vulnerable." Vivian's comfort through the tenure process came from both internal and external sources. Her dean supported her scholarship and other contributions, as did her colleagues; just as meaningfully, she developed close connections with academics of color outside of her school, saying, "I think because of the warmth and supportive nature of these people of color networks that I encountered before I started teaching, I felt very supported from outside as well—which I think was important."

Alicia also drew from supportive communities, saying, "The other piece of advice that I remember that was incredibly useful was to develop a network outside of the school." As with Vivian, mentors, sponsors, communities, and allies often help guide junior faulty through the labyrinth of academia.[11] Brianna notes, "I think mentors are really important for everybody's path. For mine they were instructive and they were instrumental in terms of the information that was shared, but also the support that was provided." Patrice also relied on mentors through the tenure process—both for practical advice and political tactics:

> I had really good mentors who were also fantastic political strategists who were able to give me the advice early on, the pitfalls to avoid, the people to be nice to, and the kind of the stuff they'd be looking for in my [tenure] packet. So I never felt I was just left hanging, and I feel so lucky for that because I've run into so many women of color who feel like they reinvented the wheel, or [had been kept] in the dark about the whole process. They had no idea what was expected of them. Everything was just really explicit [for me].

Hannah recalls that "the tenure process was wonderful," also crediting "mentorship by senior faculty members." One white female faculty member "took me under her wing, so that's the first person I think of as a mentor." Also, at

Hannah's institution, "the rules and the expectations were incredibly clear. I knew exactly what I needed to do" to achieve tenure, which facilitated both her process and successful outcome.

Hannah and other female faculty of color rely on mentors who themselves are not women of color—whether white women, white men, or men of color. Karen's primary mentor early on was "an older white man who for years was so critical to shepherding me through the process of getting tenure." He not only "read all of my stuff" but also prepared her for tenure by explaining, "'This is what you need to do. This is what you should be worried about. This is what you shouldn't be worried about.' So it was really great." Especially when there are few tenured women of color, junior female faculty of color must rely on those with different backgrounds to facilitate the process. Mariana is the first "female brown person" to earn full professor in her state; the tenure process itself was "scary and frightening because you are a woman of color and you're the only one at the time [so] you're just a little bit isolated." Yet colleagues from different backgrounds and women of color at other institutions encouraged her.[12] While she occasionally worried whether her record would be sufficient to earn tenure, "I was told repeatedly I would be fine." Her mentors were right.

Challenges with the Trifecta

While some female faculty of color enjoy relatively smooth sailing, the tenure or promotion process for others is rough. Frequently, these barriers are not purposeful or overtly discriminatory, although intersectional (raceXgender) challenges and implicit bias affect each of the tenure requirements: teaching, service, and scholarship. Some who face hostility answer with resignation; others respond with litigation.

Teaching Barriers

The many classroom confrontations and biased evaluations discussed earlier affect not only day-to-day teaching and learning but also the ability of women of color law professors to succeed professionally. Tenure denials are a common response for those who cannot meet the emotional labor required of women of color in the classroom, performing the role students expect of them regardless of their true feelings, innate style, or preferred pedagogical approach.[13] Aisha recently received word of her "unanimous tenure vote, but that's only because my promotion process [from assistant to associate professor] was so incredibly horrible." Promotion involves "a full on review of your teaching, scholarship, and service," including external review of research. Although Aisha was and still is confident that "I had met and exceeded the standard," nevertheless, "My faculty voted me down." They not only denied her promotion, but also "refused to give me any reasons at all as to why," although "rumors floating around" suggested that "the issue was teaching." Whereas her promotion subcommittee had noted that she exceeded the standards for teaching, highlighting how her evaluations had steadily improved over time, the full faculty "made a lot of hay out of my first semester in my first year of teaching" when her evaluations were weaker. Aisha's full faculty refused to see her trajectory of improvement and instead "took those [early] teaching evaluations—which were a bell curve so they weren't skewed too horribly, they were curved—and they essentially asserted that that proved that I was an incompetent teacher." This was their excuse to block her promotion.

A Native American named Mia also endured a horrific tenure process, admitting in her DLA interview, "Well, this is my tenure year and I knew that the faculty would vote no." As the first woman of color hired onto "an all-white faculty" except for two other people of color, even Mia's hiring had been contentious. When she was a job candidate, "several members of the faculty" who opposed the dean's attempts "to build diversity in the faculty" "had voted no in the hiring meeting," though Mia was hired over their objections. In response, this "contingent from day one [said] that they did not want to hire me and said they would vote no in the tenure process," regardless of her performance. Mia moved forward with her application in order to document the intersectional challenges she had faced in the academy:

> So what I decided to do was to put together a dossier as much for me to reflect on my time here and developments here, as well as to try to explain to them— because I don't think they realize how I was treated; I don't think they get it. So it was to reflect for myself and to try and explain to them how I felt I was treated, and in doing that to also create an official record.

Ultimately, "what I knew would happen, happened." Rather than formally state their opposition to diversity, her colleagues claimed that she "does not meet expectations in teaching." They reached this conclusion "even though I had positive peer reviews" from colleagues, countering early "student evaluations [that] were below average." Furthermore, even though she suggested appropriate scholars to conduct outside review of her niche scholarship, "they got nobody with that criteria," instead selecting faculty unfamiliar with her area of research. Mia considered confiding in a mentor from outside her institution but "was terrified to tell her" about the situation, confessing, "I felt like I had failed her." The intersectional challenges that plagued her from day one ultimately removed her from legal academia altogether.

Unrewarded Service

Most law schools also demand that successful tenure applicants demonstrate a commitment to service, whether to the institution, the broader community, or the public at large. Women of color faculty tend to easily satisfy this requirement, given their significant investment in caretaking on campus.[14] Yet service priorities "have an impact on productivity in other areas of faculty effort such as research and teaching," which have a greater impact on overall success in academia.[15] Though most institutions evaluate tenure using teaching, service, and scholarship, the three are rarely weighted equally. Emma's colleagues respect what "is typical in academia, which is the strength of one's scholarship" over both teaching and service. Most institutions value both scholarship and teaching significantly more than service. When asked what is valued at her law school, Alexandra responds, "I say scholarship and teaching." As a result, one of her mentors is always "saying to say no" to service work and "tells me, 'You are not going to *not* get tenure over service.'"

Service is personally important to many faculty. Emma's "personal values involve being part of a team, working with people to achieve common goals, thinking about service to others, [and] service to the public." She maintains a "public service way of thinking," from prior government work, though she sees academia as more "individualistic and very much driven on individual success." Women of color often pick up the slack of service, meeting with students, advising organizations, and serving on university committees.[16] Carla has served so long on so many labor-intensive committees—including "the appointments committee, the rank and tenure committee, faculty misconduct, and decanal review"—that she is seen as someone who has "specialized" in them all. Haley regularly works twelve-hour days, mainly because of burdensome "committee work [including] projects . . . that nobody else will do." She muses, "I only teach three days a week, but I'm in there every day for early mornings and long after [class working on] things that aren't teaching or writing that end up consuming a lot of my time." After serving on the

Appointments Committee in her first year in law teaching, Valeria was selected as chair in her second year. Proportionality again comes into play, as few faculty can be diverse representatives of their schools, and schools strive to highlight diversity when recruiting.[17] Valeria recalls, "They were like, 'We would really like for you to take this. We think you could handle it. We think you're a great representative for the school. So what do you say?'" She said yes. She does appreciate the opportunity but knows it is a huge task for a second-year professor who should be focused on building her scholarly portfolio to secure tenure.

Extra service responsibilities create a central dilemma for many women of color. Often, the tasks they are offered align with their own values and priorities, potentially improving student or faculty diversity, or bringing a unique perspective to virtually any group, as one of few people of color at their schools. Yet their extra service benefits the institution greatly while potentially hindering individual faculty whose contributions go unrewarded. Brianna suggests that "disparate 'housekeeping' requirements" performed by other-mothers who are responsible for taking care of the academic family constrain particular groups because "of the extra burdens of service that people of color carry."[18] Women of color faculty rarely receive extra rewards, recognition, or remuneration for extra service. Instead, it is expected. Grace missed an opportunity for summer funding for those developing "innovative ways of teaching," though she was doing just that; her associate dean "said to me, 'I told the dean not to give you that [funding] because you . . . would do it anyway,'" feeding Grace's frustration of "the sheer amount of service that certain groups do disproportionately" without reward.

Publish or Perish

While most schools adhere to the tenure trifecta—teaching, service, and scholarship—the litmus test for most schools is scholarship. Colleagues may make excuses for less-than-stellar teaching or lower-than-average service, but an assistant professor who does not publish will likely not be promoted.[19] Unfortunately, the realities of both teaching and service create intersectional (raceXgender) barriers for women of color to excel at scholarship. Those who excel generally do so in spite of the extra time they spend on service and managing or mitigating classroom confrontations. The cost of this "daily grind of service" is that it "actively limits women's research time."[20]

For an Asian American female law professor named Chris, "the biggest tension [involves] trying to figure out . . . how much time and energy to put into scholarship as opposed to service work." She admits that "that's the biggest criticism that I've been getting since I started my career, that I'm doing too much service work" at the expense of scholarship, likely because she gets "a lot of energy and personal satisfaction" from performing service. While "[o]n the one hand I recognize that and I do want to spend more time on scholarship," both because she enjoys it and because her institution values it, "on the other hand, I feel like I have this privilege [as an academic, so I want to] make sure that those resources make it out to the community, that we are not an ivory tower." Imani has realized that "when it's time to do scholarship, I often do that outside of the office. She must literally flee the many students, colleagues, and other service responsibilities that surround her on campus in order to write. Vivian admits that when juggling her various personal and professional responsibilities, "the thing that continually gets short shrift is my own writing." She finds time for "the teaching; I'll do the administration stuff, and I'll do the stuff I have to do at home; and it's very, very hard to find the time to write."

Furthermore, normative legal scholarship, the traditional format for law review articles, tends to be valued above identity-based work.[21] Not surprisingly, women of color law professors publish articles, essays, and even op-eds involving the interaction of law with race, gender, sexual orientation, socio-economic status, and other identity-related areas.[22] Non-traditional legal scholarship may be viewed with suspicion by colleagues who do not understand it or may even feel threatened by the work itself—and respond by derailing a junior colleague's career. Scholarship drives rewards and advancement at Cindy's institution, though highly valued scholarship is "mostly male-generated at our school," whereas the scholarship that many of the women produce "is not valued in the same way as traditional scholarship." Even with the dean voicing his support for their work, "women are still really undervalued." Armida fights the perception of "assumed incompetence" not only from students, but also from colleagues who discount her work, announcing their belief that "because I write on diversity issues, somehow it's not scholarly." That attitude results in them "diminishing the work that I do," which draws from experimental and critical theory, because her colleagues prefer "more traditional doctrinal [research]." Armida has decided to not "conform myself to fit" their expectations, sticking with her research priorities to "try and do my best . . . because that's what I want to do and that's what I'm excited about." Her first year was a challenge, but as she continues in academia "I get more confidence in what I'm doing and that comes from experience. But I still face challenges." Patrice's identity-based scholarship is similarly devalued by "white guys on the faculty who are . . . hostile to race work." Her response was to avoid presenting her scholarship to colleagues, though it "was tricky because I wanted to be able to do the work I wanted to do, but I also wanted tenure, right?" This emotional labor, hiding her true feelings to fit in and get ahead, exacted a huge toll on Patrice's mental health.[23] When asked about the tenure process she had recently gone through, where her scholarship was picked apart along with her teaching and service, she replied, "Oh my God. [Sigh.] I have post-traumatic stress disorder."

Responses: Fight or Flight

Responses to these intersectional (raceXgender) challenges range from resignation to litigation. Brianna was formally assigned a white male mentor in her first year of law teaching who offered "bad advice" including, "'Don't worry about writing for your first three years.'" Brianna believed it "was the dumbest advice he could have ever given me [and] thankfully I didn't trust him and I didn't take it, but then I knew he was trying to tank me."[24] This realization was swift and obvious to Brianna, who thought to herself, "Don't write for the first three years? The tenure-track was only six years!" Now, she tells young female faculty of color, "Don't listen to any stupid advice about people telling you that you can take it easy [even in your first year]. You can't take it easy."[25]

White male faculty may see the tenure process as easy because it actually is easier for them.[26] Carla's significant "experience on the Rank and Tenure Committee has allowed me to see the ways in which certain professors get enormous amounts of leeway." White men "can make mistakes, they can be disorganized, they can be rude to students, they can not offer question and answer sessions [before exams], et cetera, and students are comfortable with that" because they expect that "a law professor is a white man, a Caucasian man," and so will not complain in evaluations or otherwise. The students see the white male as "the gold standard and then everyone situates in relation to that," resulting in "female professors hav[ing] a narrower margin of error than Caucasian male professors" even with tenure. Leanne experienced firsthand the difference in "support given to particularly young [white] male professors" as compared to herself and other junior scholars of color. When a white male junior colleague "went up early for promotion" with the support of senior colleagues, two women who were hired the same year as he was were discouraged from applying—though, when compared to "the golden guy," they published at roughly equivalent rates. Leanne was similarly discouraged from applying for promotion by her associate dean for faculty development, who told her she "needed to wait another year or two," although she feels "it's ridiculous how long I've been waiting." Now, he "keeps saying, 'Oh you're golden. You're totally a cinch. Don't worry about it.' And I'm like, 'Really? Because [before, you] explicitly said I should not go up.'" Leanne's experience shows that even senior administrators tasked with advancing the careers of the faculty cannot necessarily be trusted when it comes to the professional development of junior female faculty of color.

These experiences contribute to ongoing distrust among colleagues at many institutions. At Alicia's school, some white faculty present a friendly face towards faculty of color, but "behind closed doors" there is the "denigration of the person's work, their scholarship or their teaching."[27] Recently, "several people came to my office and said, 'Did you know that so and so goes around speaking ill of X?' And then they said, 'And so and so is also speaking ill of Y and Z,'" where the referenced people "were two African Americans and one Latina who were up [for promotion]. All three of them were targeted." Alicia wanted to protect these junior scholars of color, but "didn't know which one was going to survive [the character and scholarly assassination attempts] because . . . it's random at some level. Everybody has weaknesses. Everybody has strengths."

Surya, an Asian American professor, applied for tenure at the same time as four colleagues. While she "was the only one who had a bad experience," she attributes it wholly to "one person on my tenure committee" who "made it a little bit miserable" by engaging in "a bit of a hazing process" involving this senior white female colleague who "didn't want me to succeed" being "very, very mean to me." On days when this colleague "would review my class [she would] storm out" halfway through, "claim[ing] that she couldn't stand my teaching and had to walk out"—this, in spite of Surya's maintaining "very high teaching evaluations" from students and positive peer reviews from other colleagues. Though these microaggressions—"subtle verbal and nonverbal insults directed toward [her]"—motivated Surya to work even harder,[28] she now attributes the behavior to jealousy, because she had multiple articles published in top law reviews while this senior scholar had none.

Few women of color react as Surya has to bullying, discouraging, or disrespectful colleagues. Most instead have a fight or flight response. When "the committee voted no," halting Mia's tenure application, she was given one terminal year to continue in her position and the option to either send her application to the full faculty—where they would likely support the committee decision and her denial "would be part of the employment record"—or withdraw her application and keep her record intact. Mia decided to withdraw her application, return to her hometown, and pursue other interests. She is the only DLA participant to have left legal academia during the course of data collection, and she did so only after being denied tenure and essentially forced out.

Others respond to hostility with the urge to fight. Lola decided to stay and accept her faculty's decision to deny her promotion last year, working to improve her teaching even further. She expects to easily satisfy the requirements when she applies for tenure next year. Yet if she is again denied for intersectional raceXgender reasons, she has decided that "all of that would have to come out" in court.

When Aisha's promotion was denied by a full faculty vote, "the dean immediately signaled to me that he wanted me to withdraw my candidacy," preserving her right to apply again later. Unsure of how to proceed, "mentors really became important." External mentors suggested she withdraw, though senior supporters at her own institution "who knew about [the internal workings] immediately told me, 'Sue them.'" She followed the advice of her colleagues: "I hired the scariest lawyer I could. I filed a complaint with the EEOC [Equal Employment Opportunity Commission] and basically said, 'You can articulate grounds for why you [denied me] or you can face a massive lawsuit.'"[29] Predictably, the dean then asked the committee to articulate grounds for her denial—but the subcommittee that worked on her application had actually "unanimously voted *for* promotion. And in fact in the teaching section they asserted that I met the *tenure* standard, which is a higher standard than the promotion standard." Though the committee as a whole, and subsequently the full faculty, did not follow the recommendation of the subcommittee to promote her, they also did not follow procedure to articulate grounds for denial. Both the university provost and general counsel joined the dean and relevant committee members, "and it was them flurrying around [in] full-on panic mode" for four months. The dean "hired outside counsel, and their lawyer was negotiating with my lawyer"—including one proposal that would grant Aisha promotion if she agreed to leave within a year ("I said no") and another that would grant her promotion if she agreed to teaching and publication conditions involving "a lot of just made-up bullshit" ("I rejected that"). Aisha believed: "I've met the bylaw standards. Nobody else has been required to do anything extra. I refuse to. Why should I leave?" She also felt that accepting their conditions would be akin to "an admission on my part that there was something wrong with my file" when she knew there was not. She admits that "if they had offered me a massive settlement I would have thought about leaving the academy entirely," given the miserable process and her distrust of faculty even before this debacle. Ultimately, Aisha says, "I stuck to my guns and they caved." The provost "read my file very carefully" and issued a report confirming that "she meets the standard" for promotion and "that was that." Over the next few years, "the dean kept asking me whether I still had my lawyer, and I said, 'I will be lawyered up until I leave.'" And she has been. Aisha believes that because she "won at that level" and created a record, that "there's already a history of discrimination" so "they could do nothing to me [afterward]." Not surprisingly, when she went up for tenure two years later, it was a smooth and easy process.

Although the tenure standards at April's institution had been "vague" for years, immediately before she applied for tenure her colleagues decided to "develop some new rules" to govern the process. April explains: "I believe in having rules as well," but the new standards put her at a clear disadvantage with no notice. Each external reviewer now "had to be someone who possessed the title of professor of law and had been tenured for at least ten years." While seemingly neutral, this rigidity "knocks out the vast majority of minority women" whose work often engages with other scholarship involving race, intersectionality, privilege, and critical theory. Her task was especially daunting when coupled with the small number of women of color in academia, let alone the miniscule number that held the professor of law title and had been tenured for at least ten years before April applied. Her portfolio was so strong that despite the new rules, the relevant committee "recommended that I be tenured." Yet "the tenured faculty voted not to tenure me, not to accept the recommendation of [the] committee." When she heard the news, April recalls, "I was devastated." Critically, the dean supported April, adopting the committee's recommendation over the objections of the full faculty. Because there was "a split decision"—"my committee says yes, my dean says yes, my faculty says no"—and April refused to withdraw, her file was then "sent to the office of the president" for his recommendation, "on advice from the provost." At that point, "the provost reads all my stuff and the president reads all my stuff and they decide I should be tenured." Their endorsement was sent to the university trustees, who, after some back and forth with the general counsel, finally "vote to tenure me." April secured a positive outcome, but endured a miserable process. That period of uncertainty constituted "the longest months of my entire life. It was agonizing and painful, full of guilt and bad feelings about how I have ruined the life of my entire family." April had been a successful big-firm litigator in a large metropolitan city before uprooting her family to move to what she thought of in those months as "the armpit of America, the backwater of life. This is where I moved my family and now I have fucked it up. What will become of us?" As you can imagine, April "was devastated for months and then I got tenure. In the process I also lost I think twenty pounds and it was just horrific." But she refused to go down without a fight. And she won.

Comparison and Contrast

In contrast, not one of the white male professors who participated in the DLA study expressed tenure concerns—mirroring the quantitative data showing that 100% of white men are satisfied with the tenure process. Matt plans to apply for his first promotion next year and says, "I actually expect it will be really, really friendly." He believes "everybody who is hired here, the expectation is that the faculty will help them get tenure as opposed to screening them out," though this may not have been the experience for his female faculty of color colleagues. John is going though the tenure process now and laments that "the committee hasn't been as transparent as I would have liked," resulting in him being "more proactive in finding out what's happening when." Aside from that, "it's been pretty smooth sailing and I don't expect to have any hiccups." He is not confused about the guidelines or worried that they will be applied unfairly, but simply would prefer his committee initiate more frequent updates. John clarifies: "I'm feeling very confident. I'm not concerned at all."

Considering the contemporary complex procedures for professional advancement in legal academia, the tenure process decades ago at many institutions was streamlined, simplified, and informal. Christopher summarizes his tenure process from more than forty years ago as follows:

The dean who hired me made the tenure decision unilaterally, did not consult with the faculty, did not have a faculty vote, did not have a formal review. Basically, you were appointed an assistant professor for three years and if you did your teaching well and if you wrote an article or two then the dean would say, "OK, now you're an associate professor with tenure." It was that simple.

While this is not the process at perhaps any law school today, one wonders how many of the older mostly white mostly male law faculty members still teaching today benefited from a relaxed process years ago, especially as compared to the women of color who have joined law teaching in increasing numbers in recent years and now face overt obstacles and covert barriers to securing tenure and promotion.

The experience for men of color also tends to be straightforward. Jack says, "I felt relatively confident." Ryan's tenure process "was at moments stressful," though "primarily because you're sitting around and you know you're being evaluated and judged for every little thing." Ryan's stress came "not because the faculty was placing stress on me, but because I was stressing myself. It was an internal stress." Yet external pressures can cause additional strain. Jorge is roughly halfway through his school's "five-year process" for tenure, which is "a little murky. They say it's a three-publication requirement, but I get the sense that it's not [laughing]." Before Jorge applies for tenure, he will have to unearth the informal requirements. His "plan for that is essentially I know that I'm going to be doing a lot of writing and it's going to be more than three publications so I'm not worried about that requirement or the teaching or the service." The one thing "that gives me pause" and "that you can't control is how other people will respond" to the research, especially because—like many faculty of color—he does not produce traditional normative legal scholarship. He "will have a lot of strong supporters," but he also anticipates push back from "people that really don't like the work I'm doing." Innovative or atypical topics or methods employed by people of color continue to be devalued by some colleagues, which could also affect the trajectory of nontraditional faculty applying for tenure and promotion.

Asim remembers his tenure process as "very straightforward, very easy, no complaints." Likely, this is because he "exceeded the number of articles required" and his colleagues were "very transparent in the sense of the process." Dwayne applied for tenure early—in his third year rather than the normal sixth year—"because I had a lot of publications" and "very good teaching evaluations." At his school, "the unspoken rule was that you had to have two articles; I had seven in my first year. So after the second year, I figured I might as well come up." Good thing he knew the informal rules.

Because Stuart "wrote a lot of articles" there were no "real issues involving the substance of my tenure application." Yet faculty mistrust and underlying hostility in interracial faculty interactions played a role. He applied at an appropriate time, though not at the earliest opportunity. As a result, "there were a lot of people who would ask why I wasn't tenured, and people started talking behind my back and it kind of concerned me." He also is disappointed that student service does not count for "anything when it comes to going up for tenure," since he and many other underrepresented faculty invest greatly in this work. Ed "felt my whole tenure and promotion process was virtually free from any drama whatsoever or tension or any types of constraints. I have had an overwhelmingly positive experience." He benefited from a mentor who told him before he applied that he should buffer his application with yet another publication "so your tenure packet will be invincible." Ed does admit to "a little bit of a worry" because he heard that "some of the older members and more conservative members of the faculty . . . had a little concern that I was not on campus enough." Being one of few people of color on campus adds another dimension to the expectation of "face time"—because their absence is more apparent than when white men, who make up the majority on most campuses, are missing. Proportionality is also relevant, with the expectation that Ed stay on campus and his absence—as one of few people of color in the building—duly noted.[30]

White female senior scholars also benefited from more relaxed tenure guidelines decades ago. Lisa "wrote one article" before applying for tenure. Her colleagues "read it, they liked it, and that was it. One article, three years, and I was at full professor." Abigail's law school "had very clearly articulated standards about the number of articles and we had a process of [reviewing] faculty evaluations of teaching in tandem with student evaluations." She met the requirements early, applied early, and "the tenure process for me was not a problem at all." On the other end of the spectrum, Scarlett's school is still "in the process of writing down standards" for tenure—though the school has been around for decades. Chloe was hired along with a cohort of other diverse candidates, who later applied for tenure simultaneously. Mysteriously, as with April, new tenure guidelines went into effect the same year that the diverse candidates applied. The process for her "was difficult in the sense that people were coming to visit classes, [though] that hadn't been done before for anyone." She is confident that these changes came about because "there we were: the women and people of color [applying for tenure], so all of a sudden you had to have [more] publications, you had to have classroom visits." Creating higher benchmarks immediately before diverse candidates apply also suggests bias, employing both race and gender discrimination.

Sydney earned tenure without the full acceptance of her faculty. Like Lola and Aisha, she says it was "a really weird process for me because I don't really know 100% what went on." Though the faculty discussion of her tenure application was confidential, she heard that some people were concerned about her writing, while others thought she "had enough writing" but questioned her "commitment to the institution." Ultimately, the faculty decided "to give me tenure but not promote me [to full professor]"—an atypical move for her school. Sydney's emotional state upon hearing the news mirrors April's: "I was devastated." She was also, like Mia, "ashamed of what was happening and didn't want to share it," so did not discuss it with mentors or others who could have provided support or advice. Family helped some: "My mother's take on it is that they're just jealous."

The year she applied, Ava "felt overloaded. I had a lot of responsibilities." She "was one of the few women in the building and certainly the only young one, and I got surrounded by students all the time [who] wanted my attention." Furthermore, the white male "hired at the same time was teaching upper level elective courses with low enrollment, and I was teaching one hundred people each semester, plus a writing course." Proportionately, Ava was overwhelmed as one of the few young women on campus, expected to other-mother dozens of students. While the male hire was supported by their colleagues and "was big buddies with the male dean," the faculty did not make Ava "feel at all supported. I felt like I was drowning," with nobody "to help guide me at all." Add to her teaching and service obligations the stress of applying for tenure, and Ava was "really anxious. I was really stressed. I was depressed [to the extent that] I ended up seeing a therapist." A white female professor "who I thought would be a [friendly] colleague was really hostile to me [and also] in charge of my tenure package." That colleague "wrote up the worst external review [summaries] that you can imagine. She took all the criticism and ignored every nice thing." Tenure committees that support the applicant "try to focus on the positives and downplay the criticism, but she basically did the opposite." After reading the summaries, Ava's "faculty as a whole said, 'We need to rewrite this

because this does not look like we're supporting this candidate for tenure.'"
Two senior male scholars stepped in "and sort of salvaged what would have
been a disastrous tenure process to say, 'Well, there's actually a lot of really
good stuff'" to focus on. Ava eventually "got through tenure, but it was miserable." Furthermore, Ava "knew that on paper that didn't make any sense
[since] I actually published pretty well." She had four articles, in spite of "not
having the time and space to [write] because of my teaching obligations" and
service responsibilities. When she "tried to work at home and get away from
the students and try to create a safe space to get work done, I was criticized by
the dean saying I need to get in the office." Once again, the expectation of face
time was used to single out an underrepresented faculty member, one who
stood out as the only young woman on the faculty.

5   Leading the Charge

M ICHELLE WAS "very interested in academic work" even as a
law student, and pursued academia "to be a scholar, [because]
that's where my passion is." When she first entered law teaching, mentors
"provided a basic support network of encouragement." More recently, they
have propelled her career as a successful Black female administrator. When a
university-wide administrative position opened up at her institution, she initially "had no interest. I didn't think it was the right thing for me." Yet multiple law school colleagues "nominated me for [the position] and wrote letters,"
and the dean "met with me and said, 'I think you would be perfect for this.'"
Still, Michelle was uncertain. Though she had always been "very committed to
the institution," she had "never really thought of myself as an internal leader,"
but instead took "more of an oppositional stance toward institutions, trying to
criticize them around issues of hiring or fairness." Michelle credits her white
male dean as "the biggest factor" in her decision to apply, since he "several
times said to me, 'You know, I really think this is something you are uniquely
situated for and I will do everything in my power to help you succeed once
you're in it.'" Ultimately, she "thought, 'This is a chance to do something new,'
so I thought I would give it a try." Senior scholars in other departments were
also instrumental in her successful appointment, including "another senior
African American woman who kind of shepherded me through the process."
Michelle's new position has "been exhausting and exhilarating." She has
learned about university operations "on an entirely different level" and met

"lots and lots of new people." She is especially grateful that being an administrator provides her with an opportunity "to develop a new set of skills" after twenty years in academia. Now, "I do a lot of problem solving both on behalf of individuals and on behalf of departments or units." Also, "it's a fair amount of collaborating [and] a lot of vision setting," plus determining how to "take a vision that's been set by someone [else] and translate that into an actual set of programs." Michelle "collaborates with all of our schools on hiring" and has the authority to "put in place things that help facilitate a goal." Overall, she is thrilled with her position and the power to create change, reflecting, "It's been wonderful."

Many scholars have written on leadership, including within law.[1] Until recently, faculty of color holding academic leadership positions have been exceedingly rare, with ABA statistics indicating that 83% of law school deans and 79% of associate deans are white.[2] Currently, as white male deans and associate deans step down from their positions in increasing numbers, women of color have a window to step up.[3] The reluctance of women to assume leadership roles is often blamed on a lack of capacity, a lack of interest, or an inability to break the glass ceiling.[4] An additional rationale holds that decision makers cannot "discern between confidence and competence" in selecting leaders, thereby frequently overlooking qualified women of color.[5] Women are less likely to be chosen to be leaders, though they are more likely to display actual indicators of leadership success—being emotionally intelligent, sensitive, considerate, and humble—whereas "men are consistently more arrogant, manipulative and risk-prone," though still preferred.[6]

Intersectional raceXgender barriers—both internal and external—prevent women of color from maximizing opportunities to become leaders in legal academia. Many women of color are reluctant to pursue leadership for various reasons, including their own priorities, previous negative experiences with colleagues, and their suspicion of taking on a political role in a climate of distrust. Data presented in this chapter also detail how some who do actively seek out administrative positions are thwarted by implicit or explicit bias. Others commence leadership positions only to see the roles shift to become more menial and less meaningful. This chapter concludes with data confirming that men of color and white women have similar leadership experiences to women of color, with white men remaining situated to maintain positions of power as law school leaders.

Getting Interested

Women of color face internal barriers that block them from assuming leadership positions—although the origins of those barriers lie with external factors. Scholars in various fields have studied the so-called "ambition gap" to determine why "women express less interest in becoming [leaders] than their male counterparts."[7] When asked if she would be interested in administrative leadership, April replies, "Dean? Ugh [sound of disgust], I don't really know that I want that job." Bianca states, "I don't think I strive for leadership. I think I have sometimes found myself in those positions, [but] it's not like something I go after." Similarly, an Asian American named Karissa assumed an associate dean position at her law school solely because "the dean asked me, and I didn't really have a good reason to say no." Though she has a leadership role, she says, "I don't really want it."

The overwhelming majority of law professors are content with their current positions (see Table 9). Few see a deanship as their ultimate career goal, including those who occupy other leadership positions (e.g., associate dean). Interestingly, white men and white women are no more likely that people of color to aspire to become dean.

Many female faculty of color cite ongoing teaching and research priorities as a key reason for avoiding leadership, worrying that these matters would be given short shrift if they turned their attention to administrative duties. Carla notes, "I don't want to be a dean because I much prefer writing." Although she has "been approached by a few institutions [asking,] 'Would you consider putting your name in [as a dean candidate]?'" she has always replied, "'No, I'm not interested.'" Natalie would "never" consider joining the administration. Instead, "I would rather do my teaching, do my writing, you know, affect things in other ways." Even new law professors plan to avoid a future in leadership. Gabrielle is untenured and states definitively, "I've definitely never been interested in administration at a law school." Instead, she would "prefer to spend my time in the classroom and writing." Melissa, one of few people of color on her faculty, ponders how joining the administration could impact students, noting, "I worry that if I moved into an associate dean role that I wouldn't be able to teach the first years, which I think is key especially [because] I'm the only person of color [available to teach] in one section." Emma notes, "I don't think that becoming an administrator or leader within the institutional setting of legal academia will serve my overall long-terms goals of

TABLE 9 Ultimate Career Goal, by Race and Gender, DLA 2013

		Business executive	Politician	Judge	Dean	Associate dean	Assistant dean	University president	Other university executive	Other legal	Other nonlegal	Law professor
African American women	n	0	0	1	1	1	0	2	0	1	2	9
	%	0.00	0.00	5.88	5.88	5.88	0.00	11.76	0.00	5.88	11.76	52.94
Asian American women	n	0	0	0	0	1	0	0	0	0	2	9
	%	0.00	0.00	0.00	0.00	8.33	0.00	0.00	0.00	0.00	16.67	75.00
Latinas	n	0	1	0	0	0	0	0	0	0	2	8
	%	0.00	9.09	0.00	0.00	0.00	0.00	0.00	0.00	0.00	18.18	72.73
Native American women	n	0	0	0	0	0	0	0	0	0	2	3
	%	0.00	0.00	0.00	0.00	0.00	0.00	0.00	0.00	0.00	40.00	60.00
Middle Eastern women	n	0	0	0	1	0	0	0	0	0	0	1
	%	0.00	0.00	0.00	50.00	0.00	0.00	0.00	0.00	0.00	0.00	50.00
Multiracial women	n	0	0	0	0	0	0	0	0	0	0	7
	%	0.00	0.00	0.00	0.00	0.00	0.00	0.00	0.00	0.00	0.00	100.00
Men of color	n	1	0	1	1	0	0	1	0	0	0	7
	%	9.09	0.00	9.09	9.09	0.00	0.00	9.09	0.00	0.00	0.00	63.64
White women	n	1	0	0	0	0	0	0	0	0	0	10
	%	9.09	0.00	0.00	0.00	0.00	0.00	0.00	0.00	0.00	0.00	90.91
White men	n	0	0	0	0	0	0	0	0	0	0	8
	%	0.00	0.00	0.00	0.00	0.00	0.00	0.00	0.00	0.00	0.00	100.0
Total	n	2	1	2	3	2	0	3	0	1	8	62

why I wanted to become an academic and what it is I'm seeking to do." Writing, teaching, and other professional priorities come first for many women of color.

Family obligations and community interests keep others from pursuing a future in administration. Imani says that "initially, I definitely had a goal to one day be a dean." However, her priorities have since shifted:

> The fact that I have a daughter [has] made a difference in thinking about what life would look like having that kind of administrative role on top of being the type of wife and mother that I want to be. Although it's definitely possible to do all of that, there's definitely conflict.

Imani's female colleague who has "just became an associate dean" has already endured challenging "experiences [that have also] made me rethink" whether a leadership position would be a good fit. While Imani can still envision a future in administration, "after seeing what it really entails, it has definitely given me pause." Patrice cannot imagine adding administrative duties to her current priorities of excelling as a professor and a parent, which already involve significant balancing:

> It's hard to imagine me leading anything and still being a present and effective parent. So it's not to say that when my kids are older ... that my priorities might [not] change. But right now they're my priority, like sort of being a leader for them. Like going to parent-teacher conferences, and there's very little time for that.

Jane realizes that "even if it means more money [likely] all that means is I'll be able to hire a nanny" to cover the extra time away from home. She and her partner have "never been able to afford one," juggling work and family on their own. While leadership intrigues her, Jane is not willing to join the administrative ranks "at the expense of my kids," especially while they are young.

In contrast, Aarti is more comfortable taking on administrative duties. She would be "happy to take on this extra work as long [as it did not] come at the expense of the flexibility of my job." The extra challenge of juggling work and family is more manageable because Aarti's "husband is a stay-at-home dad, a full-time stay-at-home dad." Obviously, work/life balance is a significant factor when considering leadership, with those who enjoy a stable, healthy balance more likely to consider additional work responsibilities.[8] As explored in the following chapter, white men are more satisfied with their balance than other law professors—which may also contribute to their greater interest in seeking leadership roles.

For Alexandra, it is "hard to think of holding a leadership position with two young children at this point in my career." While she is "not foreclosing" leadership, her preference would be to contribute to her community outside the school. Many women of color share the goal of being a community leader. A Latina junior scholar named Eliana says that institutional leadership "doesn't really interest me," though she would like to work "outside the academy in some sort of service capacity [helping] an organization." Her preference is to be a leader while "doing activism and being involved in projects" rather than assuming leadership within academia. Institution building is less important to Noriko than external service work because "I want what I do to have an impact." She strives "to make a difference in my students' lives" and endeavors "to make a difference with respect to what happens with the faculty or the school," but she has a broader goal for her work to "have actual ramifications out in the real world" without being "on view" as a leader. Jennifer is comfortable being a public intellectual, appreciating opportunities when she has "been on television, been on the radio," and participated in "national speaking engagements." Yet she has "no interest in being a law school dean or assistant dean or anything along those lines." While she does "want to be out in the world, talking about issues that are important," she does not see law school leadership as satisfying her social justice goals. Destiny is also "not that interested" in institutional leadership, although she is "more interested at this point in outside leadership," perhaps at a nonprofit where she can do "more community-based work" and make an impact at an "organization outside of the academy."

Other women of color cite a desire to avoid internal politics as their reason for avoiding administrative positions. Bianca states, "I wouldn't say that I'm interested in being a leader. You know, don't get me into [the] politics." Similarly, Danielle is not interested "because it's too political. The things that I would want to do, the things that I think a law school should do [would be impossible to enact;] it just wouldn't work." For instance, she sees legal education today as "driven by this whole notion of the stigma behind affirmative action, the dismantling of affirmative action, the whole taking a seat [that should go to a white person], the whole, 'You're not qualified' [assumption]" levied against aspiring students and faculty of color. In her experience, "when

I sit in meetings and hear admissions reports and hear what people have to say, [that creates a] cloud of negativity [that] would just frustrate me on a daily basis" as a leader—if not drive her out of legal academia altogether.

When Elaine "first started my career, I think I was much more interested in being the leader of everything." Actually becoming a leader changed her: "I've had a taste of leadership in various ways and I think what I've had has been more than sufficient [laughing]. I've been approached about being deans and stuff like that but I don't like the politics of it all." Sonia has an administrative role now but was "not particularly" interested in pursuing the position early on. She "thought I'd stay a faculty member forever," in part because her natural instinct is to "not try to draw attention to myself." When she was first chosen to direct a program on campus, she started from scratch, and "had to clear out the space, get new furniture, get decluttered. I had the junk guy come. I showed up with my Swiffer and cleaned [laughing]." Her colleagues appreciated her willingness to work hard at any task to make the program successful. Now, as an administrator with greater institutional responsibilities and influence, she appreciates colleagues who have "been very supportive of me at times when I really needed it." Yet politics dog her. Conservative faculty had certain demands, while liberals "were after me for not [doing] enough." She sees this conundrum especially for women of color administrators who have to navigate the expectations of various communities because of their intersectional raceXgender identity. Sonia senses that various parties "felt that they had the right to appropriate my identity and judge me on my authenticity, but in different ways. But the left and the right both." In this way, politics also draws from intersectional bias, complicating leadership for women of color.

Structural Roots of Individual Barriers

Although the reasons women of color provide for avoiding leadership may seem individual, they have deep structural roots. Global research involving more than 200,000 respondents found that "existing gender diversity had a big impact on how workers felt about pursuing more senior roles."[9] When female faculty of color state that they prefer writing and teaching, they may be echoing what others have told them is their appropriate place in legal academia, as well as responding to a lack of opportunities for women in leadership. Research indicates that when women "receive signals" from higher ups that they will not "make it to the top," they make the "reasonable decision" to pursue other interests to maximize the likelihood of success.[10] Preferring to focus on family and community also is unsurprising given the distrust and lack of belonging that hounds many women of color law professors on campus. Political battles are both more costly and less effective for women of color administrators who are alienated even as traditional faculty. Additionally, few women of color faculty have role models or examples of successful deans or other administrators who look like them, have experiences like theirs, or share their backgrounds.[11]

In an interesting parallel to barriers to entry, indicating why women of color are reluctant to seek out faculty positions, senior women of color faculty avoid leadership thinking it is not their place.[12] Michelle was persuaded to apply for a university-wide administrative position only after her dean and senior colleagues encouraged her to do so multiple times. Mariana's path was similar. One summer day, Mariana was in her office "writing articles, [and] the call had already gone up [over email] from the interim dean whether anybody wanted to be associate dean, and I didn't even respond." Nevertheless, the interim dean "came in my office and asked me to do it," convincing her that she could play a critical role in the future of the institution and cajoling, "'Come on, it's only going to be for one semester.' Well, that semester turned into almost two years." Without this nudge, and the interim dean's direct support, Mariana would never have considered pursuing the position. A Latina named Carolina describes herself as someone who has "a natural tendency towards leadership" but nevertheless "was not seeking out a leadership position at the law school." Quite the opposite, she considered requesting a workload reduction after three years of a personal and professional "nonstop whirlwind" when her dean asked her to become associate dean. Although "I certainly wasn't seeking that" and his offer "caught me off-guard," she ultimately felt ready to take on greater responsibility and accepted the challenge. She reached this decision only "after months of deliberating, and praying, and trying to figure out [whether it was] a good fit." In part, family considerations prompted her to take the position, as she hoped the job would provide her with "growth opportunities" while allowing "my kids to become a little more independent."

As "preexisting relationships" significantly determine the ability of a leader to connect with followers, the challenging faculty interactions that many women of color endure may also dissuade them from pursuing leadership.[13] Cindy does not "do well trying to manage and dealing [with faculty] as an administrator, negotiating anger and managing complaints, which is what I think a lot of administrators end up doing." Earlier in her career, Cindy "really wanted to have leadership, [but I] didn't get those positions." Because of this rejection, "for a time, I was really unhappy." She came to terms with remaining a professor instead of an administrator, but at a cost, realizing that "yes, I want leadership, but only where my strengths will serve the institution well [though] it's been difficult to learn that there are lots of things I don't do well." The experience of applying and being rejected changed Cindy's opinion of herself to match how her colleagues see her, such that she now believes she would not succeed as a leader. Whether she truly is not suited to an administrative role or her colleagues simply crushed her desire to fulfill this dream remains unclear and may never be answered.

Annie suffers from a similar lack of confidence in her leadership abilities based on past experience in administration. She has "an uneasy relationship" with leadership, though she sees herself as "extremely goal-oriented, [and] somewhat ambitious." After tenure, Annie wondered, "'OK, what's the next step?'" and saw administration as a logical progression. Although she served for a time as an associate dean, her efforts were neither respected nor appreciated by colleagues or superiors. Because of their collective reaction of indifference and disdain, "I realized I'm really not cut out for that type of overt leadership for lots of different reasons. I mean that's not to say other women can't do it, but I just felt like it wasn't me." She felt unsuccessful in her previous administrative position partly because "when I assumed that role, people respond[ed] to the role rather than to the person; [they began acting] defensive, hostile, all sorts of other [negative] responses." This experience mirrors that of other leaders, who note how colleagues' interactions with them change as they transition into their new role, sometimes turning hard-earned "trust into resentment."[14] Women of color rarely start with that trust. Like Cindy and other women of color, Annie internalized her colleagues' negative responses to signify "I just was not good at it," determining that "I don't really belong in this [type of role]," whether or not that is actually true.

Mariana realized only when she assumed an associate dean position "that there was this dark side to faculty that came out more, because now they have to go through me." To be a woman of color in charge, with increased power "comes criticism." Even when Mariana enforced basic regulations, saying to colleagues things like, "'No, [you can't] go have a massage at ten o'clock in the morning; you have to teach a class,' [my colleagues] would get very angry at me." Carolina also believes that her faculty colleagues assume that she is "on the dark side—even though I am still a faculty member" in addition to an administrator. They engage in "a much more distanced relationship" with her because of her leadership role, further deepening the gulf between her and the majority white faculty at her school.

In addition to negative experiences with colleagues, women of color administrators also have few role models. At Sofia's school—like many others— "the actual leadership at the school are all white men, and the few [white] women who are [associate] deans are not as visible [or recognized as] the face of the institution." The few women of color administrators do often literally stand out among a sea of white male leaders, highlighting again how proportionality singles them out.[15] Laura is proud that by taking on administrative roles, she has "been an inspiration to other women who didn't have very many role models or as many role models in [those] position[s]."

While a limited number of women of color have been deans, some of those pioneers have endured highly publicized trials, sometimes based in intersectional discrimination or implicit bias, that also dissuade other women of color from pursuing leadership. As Melissa notes, "I don't ever want to be a dean. Deans are treated pretty horribly." When particular incidents are directly attributable to the intersection of the leader's race and gender, women of color faculty take note and change plans.[16] Patricia admits, "I have wanted [leadership] in the past," but now, given how nontraditional leaders are so frequently undermined, "I don't know about leadership." She adds:

> It's complicated being a woman of color and being a leader. It's very complicated. I'm not sure that the world is ready for women of color deans. There are successful women of color deans, a few; there are many more that go down in flames and the stories about women of color as deans, some of them are just so ugly. And I'm not sure that I want to subject myself, my family, to that sort of ugliness. [By "the world," I actually mean that] it's American law faculties [that] are not ready, meaning race is still such an issue that law faculty members don't want women of color, Black women especially, in positions of power over them. I didn't say "in control" because you're not really in control of these cats [even if you're dean].

In many of the same ways that female faculty and faculty of color are challenged in the classroom and hyperscrutinized on evaluations, nontraditional deans are presumed incompetent as leaders.[17] Brianna has seen it in action as a Black administrator, noting that "just as women and people of color understand the literature and the experience of being disparately situated in the classroom, [many] faculty members of color and women tend to understand that's probably the case for the dean as well." Brianna is grateful for "faculty who are critical in terms of their consciousness, who are well-read in terms of critical race scholarship and the scholarship of outsider theory, queer theory." She has "really benefited from those faculty having my back [and helping] with some of the people who will be particularly racist or sexist."

Sonia laments that being an administrator is "not the same as being on the faculty because as a faculty member you really can express very much your personal views that you back up with research and you speak for yourself. But when you're [an administrator] you speak for the institution and speaking in an institutional voice is very different." This self-censorship creates unique challenges for women of color who are used to being more oppositional than acquiescent to achieve success.[18] The emotional labor inherent in guarding one's own perspective when it is frequently in conflict with institutional goals is also too high of a price to pay for many women of color.[19] Silencing comes at a cost not only to women of color who endure negative health effects from the trauma of silencing, but also to their colleagues whose assumptions that women of color have nothing to contribute are validated, and to the institution as a whole since the novel ideas and perspectives these women could add are not shared. In these various ways, even seemingly individual reasons including a lack of interest or unwillingness to consider leadership responsibilities come from broader structural intersectional constraints keeping women of color from advancing in legal academia.

Bias as a Barrier

Despite these anticipated intersectional challenges, some women of color are interested—and even passionate—about becoming leaders. When asked if they were interested in future leadership positions, some DLA participants answered "definitely," "absolutely," or, as Kayla notes, "I would love to be a dean someday." Perhaps Kayla and those sharing her ambitions will step forward to fill the void left by the white men currently leaving these positions. Laila exclaims, "I would love being the first Arab American dean of a law school!" Some of these women see leadership as a duty, specifically because of their identity and experiences. Karen says:

> There's a part of me that wants it because I think it's really important for people like me to be in leadership positions in law schools. . . . "People like me," meaning women, people of color, people who are accomplished scholars, but also are very focused on teaching. People who are appropriately skeptical of the law school enterprise, but also respected.

Balanced against this responsibility to lead, Karen is aware of the challenges she would likely face, noting, "On the other side of it though, on a personal level, I'm not convinced it would make me happy."

Administrative success is especially complicated when the dean is new to the institution. Josephine, a Black administrator and professor, "always wanted to be a law professor" and has "mostly been in leadership positions" during her three decades in law teaching, including both internal and external (e.g., ABA) roles. She believes opportunities arose because she is "a big team player" interested and available to assume leadership at a time when many were "looking for a woman of color to promote the diversity of the profession." Initially, she had "absolutely no interest in being a dean," though she "began getting a lot of outreach from people who were suggesting my name or who nominated me for deanships." As a finalist for multiple deanships, Josephine was turned down by people saying, "'You know, you don't really have the administrative experience,'" since she had not previously been a high-level administrator. When she began her first deanship as a new member of the faculty, she discerned internal politics at her law school while acting as its leader, which "affects the dynamics of the faculty." An unsuccessful internal candidate for dean and some supporters were disappointed by the process; in addition, she notes, "I went to that deanship without knowing that there had been a cloud over the last dean, so some of that has also affected what I have been able to do because there was a real division in the faculty about whether they should support [that dean or not]."

For many women who are interested in pursuing leadership, ongoing discrimination remains an obstacle. Research suggests that the "biggest challenge" for diversity in hiring "seems to be figuring out how to overcome unconscious biases," since even purported supporters of diversity perpetuate white male dominance.[20] Those selecting leaders frequently mistake confidence for competence, resulting in men being promoted at higher rates than women.[21] Yet "what it takes the *get* the job is not just different from, but also the reverse of what it takes to *do the job well*."[22] These overlooked women of color could actually be the most successful.

When a white male dean started at Jane's law school a decade ago, he selected a white male as associate dean. Recently, when Jane's faculty was involved in another dean search and a new associate dean was being chosen, "it occurred to me and [another woman of color on my faculty] to say, 'We already do a lot of this work, but we aren't getting any of the recognition.'" Yet again, a white male was selected as associate dean. Likely through implicit bias, rather than purposeful discrimination, colleagues overlook women of color for formal leadership positions, even when they already do the work and are eager to take on more. Jane noticed a similar attitude among her faculty toward a woman of color candidate for dean, recalling, "I don't think anyone ever really saw her in that [role], saw that, 'Oh, this could be a dean. This could be someone in administration.'" Gender bias held that candidate back. Similarly, Laura "never felt like I was a part of" the power structure at her school, until she was appointed to an associate dean position. Before then, "I felt like I had been passed over for the administrative jobs [because my colleagues simply] see me as the academic and not the administrator." After multiple disappointments, Laura "gave up on that line of [professional] development," so it "was kind of a surprise to me" when she was recently selected. The presumption of incompetence facing nontraditional faculty in the classroom carries over to leadership, with colleagues assuming that women of color could not succeed.

When asked how powerful positions are filled at her school, Imani responds, "I don't know [whether] it's fair to say that it helps to be a white male, but when we got a new dean, the first offers for the associate dean position went to white males before it got down to a faculty female of color. [This may be because white men are] the first people that people think of" for leadership. Bianca's new dean "appears to be moving in the same direction as the prior dean: essentially, keeping primarily white men in the positions of influence and power." To hold power at Corinne's school, she notes, "It helps to be male; it helps to be white. I suppose that's it." Research bolsters Corrine's experience, indicating that unless multiple women or people of color are considered for positions, a lone nontraditional applicant is unlikely to be selected. One sample of almost six hundred job finalists determined "that when there were two female finalists, women had a significantly higher chance of being hired" than if there were only one; similarly, the "odds of hiring a minority were 193.72 times greater if there were at least two minority candidates in the finalist pool."[23] Mariana "was the aberration" as a woman of color administrator, since in general, to become a leader at her school, "you have to be a white male." Patricia has determined that to attain a position of power, "it helps if you are a white guy, a white guy who acts like he knows what he is doing," since "that's what leadership looks like [here]." Her experience also highlights a preference for confident candidates, even over those who are competent.[24]

Overt bias also plays a role thwarting the leadership success of women of color. Trisha had been interested in becoming a dean for decades but was never successful. As a mid-level tenured faculty member, she took on prestigious volunteer positions with AALS and other legal academic organizations because "I thought that it would be a career path towards a deanship. It wasn't. It has been for white women, but not for me." Racial bias may have played a role, since a traditional path to power for white women did not yield the anticipated outcome for her. Trisha has resigned herself to never fulfilling her dream of leading a law school. She concedes, "I think that in my case my desire for leadership in law schools ran contrary to the time and so I'm in my own way trying to make peace with that." Lola has similarly "always been" ambitious and "always kind of thought of myself [as a leader] and I conduct myself that way." Yet she sees the path as uncertain for her as a woman of color "just given the reality of what that job is."

June has served as associate dean and the chair of multiple powerful committees; she has been a finalist for dean multiple times, but never been hired to lead a law school. The loss of not fully harnessing her energy and talents is especially poignant when considering the trajectory of her life, her natural tendencies, and her long-term ambitions. June shares: "I have been a leader since I was a little girl. . . . My whole life, literally since elementary school, I was always a leader. I was a natural leader . . . all the way up to now." In her view, bias leads others to view a candidate of color "as a trouble-maker, sore thumb, [or someone with a] chip on your shoulder," which makes her "dead in the water" as far as leadership goes. Gaining leadership duties requires "you having a personal relationship with the people who [make] those decisions," yet implicit bias encourages those in power—usually older white men—to choose candidates like them. Additionally, if "they don't see people of color and women in positions of leadership, then they think we don't do that," furthering the cycle and thwarting progress. Because "now we have Black women deans in some numbers," June admits hopefully that "it's getting a little easier for [white faculty] to see somebody like me as their leader, so that may happen."

While leadership positions are increasingly available, women of color stepping into those roles may not get what they expect. A "glass cliff" could be waiting for those women of color brave enough to assume these roles.[25] As discrimination continues against women of color administrators, their leadership may cover only low-status areas and the responsibilities of the job may change. An associate dean named Susan acknowledges that "there are challenges with respect to being in a leadership role in the law school," especially involving confrontational faculty. Although many faculty are respectful, the few that create conflict alter the experience entirely—just as the few students confronting women of color in the classroom damage the learning experience for everyone. In Susan's experience:

> most people are used to and comfortable with women in leadership positions, but I have a couple males on my faculty who clearly have difficulty with women in leadership roles, one of whom makes inappropriate comments not only to me, but that has been recently reported to me by a female colleague [for making other improper remarks].

Some of his comments are "embedded with sexual overtones," while others "suggest that female colleagues are inferior." Because Susan is also the "EEO/affirmative action person on our campus," she faces the "big challenge" of navigating how "to deal with this in a way that respects both the wishes of the person who was victimized by this, but that deals with the problem as well." When Melissa became chair of a committee, two colleagues "actually mounted an attack against me," trying to derail the committee goals and thwart her progress—responding as ignorant students do to an unexpected woman of color authority figure. Melissa "actually had to have the dean step in" to calm things down. She also reached out to her external network of women of color mentors to "say, 'I've never seen this before. What is this?' And they say, 'Well, it's probably [that] they see you in a position of power and they are looking at wanting to be in that position [themselves].'"[26]

Many women of color who are successful in leadership realize their voice is heard only on low-priority items, creating the illusion of inclusion while saving real power for others. This *symbolic progress* maintains an unequal status quo by providing women of color the impression that they are part of the power structure without much cost to the establishment.[27] Zahra sees through this façade, noting, "I don't feel like I'm a part of the decision-making process—unless it's on tangential things [or] noncontroversial things." She admits, "On things that are of less importance, I have a voice. With appointments, and the direction of the law school, what kinds of people we will hire, how we are going to move forward, that kind of stuff, I don't." While Zahra may be interested in more meaningful leadership in the future, she doubts that the opportunity exists for her at her current institution, lamenting, "I don't see a path for that actually, just given who I am, [as] a nonwhite woman."

The leadership role itself sometimes shifts as women of color assume the job, especially when colleagues resist them wielding power. This *feminization* of the role of dean parallels other positions that have lost status as women join in increasing numbers.[28] Destiny asserts that "as you get into more leadership roles, there seems to be a lot more resistance to us occupying positions of power and being able to exercise that power." She sees a correlation: "As we begin to take on more leadership positions, [those opposing women of color in these roles have less] tolerance for us." June also sees the increase in women of color deans as directly correlated with the fact that "the economy and everything is bad." With fewer white men interested in navigating the current "time of crisis in legal education," more opportunities are available to women of color—who then must deal with constant emergencies, running the risk of going over the glass cliff and taking the institution with them.[29] Sonia similarly believes that many whites "who are distinguished scholars don't want to be deans," in part because many institutions are facing "lots of problems right now." She senses that "the model of leadership is probably changing," from visionary influential leaders with significant power and little outside interference, to crisis managers micromanaged by university officials or boards beholden to the bottom line and external regulators. Recently, when Carla "was supposed to be on research leave," she found out just weeks before that the promise was being rescinded. She recalls, "My academic dean called me and said, 'You can't go on research leave. You have to chair [a particular] committee.'" While some may have been flattered by the request, Carla saw the situation as a demand that she perform institutional housekeeping, noting, "I've been in this long enough to know that's not really a compliment; that means someone needs to stay and clean the house [and] it's going to be you." She decided to grin and bear it, as she is wont to do, even if that performance of ongoing emotional labor exacts a toll.[30] A role that had previously been prestigious was reduced to what Carla considers clean up, just in time for her to miss her leave and take the helm. She continued in her role of "taking care of the academic family," providing the extra service expected of her.[31]

Comparison and Contrast

As with all other facets of the law faculty experience, women of color who aspire to leadership face unique challenges as compared to their white and male colleagues. In leadership, the interests, priorities, and experiences of white women parallel those of women of color, again highlighting the pervasive quality of gender privilege in legal academia even beyond the importance of intersectionality. Men of color have similarities with women of color, too—indicating ongoing racial bias. White men, on the other hand, enjoy more streamlined and straightforward opportunities for law school leadership.

Ed says, "I have no interest in administration whatsoever. I would never have an interest because I think I would be a terrible dean or administrator." Ed, like Melissa, has been conditioned to believe he could not succeed as a law school leader. Like other people of color, he also is more interested in being actively involved in the community, participating in "a lot more public intellectual platforms," where even one popular news article might "have more response [and impact than] all my law review articles." Stuart's previous committee leadership "was something the dean talked me into and I didn't enjoy it at all." His own negative experiences, especially while working with difficult colleagues on faculty recruitment and hiring, have now turned him off of leadership altogether—as similar experiences did for Cindy and Annie. Like women of color who prefer to write and teach, Dwayne is "not really" interested in pursuing a deanship since his primary identity is "as a scholar." Yet while he "never really pursued them," some leadership opportunities were presented to him. Family is Asim's main priority, though he could perhaps be convinced to become "an associate dean for research, but even that I'm ambivalent on." His hesitation stems from his conviction that succeeding at the job would mean "I would have to not put family first," just as Imani, Jane, and many women of color assert. While Ryan "always thought perhaps I could be a law school dean," he is "not so sure about that anymore," given ongoing challenges in legal education and the shifting role of the dean. In addition to wanting to prioritize his scholarship, he also believes he has not "developed skills to have the patience" that a Black male dean would need to successfully navigate the role. The politics dissuade him, as they do for Bianca and other women of color.

White women express comparable negative sentiments regarding leadership. Marybeth declares, "I certainly don't want to be any kind of dean, ever."

She sees it as "the job from hell," especially since she prefers to spend her time writing and in the classroom. She emphasizes, "I don't like administrative work at all. I think I'd hate that." Similarly, Isabella calls herself "a reluctant leader," and only for positions guiding and advising students. She has been "offered to be an associate dean twice" but "turned it down because I want to be a teacher and not an administrator." The leadership responsibilities she has accepted are more service oriented, furthering her role of "taking care of the academic family" as an other-mother.[32] Madison, a junior faculty member, feels "conflicted" because she "would like to play a leadership role," but she prefers "scholarship and teaching." She hopes to take on "leadership along the lines of scholarship and/or teaching" to merge her interests. In this way, white women's priorities to teach and write parallel those expressed by Carla and other women of color. Ellen's previous negative experiences in leadership, like Annie's, have dissuaded her from pursuing it further. As the current chair of a high-powered committee, she admits that "some parts of it are really interesting," although "faculty politics [have] just been ridiculous." Other committee members contested her authority, much like students in class, by "using procedural delays to interfere with [voting, as well as] a lot of aggressive behavior" which left Ellen "feeling totally blindsided." Though she enjoyed certain aspects of the position, she affirms, "Is there any way I'm going to serve on this committee next year? No. It's such an absolute pain." Chloe is one of few white women who would consider serving as dean. Her past leadership opportunities grew out of other people encouraging her after "seeing something in me," rather than her actively pursuing a position. Yet she worries that a deanship would involve too much struggle "to juggle work and family," as she expects deans to be "out every night" working rather than home with family. While not all male deans have a hard time balancing, and not all deans work every night, she worries "that would be how I would have to do it," and the compromises would not be worth it.[33]

White men, in contrast to all others, are more direct about both their interest in leadership and pursuit of it.[34] Since they portray themselves as confident in their ability to do the job, their competence matters less.[35] Some white men see themselves in the role of a leader even when they are not currently pursuing positions. Critically, those in power see white men as a natural fit for leadership positions too, as Jane, Surya, and other women of color note through their own experiences. For Christopher, "through high school and college I was always the class president or fraternity president, all of that sort of thing. I was one of the two top officers on law review. [Leadership] seemed to be something I naturally gravitated to." More important than his own interest is that "people sort of acknowledged I was somebody that would be an appropriate leader for whatever they were doing." This external validation likely cemented Christopher's interest in leadership, as contrasted against Annie's internalization of the belief that she does not belong in leadership based on her previous experiences in those roles. Christopher became a dean early on, and continued in that role for many years. He had few personal obligations at home, as his wife managed their household and raised their children primarily on her own, which freed Christopher's time to focus completely on faculty and administrative duties, facilitating his professional success.[36]

Justin is ambivalent about a leadership role, admitting that he "would do it if called upon, but it's not something I would actively seek out." Some white men are called upon to fill these roles even when not seeking them directly. Joe is in the early stages of his law faculty career, but is "not ruling a dean[ship] out [since] maybe this opportunity will become available down the road." He recognizes leadership as a possible outcome, even without "plans to pursue that," because he has seen white male faculty who "become an associate dean and then they'll go for a deanship somewhere." He admits that "in some ways I've been surprised by some of the people who've done it. That's why I said, 'I'll never rule it out.' Down the road I might go for something like that." Contrast Joe's straightforward belief that a leadership position may be in his future, whether he actively pursues it or not, with Trisha's direct pursuit of leadership without success.[37] Joe also sees the role of dean as within his *habitus*, that is, an attainable outcome for his future; not only has he not ruled it out but also he has seen other white men who he believes are less qualified attain those positions with seemingly little effort, which further inspires him.[38]

White men see themselves in leadership positions—and others do too. This feeds into a system that not only prioritizes confidence, but also "rewards men for their incompetence while punishing women for their competence, to everyone's detriment."[39] Ken is not directly pursuing leadership but sees it as a personal goal to help "the people around me and the whole place to succeed, and so I invest a lot of energy and time in [the school], which I guess sometimes leads to leadership-type roles." Those with power notice Ken's efforts and reward him with formal leadership roles. Ian also began law teaching deeply invested in service work and "heavily involved in just trying to be a work horse in most of the committees I was on." As the service became overwhelming, he considered doing less. Yet his dean had taken notice and suggested that instead of scaling back, Ian could "continue doing what I'm doing and maybe do a little bit more in terms of harnessing some of the energy of the faculty and helping them move forward." He was offered an associate dean position as formal recognition of his service work, with the expectation that he would continue and expand it in exchange for fewer teaching obligations and greater pay. This recognition and reward is in direct contrast to Jane and other women of color who devote significant hours to service with no acknowledgment before being passed over for leadership in favor of white men.

6 In Pursuit of Work/Life Balance

S URYA IS ONE OF THE RARE WOMEN of color who "applied to law
school wanting to be a law professor." Two female faculty mentors offered guidance "on my writing all through law school" and "were very
helpful" when Surya was on the job market, providing advice "on my FAR
form" and even organizing a mock job talk. When Surya and her husband
were first employed in demanding yet flexible careers they "used to work on
the weekends, and like stay at the office until 8 p.m. I mean, we used to work
all the time"—but that was "before we had kids." Now, with young children
at home, "you want to get home by six [if possible, and] I don't work on the
weekends, because you're with your kids." With two full-time working adults
in the household, "there is nobody like the dedicated full-time housewife" to
tend to the home and family. So Surya picks up the slack, "figuring out laun-
dry, groceries, kids' afterschool activities, and their schedules, their homework." Because "you can't fit all of that in just [from] 6 to 10 p.m., some of that
creeps into your daytime." As a result, Surya recognizes, "I don't necessarily
have the full nine-to-five [day] just working on my article [or] just working
on my teaching." Though her husband contributes, Surya states, "I for sure
do more" of both the hands-on childrearing and the planning. Surya is "more
like the manager, and he is the employee," meaning that "everything has to be
in my head of what needs to be done and on what schedule and what's happening when." After organizing it all, "then I tell him what to do, so I think
that makes it a little easier on him." His job is simply to "get the task done

when I tell him to do it, but I have to know, 'What are the fifty tasks that have to be done this week?'" Her husband has been a supportive partner and dedicated father, encouraging Surya's visiting appointments at various schools. When Surya had her first child, she was so overwhelmed that she worried, 'Oh my God! I'll never write again!'" Over time, however, she has taken the long view, noting that "it helps to see, 'What did I do in the last five years?' because then suddenly it's like, 'Wow! I accomplished a lot of writing. I did a lot in five years.'" She acknowledges, "It's a lot to juggle," but she has found a way to excel.

There is no one-size-fits-all, ideal work/life balance. Yet most women of color law professors concede that they could do better. Some researchers define work/life balance as a "comfortable state of equilibrium achieved between an employee's primary priorities of their employment position and their private lifestyle."[1] Others suggest that "balance is achieved when one feels fulfilled both at work and in [one's] lifestyle."[2] This chapter discusses DLA participants' responses to questions about their work/life balance, without offering judgment, winners and losers, objective preferences, or external goals—aside from individuals expressing perspectives on whether they have achieved the balance they seek.

Race and gender variations in work/life balance are stark, with women of color engaging in a difficult balancing act every day and long term. Most women of color faculty are the default parent at home, managing the household and taking on the bulk of child-rearing duties, including the mental load. Those without children or partners often have nothing forcing them to stop working. Women of color also take on additional personal responsibilities, from elder care to community involvement. White women have similar challenges, while white men and many men of color tend to enjoy their balance— often because women are picking up the slack at the home.

Workaholics Seeking Balance

Women of color express frustration both with the extra service work they take on as academics and the extra burdens they carry in their home lives, leading to greater imbalance overall. When asked to share details of their work/life balance, most women of color DLA participants respond as Grace does: "So, 'I don't have balance,' is the answer." Haley notes, "It's always been imbalanced." Patrice laments, "I feel like already I'm not doing nearly as much as I'd like to."

Many women of color law professors are self-proclaimed or externally described "workaholics." Lola initially asserts, "I have a pretty good balance" but interrupts herself to admit, "Well, my partner doesn't think so. He says I work too much." Erin is "fortunate in that I think my [partner] understands why I'm so busy, because I pretty much work all the time, like there's no day off." Ironically, the flexibility in law teaching encourages constant work. Kayla "can totally work by myself [for] days on end without coming up for air or seeing a human," admitting that perhaps "that's not healthy, but it's a temptation." She has recently started a romantic relationship and realizes that "dating has been really challenging because I don't feel like I can devote the level of time that I want" to work while getting to know someone new. Notably, Grace, Haley, Kayla, and others lament their lack of balance—and they do not have children.

Many who are child-free note that their balance suffers since nothing forces them away from work. Just as parental leave is more than a women's issue, achieving work/life balance is more than a parental issue. Many single individuals and nonparents are heavily invested in their extended families and communities, striving to balance their personal priorities and professional responsibilities.[3] A Latina professor named Marisol notes, "I mean I don't have kids and I don't have a husband, so you'd think that I'd be able to do all this stuff. [Yet] I have a horrible work/life balance, horrible, horrible, horrible." Being an academic provides "this wonderful, flexible schedule," making it easy to "end up blurring the lines [so that] you work at home, you work on Saturdays, you work on Sundays, you're just never *not* working." Marisol believes "there's always something to do," so "you sort of never leave work," which makes balancing "my biggest struggle."

Partners sometimes complicate balance. Grace notes that "because I don't have children, it's easier to spend almost all of my time working versus deciding that I need a break." This affects her relationship with her husband, who will "get to a point of frustration" that finally forces Grace to "take a break; and then it will build up again and then he'll get frustrated and I'll take a break." Grace acknowledges that "part of the problem is [flexibility,] because on our jobs you can do so much work at home too that there's not that separation between work at the office and work at home." She stays on campus all day to teach and complete "a lot of administrative work." Then, "once I go home, the first thing is: open my computer, read my emails, and start doing more work." She does "see my husband for maybe five minutes, maybe a half hour if he's cooking and I'm talking to him. But then I'll go back upstairs to my office and then just work until my brain can't work anymore." After a few weeks of this schedule, "my husband will start making comments about how I just work too much and he never sees me [because] I'm a workaholic." When it escalates he asks, "'Do we even know each other anymore?' [and] then I feel bad because he's right." To make amends, "we'll go out to dinner. I'll try to make more of an effort and that will last a week because I'm cognizant of it . . . and then work takes over again" as the cycle repeats. Talking through it, Grace notes, "God! As I say it, it sounds so horrible!"

Those who have children, like Carla, spend their time "literally work[ing] around the clock . . . in a panic." Carla "never took a vacation. I didn't go to Hawaii. I didn't go to Europe. I didn't do anything. I just worked, worked, worked, worked." Comparing motherhood to her single life, Carla admits, "It was better to have my son around, because I would actually take more time off." Carla's experience counters existing research, by indicating that children contribute to *better* work/life balance by pulling parents away from the job, even if "life" then revolves around kids.[4] Emma's "work/life balance is work and family, period." She is "a mother of a two-year-old and I am currently pregnant with another that's due shortly." For Emma, "when I'm not at work, I'm actively engaged in my family life with my immediate family, with my husband and my kid; and when I'm not doing that, I'm working. I don't have much going on outside of those two things." Melanie similarly notes, "I have no life other than my family and my work. Friends who don't mind being on the backburner for most of the time—that is one of my main strategies. There isn't a whole lot of life." Elaine worked a lot when her children were young, but still "spent a lot of time with our kids" by painstakingly "structur[ing] everything else in our lives around the kids." Elaine "traveled a lot" to present at conferences but she and her husband "always took our kids." The result? "We didn't see as many museums. We didn't go to fancy restaurants. We did kid things." When Destiny's children were young, she also "just did not have time" to do much besides work and family. She laughingly notes that she has lived in the same city for "almost fifteen years, and I don't know it, because I'm never out in the world!" She has lived there, but until recently "was never a part of it. I never had the time. All I did was work and [manage] my household, so all of my time was spent between those two things." Her experience of a "social life out in the community [being] completely absent" is common for women of color law professors. With grown children, Destiny is "just now emerging" into the social scene, "and really getting to know people and really getting to know spaces and things and what's going on." Vivian was "gob smacked" trying to balance the personal and professional aspects of her life. While she "had a child after tenure," she is "just in awe how people would do this before they get tenure." Her own tenure process was straightforward "because I was a workaholic. I worked. All I did was work, basically . . . and I really enjoyed it."[5]

Even as women of color characterize themselves as workaholics, many enjoy working hard, lamenting their inability to be fully immersed in their work when children, parents, and other personal obligations interfere. Karen gushes "that it's actually nice to have . . . a professional space to be in," because her home life revolves around the kids. She feels somewhat balanced, though her kids are "big enough to notice when you're gone; small enough to really still want you around." As a result, "there are definitely times when you leave too early in the morning and come home too late at night, and don't see your kids all day. That don't feel so great." When Mariana was involved in the day-to-day of raising two young children, she felt "the problem is that I love researching." Reflecting on her daily routine, she says, "You wake up, go through your email, get ready for your classes, and the rest of the day you spend researching or organizing your projects." But "at some point you really need to stop." Now that her children are older, "they have their own families [and live] in different cities." Yet not having them to distract her away from work makes her "a danger to myself," as she keeps saying yes to service work and taking on additional projects, until "I overdo it on the computer and I hurt myself." The work never stops.

Some DLA participants directly compare their current academic life with previous private practice, expressing relief at the more flexible schedules they now hold. Melissa notes, "I can see the difference between being in private practice and being in academia and having the same breaks as my son, even though I may teach through them. I still have that time with him when he is off school, summer breaks." Imani finds work/life balance "to be difficult even though I have a flexible schedule as a professor." Reflecting on alternate universes, she wonders:

> I don't know what I would do if I was actually practicing law and trying to do all of this. I actually don't know what I would do with more than one [child]. Originally, we wanted more than one child [but] it didn't happen. Now, I look

back and think maybe that was a blessing in disguise because I barely have my head above water with just one!

Others see academia as creating greater difficulty balancing than legal practice. While academics generally enjoy significant flexibility in their workday, legal practice can be more family-friendly. Legal academia touts a flexible workday but does not commonly accommodate ongoing part-time, flex work, or work-share opportunities, as the corporate world increasingly does.[6] Academia rarely provides for full maternity leave (the tenure clock ticks on); the academic salary compared to corporate legal practice leaves less expendable income for childcare or extracurricular activities; and corporate perks from backup care for sick children to express-mailing pumped breast milk home from work trips are unheard of in academia.[7] Additionally, Camila notes one downside to her academic position is that it is "a solitary job." "In practice it was so easy, you were always being thrown with people, thrown with new people and there was just a lot more exposure to people and different people." As an academic, "I don't have that now. I miss that." The grass is not necessarily greener in academia.

Gendered Expectations of the Default Parent

After leaving campus, many women of color go home to work the *second shift* of managing their household.[8] Sociologists have also highlighted the ongoing *invisible work* that many women contribute to the household, in addition to time consuming chores and duties.[9] Social media, ahead of legal scholarship, has recently brought attention to the trials and tribulations of the *default parent*, the one with primary responsibility "for the emotional, physical and logistical needs of the children."[10] They are the ones their children turn to first, expected to arrange doctor's appointments and play dates, purchase school supplies and ballet shoes, and manage meltdowns and pick-me-ups.[11] Although the default parent may not be "visibly parenting during every minute of every day," tasks and to-do lists associated with their children occupy "the back of [their minds, because they are] keeping track" of it all.[12] Even when two parents "do equal amounts of chores related to children," the default parent is the one "in charge of the family's minutia," which includes knowing "what needs doing" and either doing it herself or delegating to the *back-up parent*.[13] The management responsibility of being the home "boss" adds a layer of complexity to work/life balance, as "the scope and volume of managing this many lives and details comes with a surprisingly huge emotional and mental exhaustion that is unique to the default parent."[14]

This *mental load*, usually carried by women, has been studied and discussed in both academia and popular media.[15] Women tend to "do more of the intellectual, mental, and emotional work," plus "more of the learning and information processing" to keep the home running.[16] Male partners help, but usually only after women first notice and then delegate specific tasks to them. The default parent's jobs of "thinking, worrying, paying attention, and delegating is work that is largely invisible, gets almost no recognition, and involves no pay or benefits."[17] Single parents do not have even a backup parent; instead, many hold full-time jobs while also managing the household, dealing with day-to-day issues involving their children, and responding to family crises mostly alone.[18]

Some women of color share equally with partners in parenting their children and running their household.[19] Emma acknowledges, "I rely heavily on my husband, who is wonderful, amazing . . . and has been a wonderful resource to me and an inspiration to me." She characterizes their relationship not only as "very strong," but also as "equal" and "coparenting." April gushes, "My husband is the greatest husband you could ever find. . . . I'm lucky to have him. We are in a very successful and mutually fulfilling relationship in all of the different ways you can describe it." Jane, whose partner has a similarly demanding yet flexible job, credits open communication for their parenting equality. She says, "Every week my partner and I will work out . . . what my teaching schedule is and what her [work] schedules are, [so] we can figure out who's dropping off on what days," with an attempt to "work it out where she will pick up the kids twice during the week and I'll pick the kids up twice during the week." That way, each parent "can work late on two nights of a given week [and] then we'll split the fifth day [depending on whether] either of us has a deadline." This requires "a lot of talking, 'What do you have going on?' and 'What's your deadlines?' and things like that." Even when their children "were younger and they would get sick more often," Jane and her partner would discuss "who can stay home" on any given day, rather than the responsibility defaulting to one of them. Through open and ongoing communication, they avoided the default parent trap altogether, engaging in equal coparenting. Frequently in opposite-sex relationships, however, gender norms dictate that women are the default parent; with seemingly flexible schedules, this is even more expected of women law professors. Changing circumstances affect parenting roles as well. Sofia says that initially, "my husband and I share[d] childcare responsibilities pretty easily." However, her husband now has a job that requires frequent travel, "so I have been single parenting."[20] Not surprisingly, "this is the first year where balancing work and family has been really hard because I've been taking on 90% of the family load."

Many default parents point out that their partners also contribute. Destiny and her partner, also an academic, had no friends or family nearby when they first moved to a new town for his work. Instead:

> [It was] just my spouse and I and we basically had to switch off. When he was at some function, I was not there because I was home with the kids. When I was at some function he was not there. So we spent years and years never traveling or attending the same functions because we really had to deal with these kids!

While her husband did contribute, Destiny admits, "I actually ended up bearing much more of the weight of children and facilitating my household than my spouse." Because her husband "was very active academically" and often traveling, Destiny had to "carry that weight, and carry that weight by myself" for much of the time. She is aware that "one of the consequences of that is [that] I probably was not as productive as I could have been," while her husband's career took off. Karen appreciates that the flexibility of being an academic means that "if my kids need to go to the dentist at 1 o'clock, I can take them. It also means I have to leave work and take someone to the dentist at 1 o'clock, which is not necessarily the best use of [my] time."

Imani uses the flexibility to get her work done during her child's regular school hours, so that after school is out, "I can focus completely on [family] and helping with homework, and helping with reading, and things of that nature." She says of her husband, "I try to devote my time to him, not constantly working at home." Her main challenge involves producing scholarship, as she "just can never really find the time or space to do it while I'm here in the office," with excessive service and student demands on her time.[21] Yet "it becomes difficult" to write from home when "I'm up in a separate bedroom and my daughter constantly comes in and is asking, 'Why can't you play with me?' and 'Why do you have to work?' And I hate that, to be quite honest with you." Imani admits, "I struggle with [balance]. Sometimes it makes me think, 'Why am I doing all this to write these articles?' And 'I'm spending time away from my daughter.' And 'Is it all worth it?' So I definitely have that conflict."

Like Destiny, she notes frankly, "It could be why I'm not as prolific a scholar as some people are, because I do place my family as a priority over my work." With added gender expectations of managing the household and being the default parent, it is no wonder Imani is stretched thin.

Women of color law professors also tackle the brunt of household management. Surya considers herself the "manager" for her family's home life, while her husband is akin to an "employee." Their circumstances mirror research indicating that male partners "may do more housework and childcare than before, but women still delegate" their tasks after listing, planning, and organizing.[22] Natalie and her husband, who also works full-time, pay a nanny for childcare from 9 a.m. to 5 p.m. on weekdays, while on "the weekends, we coparent." She remembers: "When I was pregnant and nursing it was very hard. That first year [after having a baby] it's very hard to be productive, get things done." Still today, she contributes more than her partner at home, explaining, "I cook, I make major parenting decisions like how to discipline, I buy all the clothes." She is also "more like the boss of it; like, if I tell him to do something, he will do it." Otherwise, it may not get done. She "take[s] charge of the domestic realm" to such an extent that "in terms of gender roles, I cannot pretend that we are totally there," in an equal split of household and childcare duties. Although "he's better than almost every guy I've met," Natalie carries a heavier mental load and contributes invisible work as the default parent.

Managing the realities of work/life balance can create conflict both when women become frustrated by the extra load and when their partners do more than they expect. When Annalisa "first started teaching, I was basically by myself [with the kids,] with my husband commuting. The commuting created a lot of tensions in the family, in our marriage, and also within our parenting." Once her husband found a job nearby, "life was much better." However, when he switched positions again, Annalisa "had a whole year just by myself with the kids during the week days [while] my husband flew back and forth." Ultimately, they moved to a new location where they both found mutually fulfilling work and which also eased the tension in their relationship. Laila pays for "day care for my kids nine to five, and then if I need anything I have my parents [nearby]." Yet when she recently traveled to present at an academic conference, "that created a little bit of tension [with] my husband because he had to take care of [the children]." In addition, at Laila's law school "we have to teach at night every few years," as it is a rotating responsibility among the faculty.[23] Laila knows firsthand that "especially when you have young children, that is harder, because the only time you get to see your kids is at night," since they are in school all day. Those semesters when "I'm in class two nights a week, I don't get to see them pretty much all day for two days a week" including at bedtime, which also creates "a big burden on my husband" who steps in as the primary caretaker. This juggling increases family tension as well.

Class privilege helps many women of color law professors achieve balance. As Natalie bluntly states, "I pay for childcare; that's how I balance. I'm privileged enough to get my money, and hand it over to the person who cares for my child." Imani's daughter's "school ends at three, but she goes to after-school care that ends at six, [though] I try to pick her up at four or five so we have homework time before she goes to bed around eight." Vivian's young child "is in after-school care until 6 p.m." Her guilt at his "late" pickup is assuaged by reminding herself that "he actually really likes it." April's children benefit from having "two really great sitters that are adult women, and I pay them very well"—a benefit of her class privilege.

At the end of the day, whether partners, nannies, or day care is available, women of color manage work/life balance by juggling personal and professional priorities. Carla "got comfortable . . . existing on very little sleep." Though her partner was the primary caregiver, she still contributed a significant amount of daily attention to the family. On a typical day, Carla would start off early in the morning with exercise, then "I go home, get ready for work, go to work; I would come home at three [to] be with my child, cook, get him to bed, [then] work until eleven," repeating the process "seven days a week." Laura also "would work a lot after [my kids] went to sleep," which meant, "I did a lot of work between 10 p.m. and 2 a.m. That was my work period." Working late into the night freed up weekday time for family, while she "also reserved pretty much the [entire] time on the weekends to do things with them," especially culturally significant events including powwows and musical performances. It was important to Laura to do "a lot of things together as a family," so she structured her work time accordingly. Laila also does "work more at night. I do work more on weekends [but then] I have to sneak in work when my kids are doing something else." She says, "I try to be as efficient as possible during the day," so she has time with her kids in the evenings before staying up to work again late into the night.

Many of the mothers in the DLA study start the second shift after getting home.[24] Laila "knew when I got home [from campus] it was job number two," taking care of the household, even if "there was no time for it." Gender norms often compel women to incorporate these duties into their professional lives, though men rarely do. Destiny "found it very difficult [to] teach, and keep my household stable and things moving, and then try to write during the year." Instead, she "did most of my writing during the summer," when service and teaching responsibilities ebb. Haley, like many others, is "usually reading for class in the car while [my child] is practicing" sports. Zahra's husband works nights; managing their two children, especially with "conferences, over-nights, and things" requires constant "juggling." They "rely on a lot of help from friends, babysitters," and family. However, Zahra tends to do much of the work herself, saying, "Generally I'm able to, kind of, take my kids to school and pick them up and be there for them, given this job." Though she admits that "there are stressful times, and periods where it is difficult," overall she appreciates that law teaching allows her to "maintain a good work/life balance."

There's More to Life

Many women of color have obligations and interests beyond partners and children, providing financial, emotional, and even legal aid to extended family and community.[25] Erin sees a gender component to this support, noting, "I think that's true for all women. We have responsibilities to our [extended] families oftentimes [that] will take us out of the [law school] environment." Aging and ill parents are a primary source of concern and dedication. Mariana accepted a job at her current institution "to be closer to my father" when he became "very sick." Although she does "have siblings [near] my dad, they're barely functioning as adults" themselves, leaving most of the caretaking to her. Gabrielle's situation is "difficult at the present time because my husband's mother was having some medical issues," causing her and her husband to commute between their home (near work) and her mother-in-law's home out of state. Now, Gabrielle has "a lot less time to get the balance right," juggling desires "to spend time with my husband, and to get these articles done, and everything else I need to do, and prepare for class." Lately, "it hasn't been a very good balance." Vivian helped out when her mother was sick and later passed away, which "was super intense and preoccupying." She now cares for her father, though she is relieved that "so far, my dad is not in eldercare crisis." Many women are part of the *sandwich generation*, expected to be the primary caretaker of aging parents at the same time that they are the default parent for young children.[26] Annie recalls, "My parents aged around the same time my kids were teenagers. That was hard. It was a very hard time in my life." When her father moved nearby, she began "going over to his house to clean and cook and chop [vegetables] once a week or more, and then trying to do things with my kids." It became impossible to juggle all of that while "trying to be an overachiever at work still." Yet Annie was not comfortable relaxing her professional focus because "I was so afraid of not being taken seriously at work." Again, gender bias and the presumption of incompetence fueled her drive to do more at work while simultaneously doing more at home. Trying to prove wrong those who have low expectations of women of color is a common, but exhausting, response to these challenges.[27]

Hannah is single and child-free, "so I don't have as many obligations as others do. On the other hand, my parents" and sibling take up a considerable amount of time. She provides both "emotional support and some financial support," and recently traveled to a hospital out of state to help family with "health issues." Hannah's family members "come and visit quite a lot and spend a lot of time here and we spend a lot of time on the phone and things like that." Martha supplies both emotional and financial support to an uncle who "depends on me as his main surrogate daughter." In addition, "when my sisters have legal problems, I usually hear [from them] on the phone." Bianca acknowledges that "my mother was very dependent on my help, on my financial aid."

Alexandra also has "small financial obligations to my husband's mother," though greater responsibility looming on the horizon "informs my decisions" even now. She and her husband are renting "a tiny two-bedroom" apartment where "there is no good place for me to work." Although they "would love to buy a house . . . I'm uncomfortable dumping all of our savings into a down payment when we have aging parents and we have my mother-in-law ([who] is basically on welfare)" to care for, along with their children. As the primary earner in her nuclear family, and likely for extended family in years to come, Alexandra is "much more tempered in my financial decisions because I know it's not just about me." Similarly, a woman of color scholar and administrator admits that "work has been all consuming. I don't think I've struck a particularly good balance. I decided not to get another dog because I just could not imagine the dog getting a fair shake with my schedule." Nevertheless, she does prioritize exercise, and tries "to eat right and to sleep" because "my health is important to me." Although she does not currently have responsibilities associated with a partner or children, she does provide both financial and emotional support to various extended family members. While she enjoys her job and is not particularly worried about her balance, "I would never ever do it at the expense of not being there for my mother, [who] might need me at some point." As a Black administrator and professor named Josephine confirms: "My job is always on my mind. It's not a good opportunity for balance. I don't think any dean has that luxury."

For some, duties extend beyond partners, children, and parents to extended family and communities. Marisol is not responsible for a partner or kids, though "I have a ninety-two-year-old grandmother and a ninety-year-old great uncle" who live nearby. When other extended family have health crises, "then I have to go fly home and help out." They all depend on her to also "do the legal work; since you're the lawyer of the family you're always being called and asked to do stuff." This is true for many faculty of color, connected to families and communities who need legal assistance but lack meaningful access to justice.[28] Marisol's juggling is compounded by the fact that her extended family has no clear understanding of her career. Part of why it is "really hard to balance work and life is because . . . they don't see you going to work eight to five, [so] they think you just have [lots of time] off." April warns, "The list of things I have to do is long." In addition to caring for her husband and children, a number of extended family members moved nearby. "Every one of them needs something" and April tries to provide it. In addition, she says, "I am an active church member. I am the lawyer for all the little church ladies: this one needs a divorce, this one needs a will, this one needs a this, this one's husband is dying and she needs a power of attorney." She sees all of their needs as her personal obligations. Plus, "I have a depressed and oppressed African American community. I try and help them when I can." Also, "I am a member of a sorority and a service organization and I participate actively in those things as well." In short, "I got a lot of shit going on all the time," and she juggles it as best she can.

Comparison and Contrast

Few faculty, regardless of their racial or gender background, believe themselves to be experts in work/life balance. Yet on this topic perhaps more than any other addressed in this book, gender differences are stark—surpassing even intersectional bias. White male professors are generally comfortable with their balance, as are most men of color, while white women struggle with many of the same challenges facing women of color. Most faculty are workaholics, but few are as involved in managing their home life and supporting their communities as women of color. As Cindy notes:

> [A] lot of us [on the faculty] have young kids—both the men and the women. But most of the women who have families on our faculty, we are primary caretakers if not coparenting, whereas a lot of men with families have their wives home who do most of that work.

The balancing act is easiest for those white men who have less to balance, who have partners with less demanding or time-consuming jobs, or whose partners stay home to manage the household and take on primary parenting duties. Few, if any, white male faculty are the default parent; instead, the default is for the careers of white men to accelerate in part because their partners manage the home life.

A former dean named Christopher acknowledges, "I probably would not have achieved the professional success I did if I was not a workaholic with my professorship and my administrative job." He also credits freedom from child rearing as directly related to his professional success. While he now regrets spending little time with his children, he also believes he had "a saint for a wife who raised our kids until they were in junior high school, then went back to the workplace." Research shows partner managing the home life "allows everyone else the freedom not to."[29] When Joe was single, he was "one of these guys [who was] always at work, 24/7." Once he married, he made an effort to spend time with his wife. His next hurdle will be managing with his first baby, due in two months. When pressed on how the baby might alter his work/life balance, he responds, "I don't anticipate any changes. I'm not going to take any leave. [In fact,] it never occurred to me to do any of that." Joe "might cancel a day of class," though he has not "talked to my wife about that. Maybe she's upset." His priority is to continue working just as he has in the past, including "teach[ing] at night. I love teaching the night students and I'm not going to change that." Few new mothers who are academics could say the same.

Most white male law professors do contribute at home. Ian and his wife "have three young children." Echoing Emma and other women of color, Ian notes, "There's not a lot of social life. My social life revolves around my family and job, and I'm happy with that." He and his wife, who works full-time as a teacher, share parenting duties. Ian says, "I love that I have the opportunity almost always to come home and cook for my family and help provide for them in that way and play with them and enjoy them in that way." John, whose wife is also a teacher, is "responsible for getting [my child] to school in the morning," which is "easy to do, given I don't teach until the afternoons." He appreciates how "mobile" his job is, "so you can do it from home if you're not teaching." John's conference travel is "more of a pain" for his partner, who then has to wake their child to drop off at child care before her own work-day begins. John is "also responsible for my [child] many nights and weekend days" now that his wife is pursuing an advanced degree.

Ken has pushed back against his law school's "norms about parent-ing[, which] are completely gendered." His wife gave birth to their first child "within four days of a colleague of mine, who gave birth to her baby." While "it was unquestioned" that his female colleague would receive a semester of leave, Ken's request to do so "was denied." Ken's wife planned to take time off immediately after the birth of their child; when Ken told his dean that "'when she goes back to work, I may choose to stay home and be the full-time care-giver so one of us can be home for the first nine months,'" his dean "basically was like, 'No.'" With a new dean in place during his wife's second pregnancy, Ken decided that "this time I'm going to demand a leave and I'm going to ex-plain to the dean why men and women should not have different rules." With-out Ken having to insist, the dean immediately agreed to the leave, though Ken is unsure whether "that signals a change in policy or the fact that he's a new dean and he hopes to make me happy in this instance; [either way,] that was refreshing and really great." Other problematic gender norms persist. Ken had agreed to participate in a series of student-faculty meetings before they were scheduled for evenings; when he asked if there were "any way we can move this program, what I got back were bewildered looks," with everyone "baffled when I said I couldn't do something in an evening," since they ex-pected a male professor to be free. When "they refused to move it," Ken re-signed. Ken sees this as part of a larger pattern, also evident in the DLA data, where most of his male colleagues "have spouses that stay home and take care of the kids full-time," giving them the freedom to "work longer hours." Even when those colleagues "are not in the office, they don't have to do all kinds of other stuff because they have a spouse where it's that spouse's [responsibility to spend time] organizing play dates or buying groceries." Pervasive gender expectations for women at home propel their male partners forward while holding back not only women but also the men who push back.

Other white men who are single or have no children note few personal obligations competing with work. Matt says, "I adore my wife, we don't have kids, so childcare is [not an issue]. We haven't had significant elder care or other family care responsibilities yet, thankfully." He is aware that "in terms of family commitments, there are fewer demands on my time than many colleagues." The flexibility of his job helps him to "take on more of the housekeeping" or be available if "we need repairs done or something." Justin's life is "pretty much all focused on work." He may "see friends every once in a while" or "watch a movie" when he travels to visit his partner out of state. Otherwise, he is working. Adam's work/life balance has "been a real struggle" because of his deep commitment to students and his husband's more demanding work schedule.[30] The "risk of doing too much" is a big concern, as "the burn out issue [is] always on the horizon and always looming." He believes this is exacerbated by colleagues "who have a great work/life balance" but are "not respected at all" because they "only work fifteen to twenty hours a week," teaching classes with old notes, avoiding service duties, and not fully meeting their students' needs.

Like white men, men of color are more comfortable with their balance in part because they juggle fewer responsibilities. Dwayne took efforts to attend his children's soccer games on weekends (working on research during halftime), but was not involved in day-to-day child rearing. Like Christopher, he acknowledges, "My wife was very good. She took care of the home life and all, which freed me up to really focus on my work." Fermin works "about 80 hours a week" and "treats every day as a workday," including weekends. His wife works long hours too, though she also "spends family time" with extended relatives nearby. They do not have children and "split the chores" for the household. He admits, "I'm not sure I recognize balance. I probably don't have it, but I'm very happy doing what I'm doing." Again, the goal of this chapter is not to suggest a particular balance as appropriate or optimal, but instead reveal how participants themselves reflect on their lives, noting intersectional and gender-based patterns.

Jack, who was child-free until tenure, is "not sure I would have been able to [raise kids] pre-tenure." With his infant in university day care at the institution where he and his wife both work, they are "just figuring it out," including Jack "getting sleep where I can." He is on a previously scheduled leave—not parental leave, though his school does offer course relief to new parents. Like Joe, Jack requested no accommodations to care for his newborn. While it is

Jack's prerogative to accept institutional help or not, equal gender participation in family-friendly policies would both make them appear and become more gender-neutral.[31]

Ed says he has "a great work/life balance" mainly because "I just really like doing what I do. He has "been able to maintain a good life with my partner, friends, and do things I like to do, like going to see live music." Ed is "a night owl, so after the baby goes to bed I'm able to get a ton of work done," as are many women of color. Ed also spends half of every week out of state at his law school (while his partner and her mother stay behind to provide childcare); being away from home contributes significantly to his professional success since "for three days a week it's school, a lot of school, and more school, and then when I go home there's less school." He contributes when he is home, but being away provides concentrated work time without interference from any family obligations. Stuart has "an incredibly large [extended] family" nearby. His wife has a similarly demanding yet flexible job; she took time off to care for their children and now is back at work full time. Stuart's mother-in-law also provides supplemental care for his children, including school drop-offs and pickups. He realizes that "I can't ever complain about the work/life balance here in large part because of my mother-in-law and having family around." Relying on them makes his professional life easier, since any time "you have something come up and you're in a little bit of a pinch, there's always someone to help out." While Stuart, Ed, Jack, and Ken contribute to the family as involved parents, neither these nor any other male law professors in the DLA study describe themselves as the primary caretaker or the default parent—in direct contrast to the many women of color faculty who fulfill these roles.

Most white women law professors also carry the mental load and are the default parent, highlighting the pervasive role of gender in work/life balance. After the birth of her child, Ellen took one semester off from academia before she and her partner hired a full-time nanny. Ellen is now "trying to cram my work into forty hours a week and it's definitely been a challenge." She is grateful to have no "responsibilities related to elder care . . . or any other substantial family obligations." Like Surya and Natalie, Ellen is "the organized person" and "the planner" in her household. Her husband "is very happy to let me do all of the organizing, planning, remembering it's Thursday so trash needs to go out." These are classic examples of default parent responsibilities, and indicators of the burdensome mental load that Ellen carries. As for many women of color, this invisible work became "really frustrating" for Ellen, "especially after a year of working full-time [with an infant] and having all those additional child things clutter my brain." She discussed the problem with her husband and now, "I set for him a recurrent iPhone reminder" to get weekly tasks done. Coupled with Ellen "pulling back," she also recognized both that "there are a lot of different acceptable ways to have something done [and also] that if he does it at the very last minute that's just the way it is and I'm not responsible for it and it's not my problem." Just as for Jane and her partner, communication was key for Ellen to overcome gender-based expectations and find better balance.

Many white women strike a precarious balance, constantly juggling work and family. Scarlett has been the primary caretaker for her two young children since they were born, working full-time at various academic positions but able to afford only part-time childcare. Finally on the tenure track, with the ability to cover full-time care, "this year is the easiest it's ever been" since she has "some breathing space right now that I never had before," including time "to be at my desk all day and [even] travel" for work when needed. She is still the default parent, with a marriage "about to dissolve," in part because there was "a lot of stress" when she was on the job market. The constant juggling of "working my butt off to write enough or be good enough to get a job, and then take care of the kids at the same time" without much support from her partner "basically made [the relationship] fall apart." In contrast, Abigail's husband—whom she credits as being "better with babies than I am"—"took the first year [after each child's birth] off from his [law] practice to stay home." Abigail's father also lived with them, "so we had a third parent" for "much of my children's youth." Abigail "did not get any maternity leave whatsoever," though she found a way "to create my own maternity time" by trading class time from the next semester with another professor teaching the same course. She was comfortable making special arrangements only because "another faculty member—male—had done the same thing" the year prior. In these and other ways, men creating and utilizing family-friendly policies pave the way for women to do so and normalize the need for balance.

Jordan is a single parent to her children, who "are with me exclusively." When she was married, her partner "was able to assist, [which] enabled me to do a more robust amount of work than I'm able to manage now." Her mother moved in for a year after the divorce, but now, without a "support structure," Jordan feels she is "just on my own here, trying to do everything." Her scholarship has "really taken a hit" as she "could barely get anything done except keeping up with the day-to-day." A partner managing the home life would free her to be more productive at work. Ava agrees that "work/life balance is a hard one." While she laments that some "do it better than I do, being much more productive scholars," she suspects what the DLA data prove: that many male colleagues "have a wife at home taking care of the kids; I get a sense that they get a lot done in part because they are just so well managed." Just as Surya and Natalie do, Ava applies employment terminology to this gendered arrangement: women are the household "managers," while men accept limited tasks at home, freeing their time for professional advancement.

Chloe, whose son was a high school swimmer, notes wryly, "I've written a lot of articles by swimming pools." Without a leave policy, she was back in the classroom just six weeks after delivering her first child by cesarean section. "I'm working, and they're little," was a frequent concern when her children were young, as she did not want to "feel like I wasn't there" for their childhood. Chloe echoes many women of color, admitting, "Sometimes on the bad days, I feel like I missed it all because I was at work." Chloe's children have grown into adults "taking care of themselves," though she now makes weekly trips to visit her elderly mother nearby. Her pregnant daughter has also asked "each grandparent to take an afternoon" to provide childcare for the new baby; Chloe's response: "I signed up for Monday."

Some white women without children appreciate that this creates opportunities to work more, in a parallel to men whose wives at home facilitate their success. Lisa, a senior scholar and former dean, says bluntly, "I never had any babies to take care of, so that was a big help [professionally]" as "I didn't really have the work/life problem that a lot of [women] did." Early on, she and her husband "ate out a lot," and even now, "I send out or buy things and bring them back or have them delivered." Similarly, Sydney enjoys her balance, observing, "I go to bed at a normal time. I sleep like eight or nine hours a night. I don't have kids. I have [pets]. I have a girlfriend; she works, too. We don't have kids. I do a lot of yoga." Isabella also feels "really fortunate. I don't have children, so I don't have to worry about childcare issues. I have a spouse, but my job frees me up to do a lot of things. I think that makes life a little easier at my house." She regularly tells "a lot of my friends and family, 'I'm rich in time.' I get to sit and ponder about life'"—in contrast to the many mothers who have no time between work and family. Academics defines much of Marybeth's life. She says, "I don't have a problem balancing. I don't have kids, so that makes it easier." When pressed, she admits that she does little besides work: "That would be key. I have no life and I do nothing else. That's actually true." Outside of work, Madison spends time with extended family, including helping her father with a recent medical crisis, yet she is grateful to "not have the demands of being the primary caregiver for anybody other than a dog." She is careful about her balance, though, noting: "I still try to actively manage my time because otherwise I will work too much and not do enough life." Overall, women from all racial backgrounds take on more not only at work but also at home—highlighting the pervasive gender privilege of men who more easily enjoy a comfortable work/life balance.

Conclusion

Implementing Support, Strategies, and Solutions

T HIS BOOK HIGHLIGHTS VARIOUS opportunities and challenges based on raceXgender privilege, obstacles created by overt and implicit bias, and intersectional barriers that prevent women of color law professors from maximizing success. This concluding chapter offers strategies and solutions to ameliorate these inequalities, as well as detailing sources of support.

The overwhelming majority of women of color, in addition to white men, white women, and men of color, see their law faculty experience as positive. More than 90% of Black women, 87% of Asian Americans, and 75% of Latinas see their professional experience as positive, compared to 91% of men of color, and 100% of white men and white women (Table 10). In addition, and despite ongoing challenges, most women of color along with white and male colleagues plan to remain in legal academia—though higher percentages of Black women (24%), Latinas (25%), and Native American women (40%) are uncertain about their future professional plans (Table 11). A few are more certain about leaving law teaching, including Carla who notes, "As soon as I get my kid through college I can walk away from this."

The overall positive experience and intention to remain in law teaching are a direct result of the support that women of color draw from various sources. The individual strategies discussed here could serve as best practices to assist other marginalized faculty surmount inflexible barriers that prevent them from realizing their full potential. Academics in other disciplines and other countries could also implement these suggestions, along with other

TABLE 10 Overall Experience in Legal Academia Is Positive, by Race and Gender, DLA 2013

		Strongly agree	Agree	Neither agree nor disagree	Disagree	Strongly disagree	Total
African American women	n	10	9	0	2	0	21
	%	47.62	42.86	0.00	9.52	0.00	100.00
Asian American women	n	8	5	0	2	0	15
	%	53.33	33.33	0.00	13.33	0.00	100.00
Latinas	n	5	4	0	2	1	12
	%	41.67	33.33	0.00	16.67	8.33	100.00
Native American women	n	2	1	0	1	1	5
	%	40.00	20.00	0.00	20.00	20.00	100.00
Middle Eastern women	n	1	1	0	0	0	2
	%	50.00	50.00	0.00	0.00	0.00	100.00
Multiracial women	n	2	2	0	3	0	7
	%	28.57	28.57	0.00	42.86	0.00	100.00
Men of color	n	8	2	0	1	0	11
	%	72.73	18.18	0.00	9.09	0.00	100.00
White women	n	6	5	0	0	0	11
	%	54.55	45.45	0.00	0.00	0.00	100.00
White men	n	6	2	0	0	0	8
	%	75.00	25.00	0.00	0.00	0.00	100.00
Total	n	48	31	0	11	2	92
	%	52.17	33.70	0.00	11.96	2.17	100.00

marginalized employees in traditionally white workplaces. Yet law schools must institute structural changes—including those proposed here—to fully overcome the challenges that currently stymie nontraditional faculty and encumber legal education as a whole.

Sources of Support

Women of color rely on various sources of support to overcome the many obstacles they face in legal academia (see Table 12). Valeria gets "a lot of emotional support from a lot of different people in my life," including "a great family," "parents," and "a significant other" as well as "two really great friends from law school [and] a mentor/best friend." April also has multiple support mechanisms:

TABLE 11 Certainty of Remaining in Legal Academia, by Race and Gender, DLA 2013

		Yes, at current institution	Yes, at different institution	Not certain	Total
African American women	n	4	12	5	21
	%	19.05	57.14	23.81	100.00
Asian American women	n	9	5	1	15
	%	60.00	33.33	6.67	100.00
Latinas	n	6	3	3	12
	%	50.00	25.00	25.00	100.00
Native American women	n	2	1	2	5
	%	40.00	20.00	40.00	100.00
Middle Eastern women	n	0	2	0	2
	%	0.00	100.00	0.00	100.00
Multiracial women	n	3	4	0	7
	%	42.86	57.14	0.00	100.00
Men of color	n	7	3	1	11
	%	63.64	27.27	9.09	100.00
White women	n	8	2	1	11
	%	72.73	18.18	9.09	100.00
White men	n	4	3	1	8
	%	50.00	37.50	12.50	100.00
Total	n	43	35	14	92
	%	46.74	38.04	15.22	100.00

We are active members of a church and I have a couple of good girlfriends, so I feel like I have good support. When I was in my work crisis with the lawsuit and everything I started seeing a psychiatrist. I am very thankful that I have insurance that helped to defray the cost of that. We have ample savings [and] make enough money, so I can travel and that makes me happy.

Virtually all DLA participants, regardless of racial and gender background, rely on family, friends, and mentors to support them through difficult times. Professional organizations focused on personal identity are helpful for particular faculty, as is religion.

First and foremost, law faculty draw support from family—including partners, parents, and even children. Elaine appreciates her "good fortune" at finding "a very supportive partner who not only views things like family life

TABLE 12 Support from Various Sources, by Race and Gender, DLA 2013

		Family	Friends	Internal faculty	Other mentors	Professional orgs	Religion
African American women	n	21	20	21	20	17	12
	%	100	95.23	100	95.24	80.95	57.14
Asian American women	n	15	14	15	14	11	6
	%	100	93.33	100	100	73	42.86
Latinas	n	11	12	12	12	10	4
	%	91.67	100	100	100	83.33	33.33
Native American women	n	5	5	4	5	4	1
	%	100	100	80	100	100	50.00
Middle Eastern women	n	2	2	2	2	1	2
	%	100	100	100	100	50.00	100
Multiracial women	n	7	7	7	6	5	2
	%	100	100	100	85.71	71.43	28.57
Men of color	n	9	10	10	9	8	4
	%	90.00	100	100	100	80.00	40.00
White women	n	11	11	10	9	9	4
	%	100	100	100	90.00	81.81	36.36
White men	n	8	8	8	7	6	0
	%	100	100	100	87.50	75.00	0.00
Total	n	89	89	89	84	71	35

as something he *should* partner in, but actually probably enjoys it more than I do." Because both of them are invested, Elaine can be both "real active with my kids [and] real active with my work life." Patrice and her husband are "essentially fifty-fifty" at home, including her husband doing "a lot of childcare, a lot of housework, grocery shopping [and] at least 80% of the cooking."[1]

Women of color also rely on extended family for support. Life is "exponentially easier" for Laila now that she lives close to extended family who "help a lot" by providing personal support and backup childcare. While many women of color—especially Black women—provide financial support to extended family, some receive it. Aarti's primary source of support is her husband, but "both sets of parents give us a lot of financial support." Vivian feels "really lucky my sister lives in town with [her] two kids, [plus] my dad's been supportive too." Camila, who was a single parent in her early years in legal academia, says, "Probably my biggest source of emotional support are my children," who are now grown and live nearby. Destiny describes herself as "a big family person," clarifying:

When I talk about family, I'm really talking about my extended family [includ-ing]: my parents, my sister, my brother, my sister-cousin, the people who raised me, grew up with me and helped propel me to this point. Those are the people I rely on, and very close friends.

Destiny, like many others, incorporates close friends into her definition of family, including "people I have grown up with," plus a "cadre of friends from college that I'm still in touch with," her "closest friends" from law school, and newer local friends. She emphasizes, "My support group comes from outside of my particular faculty." Similarly, Vivian depends on family and a "wonderful network of [local] friends," though her faculty is not particularly supportive. Lola has "a small group" of her "closest friends" whom she has trusted and relied on for decades. She distinguishes between true friends and the superficial relationships she has with faculty colleagues, noting that when she was denied promotion the year before, she hid her true feelings from her coworkers, opening up instead to these family and friends.[2]

While many women of color law professors note how friendships have sustained them through difficult times, others lament their lack of close friendships. Camila is "not exactly a loner," but because she does not rely much on others, "friends are something that I probably sacrificed, not inten-tionally but . . . well, by default." She does "have some friends I rely on for limited things, like, you know, to do exercise-type things," but not whom she would turn to for emotional support. Hannah also has few close friendships, saying, "I don't really hang out with friends on a regular basis. I probably go out maybe once a month and talk with people on the phone maybe once a week." Elaine "relied mostly on my husband" for support but notes, "I regret not having more of a friendship group; that's something I'm trying to sort of remedy these days." When exploring why she does not have close friends, she tearfully suggests it may be because in academia "you felt like you had to be so strong you couldn't share . . . so that means you couldn't have friends."

Many other women of color are clear that outside mentors provide sup-port. Sofia has "learned that mentorship relationships matter a lot, and that's why I've done a lot of mentoring myself." She reminds junior scholars that mentors take all shapes, sizes, and backgrounds and don't have to be "mentors like you." For her, "the critical mentor who sort of made my career was a white man who took me under his wing." Brianna took on her administrative posi-tion only after multiple "faculty of color and outsider faculty [told me], 'Yeah, you should do this!'" Thus, "it wasn't as much people who were already advanced in their careers who were reaching back" to propel Brianna forward—although she believes that "is absolutely essential. I'm trying to do a lot of that now"—but rather "colleagues who were supportive of me pursuing opportunities." These *near peer mentorships* are prevalent throughout legal academia, especially for and by women of color.[3] Marjorie, a Black professor, appreciates not only gentle encouragement from mentors but also "tough love." When a white male colleague was dismissive of her work early on, Marjorie's mentor "was like, 'This will not be the first time or the last time that some white man annoys you, you know, or somebody dismisses your work because of the work you do. Suck it up and get back out there! [Don't] let them make you stop!'"

Jane met one of her most influential mentors before starting her first teaching position when both attended an academic conference geared toward people of color. When that senior scholar discovered that Jane would be teaching the same first-year course that she taught, "she immediately offered me all of her stuff—meaning her lecture notes, syllabus, old exams—and made herself available to me to talk about any [substantive] questions that I may have when I was prepping that class." Jane took her up on the offer, admitting that "there were times when I called her more than once a week, and she was always available, and she spent whatever time she needed to help me." That experience and relationship for Jane were "invaluable, absolutely invaluable" to her success as a law professor.

Like Jane, many women of color create connections with mentors while attending academic conferences, especially those that merge personal identity with professional research. Grace is thrilled that "some of my closest friends are within the academy, not within the same school necessarily, but in other schools." Destiny's supporters include "a cadre of faculty at other academic institutions," as well as "organizations that I'm associated with." She credits the LatCrit network and annual meetings with offering "a world of support for my scholarship as well as general support in terms of keeping me stable or having people to talk to about what's going on on my faculty." Her mentors include serious scholars "who you can send that first shitty draft to who won't judge you" and also offer personal support. Jane similarly explains, "When we are at CAPALF [a meeting of the Conference of Asian Pacific American Law Faculty], I feel comfortable with those people because they look like people I grew up with." Familiarity makes legal academia more welcoming for Jane and others who participate in meetings hosted by CAPALF, LatCrit, and other identity-based groups. Annie draws significant support from "coming to these conferences. Honestly, I think I couldn't have done it without [the many faculty who] have just been strongly supportive over the years."[4]

Many senior Black scholars, including Josephine, credit the "Northeast Corridor of Women"—an informal group of "women of color, mostly African American but not all, from New York down to Washington, so we'd go up and down the corridor [to meet]"—with keeping them in legal academia. The group was "a way for me to have a larger network of [academic] women of color," since there were few at her school or locally; these meetings not only were "a nice resource," but also provided vital introductions to "people who modeled for me what it meant to be a woman of color in academia." The same group inspired Karen to participate in a "very casual" biannual dinner for women of color that creates a "really nice opportunity to talk about what's going on at our law schools, talk about what's going on with us professionally, talk about what's going on in the world." This informal gathering has become a "great support system, particularly because there are so few people of color" at each institution. Grouping the few women of color in a region together creates a critical mass where women of color faculty share stories, commiserate, and support one another.[5] Alexandra agrees that "groups like SALT and LatCrit and these conferences aimed at supporting people of color are absolutely critical" for retaining women of color in legal academia; her participation in the annual Lutie Lytle "Black women's writing group" includes "not just time to socialize," but also exposure to "critical sources of information" that she cannot get elsewhere.[6] Imani also attends the Lutie workshop "as often as I can," noting, "I'm definitely going this summer because I need that boost. I need that recharging of people who have experienced similar things that you have, just reaffirming you and helping to get you through it." Imani, Alexandra, Jane, and others appreciate the gathering of scholars at ethnically geared national academic conferences especially because they cannot find this support on their own campus.

Most institutions today do offer various forms of faculty support, ranging from funds for conference travel to workshops on scholarship or teaching. Parental leave is one way schools can show their commitment to supporting faculty as individuals, not just workers. Emma is pregnant while teaching this semester but "will have a parental leave semester which will relieve some teaching and some service," though her tenure clock does not stop. She is grateful for the partial break, offered through "a university-wide policy for faculty, male and female." Natalie was fortunate to have "a semester off" and "went back to work four months after [my child] was born." For a year after she returned to work, she was "nursing and pumping and stuff. I wasn't my most productive, but I managed to write a couple articles." Some women of color need extra prodding to accept support. Patrice was on the AALS job market while she was pregnant with her second child. Once she had accepted an offer and told administrators that she was pregnant, "they gave me maternity leave for the first semester." Although she initially planned to decline, a group of senior women scholars at her new institution "found out I was pregnant and they did an intervention [telling me], 'You can't start [teaching] in the fall.'" They urged her to think about the "women coming after you," explaining, "'If you don't take this leave, it's going to be harder for [future] women.'" These senior scholars worried that colleagues who did not support parental leave would use Patrice as an example for why it was unnecessary, or hold all women to her standard; once they explained how opponents could "say, 'Patrice didn't take this leave; why did you?' [then] that was really the kicker for me" in deciding to take it.[7]

Institutional struggles are unfortunately more common than institutional support. Elaine was the first pregnant law professor in her institution's history, though "there were men, obviously, whose wives were pregnant." Too afraid to "even look into the school's . . . maternity leave policy," she "had my baby one day and I was back to work the next week." Over twenty years later, she thinks "that was kind of silly, but it was important to me to do that because I didn't want anyone thinking that I *couldn't* do that." Her response to microaggressions was to prove them wrong, though it came at a cost of exhaustion.[8] Carolina had no maternity leave option "when I had my first child, [so] my last class was Friday and I gave birth Monday." Carolina's second child was born weeks earlier than expected; initially, "I had colleagues cover my classes," but then "I came back and I finished the semester two weeks after [my daughter] was born." Carla also "didn't have a maternity leave; I had a reduced activity[, meaning,] I didn't teach but I had full committee work . . . and, of course, the tenure clock did not stop." She wanted to spend time recovering from giving birth and bonding with her newborn; instead, "my experience was that the work became more intense."

Some institutions mangle application of their own leave policies, highlighting at best a lack of commitment to equality and at worst direct discrimination. For Sofia, "the whole thing worked differently than what I was told it would work." At her school, "everybody gets one semester of pretenure leave" and "there was no paid maternity leave, but you could take your research leave as maternity leave." After some negotiating, "the dean offered me a reduced course load for spring" in addition to her pretenure leave in the fall. She admits, "I could have taught one class, [but my problem was,] what happens to my research leave, which everyone else got?" When Sofia approached the university human resources officials to discuss taking Family Medical Leave, they admitted that the institution was required to offer her more. Armed with that knowledge, she marched back to the dean "and said, 'Actually, I'm going to take the fall as Family Medical Leave . . . from the day of [my child's] birth and I would like my research leave in the spring,' so that's how it worked out." Ironically, Sofia says, "Now the cat is out of the bag and everybody on the faculty knows the Family Medical Leave [Act guarantees leave] and so one of my other colleagues, a man, took Family Medical Leave this semester." The time and effort Sofia spent to discover and rectify this injustice has paid off not only for the other female faculty, but for men as well. Like Elaine, who was the first pregnant faculty member at her school, Sofia says that "up until now, the only tenured and tenure-track faculty to have had children were men and they were happy with the dean's offer that they can just take their research leave as paternity leave." Fathers' experiences with childbirth, physical recovery, and newborn care rarely mirror mothers'. Because men who take leave often do so months after the birth of a child, when "they had a four- or five-month-old who's probably sleeping through most of the night and who took relatively long naps," and often relying on a partner as the child's primary caretaker, Emma worries that many men spend significant "leave" time on scholarship.[9] On the other hand, Sofia "was faced with writing [scholarship while the primary caretaker for] a newborn," which she laughingly acknowledges, "is not gonna happen." There ends what Sofia calls her "saga of maternity leave," problematic, yet not unique.

Church families, religion, and spirituality also provide key support for particular faculty. When asked about sources of support, Imani responds, "Well, first and foremost I'm very religious, so I definitely rely on God and my spirituality for support." Specifically, "I try to pray very often. We go to church every week as a family, so that's definitely a great support system for me." Similarly, Kayla's "spiritual practice has definitely been a source of support," including "yoga and meditation." Annalisa's family is also "becoming more engrained in our church, and that's important to us" as a source of spiritual support.

Individual Strategies Maximizing Success

Even more than family, friends, and mentors, women of color rely on their own strength and ingenuity to persevere as law professors. Every woman of color participant in the Diversity in Legal Academia study shared personal tips on how to maximize success. This section begins where they do: emphasizing substantive and procedural preparation, and stressing the importance of being and finding mentors. Next, the chapter highlights the necessity for self-care, taking time away from professional endeavors to reconnect with other stress-reducing and life-affirming activities. Finally, DLA participants remind us: when all else fails, think big!

Preparation

Starting as a law faculty member takes enormous preparation. While mastering substantive course material is challenging for everyone, women of color also must prepare for anticipated student and faculty confrontations associated with the presumption of incompetence, and related challenges stemming from purposeful discrimination and implicit bias.

Elaine taught a large section in her first year and "tried hard, of course, to be super prepared." When Annalisa first started teaching, "I ha[d] to overcome this perception that a woman and a person of color is not as smart as [a white man]. You know, not a fraud, basically." To overcome this presumption of incompetence, "there's always a [pressure] on my side to over-prepare." Students challenged Susan on a daily basis by badgering her with questions in an attempt to trip her up, a common gendered reaction to seeing a woman at the podium. Instead of getting frustrated, disengaged, or giving up, Susan says:

> I responded by staying ten steps ahead of them. So I not only read the law review articles cited in the notes after the cases in the casebook, I read the law review articles cited in the law review articles so that any question that they asked me I could respond. Because I knew that when that day came that I said, "I don't know," I would lose all credibility in the classroom.

Brianna notes that it may not be enough to "know the stuff inside and out." Because "people of color and women in particular don't get the benefit of the doubt" that they are experts, "overpreparation is the norm." She believes that older, white male professors "can walk in with old crusty notes and not have really innovated their classes in a lot of different ways and can not be on the top of their game on any given day" and students will still accept that person as the authority because they look like what the students expect. DLA findings regarding the experiences of white men and men of color bear this out, as most men enjoy the support of students even in their first years of teaching. In Brianna's experience, women of color law professors are not "afforded that luxury," and therefore work much harder to earn and keep their students' respect.[10] Brianna warns that while you "have to know your material," it is equally important to "exude a confidence [through] a classroom persona." Those who do not "go into that classroom and command that classroom" meet "students [who] sense vulnerability [and] will devour you." Just as in leadership, where confidence is rewarded above competence, mastery is not sufficient in class; women of color must also exude self-assurance to succeed.[11]

Another individual strategy to combat the presumption of incompetence is to prove expertise using past experience. Hannah incorporates practice-related insights into class lectures specifically to "demonstrate the kind of work that I was working on and that it directly related to what I was teaching them," highlighting how and why she was qualified. Armida believes that "it's all about credentializing yourself," especially to gain legitimacy with the "white male" students who challenge her. Early every academic year, she begins "incorporating in the conversation [past] experience from [my elite law school and] large law firm. That impresses them [and] gives them a value in me. [They think,] 'Sullivan & Cromwell?! That means that she's smart.'" Carolina sees students as "brand-sensitive" consumers who want to know "that they have a good product that went to a good school," so she suggests women of color faculty use those credentials to "establish your credibility."

As a new faculty member, Eliana "spent so much time" not only anticipating classroom challenges, but developing strategies to avoid them, that ultimately "I never had a student challenge me." In class, "I immediately come in with a lot of authority, with a lot of telling [the students], 'These are my credentials.' 'This is why we are doing this.'" If any issues arise, Eliana "use[s] humor" to diffuse tension, and also "a lot of skills [from] being a mother: very sweet, very nice, very nurturing—but switching at a moment's notice and letting them know there is no messing around in my class and these are my expectations." She describes this as her "feminine approach" to teaching, with a focus on "establishing relationships where they don't want to let me down" and believes this is why "students work really hard in my class" with little pushback. Eliana's experience invokes *gender judo*, the purposeful decision by women to "take feminine stereotypes that can hold women back . . . and use those stereotypes to propel themselves forward."[12] Despite Eliana's success in employing gender judo to turn her role as a mother into an asset in the classroom, it "takes a lot of energy," "versus a white male colleague" who is assumed to be competent from the start.

Michelle entered legal academia in the early 1990s and is now also a university-wide administrator. Remembering her early days in the legal academy, Michelle recalls the ways in which she prepared for class management:

> I just decided I wasn't going to let the students make me lose my cool in the classroom. It was *my* classroom. Like, someone said to me, "I just think you are wrong." Yeah. I take a moment; I go to the board, erase the board to give myself a few minutes to calm down, and then I would sort of turn back around and smile and say, "That's really interesting Mr. So-and-So. Tell me more, tell me more." And I would do it in like a very personable way. You know I'd smile like, "Come on, tell me more. Come at me, come at me, tell me why I'm so wrong."

This put the other students at ease. Initially during confrontations:

> the other students would become so tense like, "Oh my goodness, what's she going to do?" And I learned if you ever yell or go after a student in the class, the [other] students will bond with that person because even though you don't experience it that way they experience it as someone with power going against someone without power.

By encouraging the confrontational student to explain why Michelle was wrong, and with friendly body language ("I put my hand on my hip and I kind of smile at them"), she "would break the tension, other students would laugh, that [confrontational] student would become a little bit isolated, then I'd get pretty much like a hem and haw [from the student. Plus, at that point] everyone knows that they are not going to make me crack." This detailed strategy would not only break the tension but also signal to all students that they could not trip her up.

During times when it was "very obvious to me that they were just trying to challenge my authority," Laila reminded herself that she had been a litigator who "didn't tolerate that." Ultimately the students fell into line. Imani strategically starts off strict then eases off, saying:

I also am very tough, so I come in with a very high bar of no nonsense. If you're not prepared, that counts as an absence for me. So on the very first day I kind of come off as being somewhat intimidating, as students say. Now, I always dial that back, but I find as a female and a female of color it's better to start out tough like that and dial it back.

The strategy works "because if you start out lax you can never dial it up. I don't even want to open the door for that kind of disrespect to sneak in." As a result, disrespect rarely infiltrates Imani's classroom.

Yet conflicts extend beyond the students to interactions with colleagues. Lola cautions, "Oh my God. It's worse than they tell you." Though she anticipated confrontational colleagues, "for me at least the first couple years, it was way worse [than expected]. And so being emotionally prepared for that [is key]." She stresses the mental health importance of "knowing that it's not about you, there's nothing wrong with you. You're smart. Again, you're probably just disrupting the reality or beliefs of certain people in terms of where you should be and what you should be doing." Martha was emotionally "not well prepared" to enter law teaching, coming "from the business world," where being "a rational thinker" facilitated her success. As a new law professor, she "made a lot of mistakes thinking that the merits would win." Instead of her economics and engineering background, she suggests that to better understand the pervasive intersectional motivations, implicit bias, and gender privilege, "really the preparation for law [teaching] is psychology and sociology and gender studies." She adds, "That's what I wish I would've known twenty years ago."

Few women of color faculty have the time and fortitude to educate colleagues about root causes of the challenges they face, from implicit bias to gender discrimination.[13] Instead, they find workarounds. Over many years, Elaine adopted a strategy in faculty meetings where she "thought carefully before I said things, but once I decided to say something, I said it emphatically—not like dramatically, but with a lot of conviction." She avoided being labeled as someone who was "outcome oriented" (whose "ideology shifted depending on whatever they wanted the outcome to be on a decision,") by being "authentic about being consistent with my principles and my values." After frequent silencing, mansplaining, and hepeating, she also realized that how long she spoke mattered as much as how she spoke and what she said. When she had a great idea, she "wouldn't just blurt it out," but would "talk a little longer." She will state her idea "in an organized fashion," then continue speaking to "give an example, and then maybe relate it back to something in the past." Though "it doesn't have to be long—maybe two minutes instead of ten seconds—then it seems like it is more likely that they will pay attention." She also strategically organizes "groups of people who seemed to listen to each other" into "coalitions." When one person speaks, "to the extent we think it's a good idea, we're going to say, "Oh, I agree with what she said," validating and *amplifying* both the speaker and the idea, giving the speaker credit for her thoughts.[14]

Susan had to prepare strategically to maximize her chances of earning promotion. She knew when she applied for tenure that her colleagues would critique some subpar teaching evaluations from her early years, likely based on intersectional raceXgender bias. To combat this, "I invited all of my colleagues to come and sit in on my classes—unannounced and as often as they would like. And I got excellent evaluations from all of my colleagues," creating a "disconnect between the [negative] student evaluations and [the overwhelmingly positive faculty reviews]." No advance notice was required, "because I didn't want them to say, 'Oh, well, you knew we were coming so you prepared extra well.'" She endured the extra pressure of never knowing when faculty colleagues would wander into class, but Susan is "confident that having [the peer evaluations] as the counterbalancing narrative in my tenure file was the only way I got promoted."

Mentorship

Mentorship is essential for faculty seeking to maximize their full potential, as discussed periodically elsewhere in this book. Both offering support to others and finding scholars to provide support are necessary.

Be One

In addition to the women of color discussed earlier in this chapter, many white DLA participants are thankful for mentorship. As Joe states, "I think having a mentor is invaluable, absolutely." He continues, "You learn so much from your mentors. [N]ot only did [my mentor] make me a better writer, teacher, and thinker, but also she knows how the whole game is played. . . . All the unwritten rules and subtleties of how to break into the profession, she knew." Abigail agrees: "Mentors have been hugely instrumental, [providing] a glimpse of my future self and cautionary tales and advice. I was very lucky to have superb mentors."

While many women of color are grateful for mentors, others lament a lack of guidance. When Lori, an Asian American, was a fellow pursuing a tenure-track position, her mentors "had the whole machinery set up to basically launch me," resulting in her successful entry into the profession. To facilitate the success of women of color candidates, mentors from all racial and gender backgrounds must support, nurture, and promote them. As Emma notes, "You have to have mentors. White men need to mentor people who are women and people of color just like they would mentor others." Hannah agrees, urging her fellow legal academics: "Be willing to mentor people who aren't just like you."

Sometimes, mentors provide that extra nudge pushing women of color practitioners to begin thinking of law teaching. Bianca notes that "part of how I ended up in law teaching [involves] a phone call from a Latino law professor [around] when I was thinking of maybe going into the teaching market." "Mentorship is really important," but Bianca notes that effective outreach is also key, since it is "really important to have someone who is committed to diversifying and then reaching out and finding ways to connect with the various places where you might find talented people."

Just one mentor can make a big difference. Leanne's advice came late, but helped nonetheless. She recalls:

> I called my Federal Courts professor who had been very, very supportive of me [during law school] and he immediately said, "Leanne, send me your application now! Fax it to me!" And I had already turned it in, so he called me and said, "You filled it out all wrong. You don't put Race & the Law as your first preferred course," and this is back in [the 1990s] so he's like, "That's the death knell!" He was like, "You put Civil Procedure. You put your first-year core set of courses." And I was like, "You're crazy." And he says, "Ahh it's too late. You've already submitted it."

When she did not secure a tenure-track position, her mentor "advised me [toward] taking the visiting spot" she was offered. He also demanded Leanne devote herself to scholarship for the next year: "He told me, 'Short your students. Short your husband. Short your family. Short your life. Write. Do nothing but write for the next year.'" His advice paid off, as Leanne secured a tenure-track position soon after.

Mentoring existing faculty may be just as important in order to improve retention rates and propel women of color into leadership. Yet current law faculty spend little time mentoring, whether at their institutions or elsewhere.

Data show that most law faculty—regardless of race or gender—spend under five hours per month on faculty mentorship.[15] As Zahra notes, women should make "an active effort to try and help other women, other women of color [especially]," particularly because "men have advantages because of their relationships with other men." Many "men will choose to mentor other women— and that's great—but I feel like oftentimes [women] don't mentor each other and I feel like we should." Clearly, all faculty can do better.

Find One

All types of mentors, sponsors, and allies can contribute. Vivian says the following of her relationship with a senior white female scholar:

> She's my . . . strongest ally. [T]hat relationship has been absolutely pivotal for me here. She was the associate dean when I got hired. She was my go-to person when I don't know what to do about something.

Hannah readily took advantage of the encouragement she received from two senior white men teaching in her subject area, contacting them frequently for assistance to ask, "'How would you present this material?' And I would get back answers" rather than snarky comments.

While Michelle more easily connected with mentors early in her career, now, "I'm pretty senior, so I struggle more now to find mentors." Her "early mentors were just very encouraging," understanding "difficulties in the classroom" associated with race and gender. As she progressed, they became "wonderful in terms of helping me work on my scholarship" by "helping me frame it in a way that was sophisticated and nuanced, pushing it to be better in very, very supportive ways" and even "helped me secure my second job" through a lateral move. Now, she relies more on *sponsors*, whom she defines as those "willing to do things like spend capital on my behalf," and other near peer mentors.[16] Marjorie worked for a time in a region with very few other Black women faculty, "so the four of us, we had this writing, reading, mooting, eating, and wine drinking, and massage group. The ability and willingness to take the time out and be encouraging" was vital to her survival and success.

Give Yourself a Break

While preparation is key and mentorship is critical, many suggest that faculty remember to practice self-care, especially given difficulties managing work/

life balance. Most women of color juggle too much at work—between extra service burdens, countering conflicts in the classroom, and navigating colleagues who hide hostility behind civility—and also work the second shift at home. Nobody can do it all, all the time, long-term.

Susan encourages women of color to prioritize themselves in the midst of their personal and professional obligations. So "one of the things I tell young women is, 'Think about yourself, and not necessarily your partner and your family first all the time, because [doing so] can have some setbacks.'" Annie learned this lesson firsthand by acting like "a crazy woman" when she was solely responsible for two teenaged children and an elderly parent living nearby, all while carrying a full load at work.[17] Pulled in so many directions personally, and working excessively, she says, "I look back and I go, 'Why did I go to that meeting instead of going to the end-of-the-year band award ceremony where my daughter was getting an award?'" For many of "those kinds of choices, I look back and I think, 'I was so afraid of not being taken seriously at work,'" that she could never let up. Her response to microaggressions was to work harder to prove her detractors wrong. But things fell through the cracks—including "one time, my daughter, I was supposed to pick her up from soccer, and I forgot. She was sitting there in the dark," waiting, when Annie eventually showed up. Overall, "raising children is really hard," and doing so while working as a law professor can be overwhelming. Annie admits, "I have some regrets."

Brianna is a senior administrator focused on avoiding those regrets, in part by leaning on "good support systems," including "executive assistants and secretaries who support you to protect your time." Because Brianna prioritizes family, "the first thing that goes into my calendar is my kids' schedules," which she "guards" as carefully as professional appointments. Since self-care, "especially for women, often comes last," she cautions, "Schedule your dentist appointment and your doctors' appointments, you know, try to take care of yourself."[18] Usually, women "take everybody else to the doctor and of course it's your kids ailing, but we can be there going, 'Oh my God, I've been having this pain for like two months and I haven't made *my* way to the doctor!'" Even though Brianna is "intentional about also putting my health first," still, "it's a challenge." Similarly, Mariana raised two children on her own and became "a danger to myself" after suffering an injury from computer overuse; she now warns others not to follow the path of too much work and not enough down time, declaring, "So the young scholars: pay attention to that! Are you into yoga or anything? Pilates? Do something like that now!'" Melanie draws support from "mentors definitely, my wife definitely, my son definitely, [and] my extended family very much." She also takes comfort in "being outdoors" whether she is "running, hiking, [or otherwise] being physically active and getting out of the city" to "return to my soul" and "gain some perspective."

A white professor named Ava concludes, "I think I probably do as good a job as I can do." She admits, "I look at some of my colleagues with littler kids or multiple [kids] and I think, 'I don't know how you do it.'" She envisions a fantasy life where women have greater support at home to realize their maximum potential at work, like those white men who have freedom to pursue opportunities because their partners manage the household and raise the children.[19] She notes, wistfully:

> I joke about if I had a wife at home—who was doing the laundry, grocery shopping, childcare, and everything that goes into running a house—it would free up so much of my time and I would be more productive too.

Research confirms Ava's belief that the mental load, invisible load, and default parenting hamper female professional success—just as it propels forward male colleagues who rely on partners to handle the home life.[20] Yet women must give themselves a break to survive and thrive in either realm, and ideally in both.

Think Big

It may be fantasy, but Ava thinks big. Keeping the big picture in mind is another individual strategy that women of color employ to maximize professional success, one that others can adapt and adopt to their own circumstances. A senior white scholar named Abigail wishes she had "put more towards family" rather than worrying about work early on: "If there was anything I could change I would go back and write a few less articles and spend more hours with the little people when they were little. You only see that in retrospect." Laura also worked long hours when her children were young, yet saw that as beneficial for both herself and her children, noting:

> I honestly think all of this exposure was good for them and I always thought that. It also teaches them that your mother works, your mother is a professional, and it helps them see definitely a role model of someone who is a mother as well as having a profession.

When her kids were under ten, she took a high profile job that meant "I would have to work late at night," but her children came with her and "would play in the hallways . . . and explore." She sees this early training as something that "really stimulates them in ways that you may not know for many years." It also makes children understand that they are "a part of what you're doing." Laura looks back at how she navigated work and family and sees "nothing bad about that at all," confirming current research on the benefits that working mothers pass on to their children, both boys and girls.[21]

Incorporating a global or historical outlook can also help. Marjorie reminds us to think about "the pioneers," especially the women who endured significant challenges without support. When Marjorie has a difficult day at work, she tells herself, "'You think you have it tough, girly? What about [if there were just] one of us? [At least now] there are about four of us. You can have dinner [together] at this table.'" Similarly, June says, "I don't complain" because she realizes the relative privilege she enjoys as a legal academic. In her mind, "We're not like picking cotton [or] getting whipped across your back or raped by the slave master, right? So to me, this is a global luxury." While those alternatives are deeply troubling and the distance between that reality and June's is vast, this context helps her put things in perspective.

Others think broadly about success and priorities over time, without overthinking how productive any particular hour or day may have been. Annalisa "used to feel guilty like, 'oh my gosh, the kids are in school all day, and now I have a babysitter picking them up. And I only see them at dinner,'" though ultimately she knew, "I needed to work." With a full-time job and young children, she "couldn't be the best mom . . . and be with them all the time, and [also] be good at what I did at school, so something had to give." Now she mentally separates the academic year from the summer, purposefully allocating her time differently during each period. "So during the semester, there were times when I'm doing more work and less mothering, and then my husband would pitch in." But in the summer, "I balance my life differently [than] when I'm teaching, so the kids go to summer camp from about 9 [a.m.] to 2 p.m. and then I pick them up and we hang out together afterwards." Annalisa is both hyperefficient "and diligent" about working during camp hours; afterward is family time, where "I try to turn off my cellphone. I don't check my email." Alexandra similarly "never feel[s] balanced by the day," meaning, "I don't go through my day thinking, 'OK, I did a particularly good job balancing everything.'" In response, she strives to balance more broadly, "by the week or the month or the year, what my priorities are in being a good scholar, and professor, and wife, and mother, and friend." Then, like Annalisa, she prioritizes what needs immediate attention at any given time, knowing that she will devote herself to other concerns later.

Thinking big is also useful with regard to leadership. One woman of color dean has encountered numerous faculty of color, exclaiming, "'Oh my God, you're crazy to [want to] be dean.'" While there are certainly challenges associated with women of color becoming deans, she reminds us of what will happen if nobody steps up: "Well you know what? Then all the deans will continue to be old white men. And we cannot complain about it. And that's the bottom line. Period."

Structural Solutions

Because intersectional discrimination, implicit bias, and gender privilege are institutional rather than purely individual problems, only structural solutions can truly ameliorate them. First, there must be allies in the administration who are aware of the obstacles facing women of color and proactively work to overcome them. Next, schools should work more diligently to stock the pipeline, to prepare greater numbers of nontraditional students for careers in legal academia. Yet subjective hiring procedures make clear that stocking the pipeline is not sufficient; it is also necessary to think outside the box, with regard to recruitment, retention, and leadership potential. Finally, institutions must recognize that faculty diversity and inclusion can transform legal education only with perseverance and persistence—and they must invest time, money, and effort in this endeavor to improve our unequal profession.

Allies in Administration

Former Yale Law School dean Robert Post asserts, "One of the most important tasks of a dean is to maintain faculty enthusiasm for and psychological investment in the school."[22] Doing so requires administrative support for faculty, with leaders taking active roles in protecting faculty by communicating openly, rejecting outlandish student demands, and publicizing their support for underrepresented faculty.[23]

Law school administrators should take special note of the horrific examples of gender discrimination plaguing law schools, from outright sexual harassment to other means of creating a hostile work environment for women.

Given recent controversies surrounding sexual harassment in entertainment, the judiciary, and other fields, legal academia should be especially vigilant about monitoring problematic and potentially illegal behavior.[24] Coupled with the many universities criticized for their lack of reporting and enforcement mechanisms to prevent sexual harassment and sexual assault on and around campus,[25] law schools should intensify efforts to comply with Title IX and employment law lest they draw the attention of private actors or the U.S. Department of Education.[26] All law schools should have sexual harassment policies in place, including zero tolerance for violations, clear reporting requirements, and guidelines to ensure that the documented silencing of women does not work against reporting efforts.

Even small changes can have large gender effects. Destiny's school has been working on "changing our meeting times to make them in the middle of the day" instead of at 4 p.m. as they had been for years. Why would that make a difference?

> Well, guess what? Half the women disappear at three! A couple of the men did as well, but almost all the women would disappear and . . . that is significant [because] when it came to decision-making, [women] were just not present because we were off picking up kids from school or taking them some place or that sort of thing.[27]

Administrators should also appreciate the many ways in which women of color are instrumental and beneficial to the institution, and create "institutional accountability for fixing gender service imbalances."[28] As Melissa says, "I think there definitely has to be recognition for all the many roles often women of color play in the law school; the advising and the retaining students role is completely undervalued." Women of color should receive credit and compensation for "taking care of the academic family."[29] Furthermore, administrators should do more to safeguard women of color from being overburdened with time-consuming service work that garners little credit in promotion and tenure reviews. A simple "increase in overall awareness of this issue may improve overall attitudes toward service loads, remove traces of gender bias from service expectations and enable both women and men to accept or decline service requests with equal ease and impunity."[30] Michelle suggests that leaders who want to support junior scholars "protect them from themselves. Many women of color, people of color, have a very [deep obligation to] service that can hurt them." Michelle suggests that "even if people are telling you they want to be involved in committees," administrators should "try to be very thoughtful about the kinds of things you are asking them to do prior to tenure"; even after tenure they should confirm that service "is being accompanied by scholarly production." Basically, this involves "teach[ing] people not to shoot themselves in the foot."

Administrators should also educate their full faculty on the challenges facing women of color in the classroom. Few DLA participants discussed trainings or workshops on campus that conveyed to colleagues their day-to-day intersectional raceXgender challenges. After numerous instances of gender-based student confrontations, Sofia initiated a "session on gender in the classroom" during a faculty retreat, specifically "because I felt people were not really thinking about [how] gender affected what you can do in the classroom." Yet administrators should take the lead on organizing these sessions, including hiring outside experts as facilitators, rather than adding yet another service burden on women of color faculty.

One way to have administrators who understand the experience of women of color is to propel them to these positions. Often (though not always) when this occurs, leaders are "people who get it; you don't have to explain everything from zero," as Patrice says. When she "was just going crazy" recently dealing with a particularly challenging class, Patrice approached a woman of color associate dean to discuss it, recalling, "I went to her office and was like, 'Aarrrghhhhh!' and she just got it, you know? Because she's a woman of color." Patrice "didn't really have to say much," to explain the presumption of incompetence or gender-based challenges, because her administrator "knew what was happening" through her own experiences. Yet DLA data confirm that achieving diverse leadership is difficult. Board members and existing administrators should encourage women of color to apply for these positions, promising long-term support. They must recognize that if only one woman or person of color is considered for a leadership position among a pool of white men, their efforts to improve diversity will likely "be futile"; yet if supporters manage to "change the status quo of the finalist pool [to include at least] two women, then the women have a fighting chance."[31] Once in the positions, women of color leaders must be given the freedom to succeed, not micromanaged or belittled into failure.

Stock the Pipeline

Faculty and administrators should stock the pipeline and better prepare students to become law professors. Destiny sets her students on a path towards legal academia:

What I do is mention to women in general and women of color in particular, "Have you ever thought about working in the academy? How do you distinguish yourself? Let's talk about doing some writing," you know, "Get on law review if you can. Let's talk about writing some articles. We can develop this paper—do you want to do it? Because this is going to set you apart. This can give you more options in the future, like you might want to teach. You might want to go into the academy, so let's see if we can write something that can get published."

While "those kinds of conversations" can be life changing for students, Destiny does not "think that happens much and that's part of the reason why you have so few women" law faculty. When a female student who "did really well her first year" approached Zahra to discuss a future in law teaching, Zahra "was like, 'You need to transfer to Stanford or Yale or Harvard,' and she did! She transferred to Stanford. I think it will help her." Zahra believes "we have to seek out opportunities to mentor these women of color, especially, or else they're not going to end up in those roads, they won't get a clerkship and might not try to do law review" or gather other traditional markers of success that are virtual necessities for law professors. Zahra thinks wistfully, "I wish I had that same mentoring when I was a student, and had someone saying, 'Why don't you transfer to Stanford or Yale? That will improve your chances of teaching a lot.' I just didn't have that." Vivian credits just this type of support with piquing her initial interest in law teaching. She says, "When I was in law school I was made to feel by my professors like I had something important to say," though she admits that overall "it's so easy for that message *not* to be communicated."

Jennifer also suggests beginning recruiting efforts early: "I think we should start helping people in law school think about this career." For Jennifer, "it wasn't until I was out of law school five years that anyone even approached me about the possibility." As a student, she says, it "never even occurred to me" to consider law teaching, seeing no faculty role models who shared her background. Hannah suggests, "To increase the recruitment, you need to fix the pipeline because right now there is a decreased number of women entering into law school and a decreased number of women of color entering into law school," compared to just a decade ago. Coupled with fewer openings for entry-level hires, and law schools being less wiling to take "risks" on candidates whose experiences do not match the traditional profile, opportunities for women of color candidates are miniscule. Laila suggests that schools create "a track that trains [students to become academics] rather than [assuming everyone will] just go out there and practice law." Having "a program in your school trying to prepare obviously a select few students" could be useful, especially if faculty ensured that the pool "is diverse and there are women of color." Melanie sees improving diversity as a complex problem: "When there isn't diversity, people self-select out of things [thinking they won't] be hospitable [or] there's not going to be opportunities." Yet "it's hard to diversify without [those people joining]." While fixing "the pipeline is part of it, there's something of a chicken and an egg problem." She is correct that creating a critical mass increases momentum, leading to improved diversity.

Brianna reminds us, "There has to be some pipelining that's being done towards the leadership world as well." To increase leadership diversity, administrators "should focus on creating an environment that feels fair and equitable," especially to nontraditional faculty.[32] Even "day-to-day interactions which signal to all genders that the [school] is interested in nurturing female employees may make a big difference."[33] Currently, while opportunities are expanding, Brianna would like to see the number of women of color deans increasing exponentially rather than incrementally, noting, "it's ridiculous. We gain some, we lose some." Instead of hoping the right person applies and assumes the role, Brianna warns that to increase leadership diversity, "we're going to have to be really intentional [or] it's going to continue to self-replicate," with white men being replaced by other white men.

Thinking Outside the Box

Purposeful determination is necessary to ensure faculty diversity in legal academia. Schools must change both recruiting and retention practices or risk maintaining overwhelmingly homogeneous faculty. Race and gender disparities in legal academia cannot be explained by a dearth of qualified applicants, both because the pool of AALS candidates and those graduating from law school include many diverse candidates who could succeed in legal academia.[34]

Pipelining will likely create greater numbers of women of color pursuing legal academia. To hire them, schools must expand the definition of merit beyond elite educational credentials, law review service, prestigious clerkships, PhDs, visiting assistant professor positions, and fellowships. None of these has been shown to correlate to success in legal academia. Yet most schools are unwilling to consider candidates from any but the top few law schools, let alone a school outside of the top tier, especially if the candidate has not accrued other elite markers.[35] Ironically, Imani notes, when many current white and male faculty were hired decades ago, "you could come on to the market from a good school and good background and have a good draft and you would probably end up with an offer and that's just hard to think of that happening now in the academy." Instead, Brianna suggests, "I think there needs to be greater outreach toward [women of color attorneys] who are in-house or in government positions or in firms," regardless of their other qualifications.[36] Otherwise, legal academia will continue to exclude scores of qualified candidates who could be flourishing faculty colleagues, but "don't really know how to break in to the academy," since most successful candidates follow "this traditional pipeline of law school, clerking, academy; or law school, fellowship, academy."

Sydney notes that her law school "found me through an out-of-the-box recruiting strategy" that relied less on elite credentials and more directly targeted local potential faculty candidates interested in scholarship. Mariana recounts that "the [most recent] person of color we hired" is someone that her associate dean met "at an Intellectual Property cocktail hour" for practitioners, where "they spotted her, found out who she was, and [asked whether she was] interested in teaching." Mariana conducted an initial screening interview, the candidate "was [then] given an opportunity to give a job talk, and she got a job." This candidate "didn't go through the AALS [recruiting process] at all" and "now she is a wonderful scholar at our law school." As Mariana warns, schools truly committed to faculty diversity "cannot rely on the AALS; it's not enough." If more law schools adopted strategies to reach women of color, instead of relying exclusively on traditional recruiting mechanisms that result in hiring primarily white men, women of color would likely comprise more than 7% of current law faculty.[37]

After Sonia was hired, her school "did a lot of diversity hiring in a clump," bringing in five diverse hires together. Sonia remembers thinking, "That's great. Because I was there alone as an entry-level person of color." Hiring a critical mass of faculty of color collectively is a tried and true method of improving both recruiting and retention. Otherwise, as Surya notes, "there's that one person [of color] who's always there, but [she] has no voice." When there is faculty diversity, there is still disagreement and debate, but at least "they're not disagreeing with me because of my gender or my race." Instead, when Surya has experienced faculty diversity, "our fights are genuinely about ideas and the future of [legal education]." She has held visiting positions at schools that "are not diverse at all," where colleagues "don't even see me as an individual." Instead, "they see me as a brown woman [and wonder,] 'Who is that person? What is she doing here?' They don't see me as one of them, and so that's just a little awkward. It's uncomfortable." Without exposure to other diverse faculty, "they can't even pronounce your name, so they don't even try." In her experience, "it's much more apparent that you're in the minority" when the faculty is overwhelmingly white "and then like the one or two people of color that they have are really kind of outcasts" who are "not present anymore." Tokenization of women of color leads to disengagement—hurting the individual faculty member, her institution, and legal education overall. Marjorie was hired along with "a critical mass of faculty of color, and that made a difference." There were a handful of African Americans like her, but also one "Asian [American], Latinas, a couple of feminist [men], white women [who were] feminist identified, and openly LGBT folks, so that made a difference" in terms of both recruiting her and normalizing her ongoing experience as a nontraditional faculty member.

Out-of-the-box thinking should also guide retention efforts. It is unclear whether course evaluations have any intrinsic value, as they depend on students who are by definition not well versed in the subject matter, evaluating faculty who know a great deal on the topic.[38] The comments on many student evaluations bypass substance altogether to focus on the style, appearance, racial background, sexual orientation, gender, or other personal characteristics of the instructor. Recognizing these severe limitations, administrators should consider doing away with course evaluations altogether, revising their format to account for diversity and inclusion, or decreasing their significance for promotion and tenure purposes. Most law schools do incorporate peer evaluations into the tenure file; thus, this proposal would result in less administrative work because student evaluations could be eliminated altogether, with no need to administer, analyze, or consider them for tenure or promotion purposes.[39] Because peers are in a better position to evaluate their colleagues' teaching effectiveness, this seems a better fit than student evaluations for assessing the professor. Student evaluations could otherwise be reworked to focus on the professor's skill at facilitating diversity discussions and including context in class conversations, explicitly highlighting the importance of diversity and inclusion in the classroom.

Marisol proposes at a minimum that law schools approach evaluations with skepticism, understanding the role of bias. She has seen firsthand what DLA data reveal: that "people of color don't get tenure as much because they're not supported" in the classroom or in their research—so "that's where they 'get' a lot of people [of color]." Marisol suggests that administrators "try to understand what other things are going on and [ask,] 'How can we protect this person so that they can grow as a teacher and a scholar and get tenure in the future?'" April suggests that schools interested in meaningful diversity include on student evaluation forms and even documents for school-sponsored events "a little check box that says, 'Have you considered diversity?' And you just check yes or no." That way if diversity "didn't come up" spontaneously during planning—say, when "you're putting together a panel, you call the people you know," and all of them happen to be white men—you have a moment to reconsider. She hopes "some people, they would read that question and think, 'I didn't! Let me go find somebody [else].' That would be good." Purposefully including diversity in the daily workings of the institution—standardizing and normalizing it—is an effective mechanism for effecting lasting change.

Jennifer reminds us to give due credit to service work, noting, "I think broadening the conception of what service means, might be helpful for women of color" who are overburdened by service without recognition or reward. Cindy suggests service be compensated with a bonus, similar to what some faculty receive for prominent scholarly placements, saying, "When we're doing this kind of work, why don't we get compensated for it in the way that writing an article that lands at *Yale* [*Law Journal*] gets compensated?" In this sense, even compensation may be skewed by gender bias—beyond salary critiques to conflicts involving service versus scholarship.[40]

Just Do It

The final question in the DLA interview asked participants for suggestions to improve diversity in legal academia, based on their own experiences and observations. The vast majority of respondents gave thoughtful, reasoned, and even passionate answers involving individual strategies and structural solutions that have been incorporated throughout this chapter. Others become irate, annoyed, or even angry—asserting that improvement requires acknowledgement of ongoing bias, which many faculty and administrators resist, and emphasizing that a lack of inclusion is a decades-long problem, with mechanisms to increase diversity already clearly spelled out.

Vivian stresses that "people have to deal with their own institutional bias and their own subconscious bias" before greater numbers of diverse faculty will apply, be hired, and succeed in legal academia. Colleagues reconstruct reality to explain "why the white guy hasn't written as much as opposed to the African American" candidate; she sees "completely different narratives, like, 'Oh, he's been so busy developing his economic theories' [for the white candidate,] as opposed to, 'I don't think he's capable to do the level of work' [for the African American]." Because "people tend to look for people like themselves, subconsciously," recruiting diverse faculty is especially challenging.[41] Discrimination should be addressed through focused attention on the part of the faculty and leadership, in conjunction with formal diversity training and other programming drawing attention to local challenges and suggesting institution-specific solutions to address them.

Implicit bias shapes leadership decisions and outcomes as well. While the "women's path to leadership is paved with many barriers including a very thick glass ceiling," a bigger obstacle is "the lack of career obstacles for incompetent men" who are selected to lead.[42] Annie reminds us that "the issues don't go away. I mean the permanence of racism and [other forms of bias are] so durable." Though there have been efforts toward inclusion, "it is an ongoing challenge." And the challenge itself—succeeding in legal academia while fighting implicit racial bias, male privilege, and intersectional discrimination—is unfair: "I have to constantly struggle against the feeling of entitlement that I shouldn't have to work with this. I shouldn't have to struggle. The white guy over there isn't struggling [with intersectional raceXgender bias], so why should I have to struggle?"

At a minimum, white colleagues and administrators should be aware and responsive to intersectional barriers hindering women of color from reaching their full potential, not only during the hiring process but throughout their careers. Schools also must overcome the assumption that women of color who already shoulder leadership duties, like Jane and her colleague, are not suited to formal leadership. Marisol suggests that when students are disruptive in class, administrators should "recognize that students may be pushing you in a different way because you're a female or you're a person of color or you're both." Otherwise, if "the institution allows them to do that without looking at the 'why,' then you have a lot more problems" ahead—with the institution enabling ongoing discrimination. Marisol asserts that "an institution that will support you" is one that will look at negative student evaluations and ask, "'Do your evaluations suck because you suck as a teacher, or is there something else going on?'" Frequently, intersectional bias plays a role.

Aisha suggests that administrators should "stop finding reasons to *not* hire" candidates of color. Like Vivian, she says that "oftentimes what I see in hiring situations, people will find reasons not to hire people of color and find reasons to hire white people so, you know, they give alibis to the deficiencies of white people but . . . look for the holes in [a person of color's] record to keep [her] down." If administrators "want to increase the number of women in academia, hire them, obviously. I mean, there's not a dearth of applicants out there. But you have to have a commitment to do it. It's not rocket science." Similarly, April states: "I think there's so few women in legal academia because white people won't hire them. [They] feel for some reason that we can't take a 'risk' on someone who doesn't fit [the standard] profile," even if other markers indicate a strong likelihood of success. Stuart believes his faculty has "a very 'strict scrutiny' analysis when it comes to [hiring] faculty of color." Famously, strict scrutiny has been accused of being "strict in theory, but fatal in fact," suggesting that no policy—or in this case, no faculty of color—could survive.[43] With half a dozen people of color on his relatively large faculty, Stuart believes "it's as if a quota has been reached at this school [with regard to token numbers of diverse faculty,] and that's where we're going to stay." Fermin makes clear that to improve faculty diversity, administrations should "be on the lookout all the time" for potential faculty of color "and not just expect [Professor Michael] Olivas to hand you a list of people who are ready to be hired." While the second approach is certainly easier, and available, administrators who truly seek diversity must be proactive.[44]

Many have called for leaders to go beyond "hiring chief diversity officers, establishing special endowments to support increased financial aid, launching cluster hires for faculty of color and investing in diversity programming, speakers and consultants."[45] While those are important and necessary opening steps, without a deep commitment to ensuring that diversity initiatives succeed, they may only "quiet the protesters, trustees and donors . . . while creating little systemic or transformative change."[46] Lola is direct in her criticism: "I think you always hear administrators say it's so hard to find a woman of color or minorities and I think that's a bunch of bullshit. I think they purposely don't look for candidates. It's easier to say there aren't any." Instead,

"I would say if you really are interested in improving diversity, then do it instead of saying it's hard. I think a lot of it is just lip service." Surya is similarly straightforward, asserting, "Well, I honestly don't think the problem is that administrators don't know what they can do." Instead, she believes that many agree with "the former dean of [a prominent law school who] recently said he doesn't think that there's a [diversity] problem" at his school, in spite of there being virtually no women of color on the faculty: "He knows what the numbers are. The numbers are [nearly] zero. He doesn't think that's a problem. So this is not something that they're like, 'If we only knew how to do this we could fix it.' They don't think there's a problem to be fixed." Surya stresses, "It's not my role to give them advice on how you can improve yourselves, because they don't feel there's anything to improve. They [feel they] are perfect right now. . . . I don't think the problem is that they don't know how to do it."

Ryan succinctly suggests, "If you would like a woman of color on your faculty, then you have to go and hire a woman of color." Those who do not "give it the full attention that it deserves," who merely "hope a woman of color comes your way," will rarely get results. Instead, administrators "have to go out and seek lateral moves or go after particular candidates on the market." He stresses: "To make diversity work you have to be serious and committed to making diversity work." Marisol agrees with Surya and Ryan, noting that first "you have to care enough to want to have a diverse faculty." Then, to retain women of color and ensure they are primed for leadership, law school administrators must "put systems in place to make sure that person is going to succeed."

The corporate world may be leading the way with diversity and inclusion. MetLife recently issued a diversity "ultimatum" to outside law firms hoping to work with the insurance giant: "create a formal plan to retain and promote your diverse talent by next year, or don't plan to work with MetLife much longer."[47] The general counsel initiated this effort after realizing both that the "issue is not new" and that the "problem is not recruiting diverse talent," but rather retaining and promoting diverse attorneys.[48] Social media behemoth Facebook similarly announced a new requirement that at least one-third of all staffing by outside counsel should include women and people of color.[49] If corporate entities recognize the value of diversity in employment and require it from law partners, law schools should already be on board.

After recruiting diverse faculty, law schools must maintain an environment that supports and encourages all employees to succeed. Though many law faculty describe their campus as "collegial," DLA findings reveal ugly truths lurking just beneath this mask of collegiality. Women must have a voice in faculty meetings, rather than being silenced, hepeated, and mansplained by their colleagues. When Abigail first joined law teaching, men expected their female faculty colleagues to take notes at faculty meetings—relegating them to the role of secretary rather than equal faculty member. The practice "has abated" at her institution, in part through the persistence of a white male colleague who "would say, 'Hey, why are we all looking at the girls? I'll take notes [today]. Next time, John, you can take notes.'"[50] Allies participating in educating resistant colleagues can thus be particularly effective. Ultimately, all faculty should follow Grace's advice:

> Value [women of color] the way you value the white male colleagues. Treat them in that same way, give them the space to do scholarship versus spend all this time to do service. Understand evaluations . . . are subjective and affected by race, gender, [and] sexual orientation.

Law school leaders, administrators, and colleagues must first understand the challenges facing women of color faculty and others who are nontraditional and underrepresented. This book brings those experiences to the forefront. Armed with this knowledge and drawing from a deep commitment to diversity and inclusion, we can endeavor to overcome intersectional barriers, be cognizant of our own implicit biases, and surmount the presumption of incompetence so that all faculty can achieve their maximum potential, giving law students the best chance of success, and improving legal education overall.

Appendix: Methodological Approach

THIS APPENDIX provides a detailed account of the methodological and analytical approaches used in the Diversity in Legal Academia (DLA) study, the empirical heart of this book. DLA is the first formal empirical study utilizing an intersectional (raceXgender) lens to investigate the personal and professional lives of law faculty at all stages of the career. The *core sample* of sixty-three participants comprises women of color law professors, including African American, Latina, Asian American, Middle Eastern, Native American, and multiracial women.[1] A *comparative sample* of thirty white women, white men, and men of color provide comparison and contrast. This comparative analysis allows for the data to be analyzed and organized according to various patterns, investigating racial bias (by grouping women of color with men of color), gender bias (by grouping women of color with white women), and intersectional raceXgender bias (by comparing women of color with each of the other groups).

Data collection proceeded through a novel sampling technique, employing a variation of *snowball sampling*. Snowball sampling is a standard data collection tool popularized by statistician Leo Goodman, who explains:

> A random sample of individuals is drawn from a given finite population. . . . Each individual in the sample is asked to name k different individuals in the population, where k is a specified integer. . . . The individuals who were not in the random sample but were named by individuals in it form the first stage.

Each of the individuals in the first stage is then asked to name *k* different individuals.[2]

As individuals at each stage continue nominating possible participants, these new individuals form the next stage and nominate others who can participate to grow the sample.[3] Snowball sampling is especially useful in studies where the target population may be difficult to identify or when research questions cover sensitive topics for vulnerable populations.[4] Because possible research subjects are nominated by peers, colleagues, or friends who themselves have participated in the project, these social connections encourage participation despite any initial hesitancy.[5]

While snowball sampling is used extensively in both statistics and the social sciences, it has faced some critique regarding generalization.[6] For instance, a snowball sample that began with a group of people in the Midwest likely could not be generalized to the entire US population because the social networks of the original sample, and therefore the individuals they would likely nominate, would largely comprise other Midwesterners. To combat this potential bias, the DLA study follows a variant of snowball sampling called *target sampling*.[7] With this technique, the original participants are purposefully selected to be representative of the target sample; those later nominated are selected to participate according to the needs of maintaining representation in the overall sample; the study sample is frequently reviewed to ensure ongoing representation and allow for any necessary course correction.[8] Regular monitoring allows for immediate adjustments to rectify oversampling of a particular subgroup or underrepresentation of another to ensure a final study sample that remains truly representative.[9]

The DLA project began with careful selection of a *seed group* of baseline participants that reflected diversity in a number of domains, including race/ethnicity, age, tenure status, leadership status, public vs. private institution, selectivity of institution, and region. DLA used the racial categories and percentages from AALS and ABA statistics as guidelines. The target sampling technique utilized in data collection did not seek to exactly match current raw percentages of each racial category, but to include appropriate numbers from each group to ensure a diverse range of opinions in the final study. As such, every effort was made to include a full range of perspectives, including oversampling from Native Americans and specifically seeking out Middle Eastern participants. Selections among those nominated were made on the basis of ongoing consultation with the data to ensure broad representation along each domain and the sample as a whole.

All study participants first completed an online survey covering basic demographic information (e.g., race/ethnicity, gender, job title) as well as experiential and behavioral questions (e.g., frequency of student interactions, likelihood of remaining in legal academia). After completing the survey, each research subject participated in an audio-recorded forty-five- to ninety-minute in-depth interview. The interview protocol includes questions related to the participant's pathway to legal academia, mentor engagement, interest in leadership, interactions with students, relationships with colleagues, work/life balance, professional experiences with diversity, and challenges and opportunities related to the individual's intersectional (raceXgender) identity. The survey instrument and interview protocol are reproduced at the end of this Appendix. The interviews yielded the qualitative data that is the empirical heart of this book, framed by quantitative data presented in the text as tables.

Most DLA interviews were conducted at national or regional conferences, especially those that were likely to have many women of color faculty in attendance, allowing for multiple interviews to occur at each site. Many interviews took place at the very identity-plus-academic conferences discussed in the Conclusion of this book as providing support for marginalized professors.[10] Local travel around California also yielded participants. Some interviews were conducted by telephone, specifically to include perspectives from individuals who could not travel to conferences, including faculty on maternity leave, those with health issues preventing travel, and others on sabbatical or otherwise working abroad.[11] All participants were assigned pseudonyms that are used in lieu of actual names to protect anonymity, with a password-protected code key linking participants with their pseudonyms.

Survey data were analyzed using Excel and Stata, primarily using cross-tabulations of individual responses to draw out race, gender, and raceXgender inferences from the data. Quantitative analyses are used mainly to contextualize themes, patterns, and findings derived from the qualitative portion of the study. Each interview recording was transcribed and checked for errors before being uploaded to ATLAS.ti, where they were collectively coded. The qualitative analysis technique draws from grounded theory, where data are regularly reviewed even while data collection is in progress, and familiarity with the data leads to the development of additional coding structures.[12] The analytical approach evaluated salient links between characteristics—including race/

ethnicity, gender, socioeconomic class, region, and diversity of attitudes—while considering the contextual attributes and topics of the interview. A code key analyzed and organized the data using broad strokes, drawing primarily from the interview questions themselves and early patterns from the data. Through descriptive content analyses of interview transcripts, the data revealed additional themes, as well as interpretations of findings from aggregate analyses of survey data. The resulting analyses were then further coded for more nuanced methodological investigation into various subthemes and topics explored in this book. DLA received a formal regulatory opinion of Institutional Review Board exemption from Western IRB.[13]

Diversity in Legal Academia

Survey Instrument

1. **What is your gender?**

   ☐ Female
   ☐ Male

2. **What is your racial/ethnic background?** [Mark <u>all that apply</u>.]

   ☐ African American/Black
   ☐ Asian/Pacific Islander
   ☐ Hispanic/Latino
   ☐ American Indian, Aleutian, Native Alaskan, or Eskimo
   ☐ White
   ☐ Middle Eastern
   ☐ Other
   Please also specify race/ethnicity below:

3. **What is your date of birth?**

   Enter Date. _____ /_____ /_____
   　　　　　　　　　Month　　　　Day　　　　　Year

4. **Which law school is your current employer?**

5. **What year did you complete your law degree?**

6. **What year did you begin law teaching at a tenure-track law school?**
   [Mark one.]

   ☐ 2013–2008
   ☐ 2007–2003
   ☐ 2002–1993
   ☐ 1992–1983
   ☐ Before 1983
   Please specify the month and year:

7. What best describes your tenure status at your current employment?

   ☐ I am currently tenured.

   ☐ I am currently untenured, though I have applied for tenure this year for the first time.

   ☐ I am currently untenured, though I have re-applied for tenure this year.

   ☐ I am currently untenured, though I have applied for tenure previously.

   ☐ I am currently untenured and have never applied for tenure.

8. At your current law school, how much interaction on campus do you have with . . . [Mark one for each question.]

	A lot	Some	Not much	None
a. Asian American students?	☐	☐	☐	☐
b. Hispanic/Latino students?	☐	☐	☐	☐
c. African American students?	☐	☐	☐	☐
d. Native American students?	☐	☐	☐	☐
e. White students?	☐	☐	☐	☐
f. Other race/ethnicity students?	☐	☐	☐	☐

9. On the law school campus, how would you characterize your interactions with . . . [Mark one for each question.]

	Very friendly	Sociable	Distant	Hostile
a. Asian American students?	☐	☐	☐	☐
b. Hispanic/Latino students?	☐	☐	☐	☐
c. African American students?	☐	☐	☐	☐
d. Native American students?	☐	☐	☐	☐
e. White students?	☐	☐	☐	☐
f. Other race/ethnicity students?	☐	☐	☐	☐

10. At your current law school, how much interaction on campus do you have with . . . [Mark one for each question.]

	A lot	Some	Not much	None
a. Asian American faculty?	☐	☐	☐	☐
b. Hispanic/Latino faculty?	☐	☐	☐	☐
c. African American faculty?	☐	☐	☐	☐
d. Native American faculty?	☐	☐	☐	☐
e. White faculty?	☐	☐	☐	☐
f. Other race/ethnicity faculty?	☐	☐	☐	☐

11. **At your current law school, how would you characterize your interactions with . . . [Mark <u>one</u> for each question.]**

	Very friendly	Sociable	Distant	Hostile
a. Asian American faculty?	☐	☐	☐	☐
b. Hispanic/Latino faculty?	☐	☐	☐	☐
c. African American faculty?	☐	☐	☐	☐
d. Native American faculty?	☐	☐	☐	☐
e. White faculty?	☐	☐	☐	☐
f. Other race/ethnicity faculty?	☐	☐	☐	☐

12. **Please describe your level of support from the following sources: [Mark <u>one</u> for each question.]**

	Strong support	Some support	No support
a. Students	☐	☐	☐
b. Law faculty at your institution	☐	☐	☐
c. Non-academic friends/colleagues	☐	☐	☐
d. Other mentors	☐	☐	☐
e. Professional organizations	☐	☐	☐
f. Law faculty at other institutions	☐	☐	☐
g. Non-law faculty at your institution	☐	☐	☐
h. Family	☐	☐	☐
i. Religion	☐	☐	☐
j. Other support	☐	☐	☐

12b. **If applicable, please add specifics below for the support identified in the previous question.**

a. Please specify organizations:

b. Please specify institutions:

c. Please specify academic fields
of non-law faculty:

d. Please specify relationships
(i.e., daughter, spouse, dog):

e. Please specify religion:

f. Please specify other support:

Diversity in Legal Academia

13. **Are you active with any professional groups or organizations?**

    ☐ No
    ☐ Yes, please list groups/programs:

14. **How much time <u>per month</u> do you spend mentoring law students?**

    ☐ Less than 1 hour   ☐ 1–5 hours   ☐ 6–10 hours   ☐ More than 10 hours

15. **How much time <u>per month</u> do you spend mentoring law faculty at your institution?**

    ☐ Less than 1 hour   ☐ 1–5 hours   ☐ 6–10 hours   ☐ More than 10 hours

16. **How much time <u>per month</u> do you spend mentoring law faculty at other institutions?**

    ☐ Less than 1 hour   ☐ 1–5 hours   ☐ 6–10 hours   ☐ More than 10 hours

17. **How certain are you that you will remain in legal academia for the foreseeable future? [Mark <u>one</u>.]**

    ☐ Certain that I will remain in legal academia and at my current institution.
    ☐ Certain that I will remain in legal academia, though not necessarily at my current institution.
    ☐ Not completely certain that I will remain in legal academia.

18. Which employment positions have you held or do you currently hold? [Mark <u>all that apply</u>.]

☐ Public interest nonprofit attorney

☐ Public interest law firm attorney

☐ Corporate law firm attorney

☐ Business executive

☐ Government attorney

☐ Politician

☐ Judge

☐ Law school dean

☐ Law school associate dean··

☐ Law school assistant dean··

☐ University president

☐ Other university executive position

☐ Other legal job

☐ Other job

··please specify:

19. What is your <u>ultimate</u> career goal? [Mark <u>one</u>.]

☐ Public interest nonprofit attorney

☐ Public interest law firm attorney

☐ Corporate law firm attorney

☐ Law professor

☐ Government attorney

☐ Politician

☐ Business executive

☐ Law school dean

☐ Law school associate dean··

☐ Law school assistant dean··

☐ University president

☐ Other university executive position

☐ Other legal job

☐ Judge

☐ Other job

··please specify:

20. What is your total estimated debt from law school (tuition, fees, living expenses, etc.)?

21. Did you have any scholarships or fellowships while in law school?

☐ No

☐ Yes, please list name(s) and amount(s) for each:

22. Did you work as a law clerk after graduation?

☐ No
☐ Yes, please list name(s) of judge(s) and year(s) worked:

23. Prior to beginning law teaching in a tenure-track capacity, were you employed as a: [Mark all that apply.]

☐ Visiting assistant professor of law, please specify law school and year(s) below

☐ Adjunct professor of law, please specify law school and year(s) below

☐ Lecturer in law, please specify law school and year(s) below

☐ Academic fellow, please specify law school and year(s) below

☐ Legal writing instructor, please specify law school and year(s) below

☐ Other academic position at a law school, please specify title, law school, and year(s) below

☐ Academic position outside of a law school, please specify title, institution, department, and year(s)

☐ Nonacademic position, please specify title, institution, department, and year(s)

Please specify title (when applicable), law school, and year(s) for the categories marked above.

24. **After beginning law teaching in a tenure-track capacity, did you work in any of the following positions: [Mark <u>all that apply</u>.]**

    ☐ Visiting assistant professor of law, please specify law school and year(s) below

    ☐ Adjunct professor of law, please specify law school and year(s) below

    ☐ Lecturer in law, please specify law school and year(s) below

    ☐ Academic fellow, please specify law school and year(s) below

    ☐ Legal writing instructor, please specify law school and year(s) below

    ☐ Other academic position at a law school, please specify title, law school, and year(s) below

    ☐ Academic position outside of a law school, please specify title, institution, department, and year(s)

    ☐ Non-academic position, please specify title, institution, department, and year(s)

    Please specify title (when applicable), law school, and year(s) for the categories marked above.

25. **If you have earned tenure, how many full-length articles had you published when you were granted tenure?**

26. **How many full-length articles have you published to date?**

Diversity in Legal Academia

27. To what extent do you agree or disagree with the following statements about law school? [Mark <u>one</u> for each question.]

	Strongly agree	Agree	Neither agree nor disagree	Disagree	Strongly disagree
Overall, my law teaching experience has been positive.	☐	☐	☐	☐	☐
I would prefer that there were more faculty diversity at my school.	☐	☐	☐	☐	☐
My students seem supportive when I include discussions of race, gender, or sexual orientation in the classroom.	☐	☐	☐	☐	☐
Working as a legal academic is much easier than I expected.	☐	☐	☐	☐	☐
My law school student body is as diverse as I expected it to be.	☐	☐	☐	☐	☐
I am satisfied with the tenure process at my law school.	☐	☐	☐	☐	☐
Most of my fellow faculty are open-minded and respect opinions that are different from their own.	☐	☐	☐	☐	☐
I would prefer that there were more student diversity at my law school.	☐	☐	☐	☐	☐
I would recommend my law school to people of my gender.	☐	☐	☐	☐	☐
I would recommend my law school to people of the same racial/ethnic background as myself.	☐	☐	☐	☐	☐
My fellow law professors welcome students who challenge their views.	☐	☐	☐	☐	☐
Most of my fellow faculty are supportive when faculty include discussions of race, gender, or sexual orientation in the classroom.	☐	☐	☐	☐	☐
The campus climate at my law school is one that supports diversity.	☐	☐	☐	☐	☐

28. Please <u>send a current CV here</u>. [Hyperlink to email]

29. Please list names, institutional affiliations, and email addresses for additional women of color faculty who may be interested in participating in this study. Those invited to participate may be told that you suggested them.

    Name, Institution,
    Email Address:
    Name, Institution,
    Email Address:
    Name, Institution,
    Email Address:
    Name, Institution,
    Email Address:
    Name, Institution,
    Email Address:

30. Is there anything else about diversity and your experience in legal academia that you wish to add?

Thank you for completing this survey.

Diversity in Legal Academia

Interview Schedule

The purpose of this interview is to better understand your experience in legal academia. Please be assured that your responses will be held in the strictest professional confidence. Thank you in advance for your assistance.

Before we begin I want to confirm your DOB?
I also want to formally confirm that you continue consent to participate in this research?

First, I have a few introductory questions.

1. Please state your title and your current institutional affiliation.

2. Which year and at which law school was your first tenure-track appointment?

3. How do you identify yourself in terms of race/ethnicity, gender, sexual orientation, and otherwise? [Be sure to get race/ethnicity and gender]

Now let's talk about your professional trajectory.

4. Can you describe for me how you became a law professor? Please include specific events or circumstances that brought you to the profession. [Probe for family.]

5. How have mentors affected your professional trajectory?

6. Is leadership something you've wanted or want for yourself? [Please elaborate.]

I also have some questions about your experience at your current institution.

7. What was the tenure process like at your school, or what will it be like?

8. Please characterize your relationship with other faculty at your law school. Do you have especially strong relationships with anyone? Any hostile ones? Please elaborate. [Probe for race/gender of other faculty members mentioned.]

9. Similarly, please characterize your relationship with students at your law school. Tell me about your first semester teaching. [Probe for race/gender of students.]

10. What do you see as valued (in terms of rewards or advancement) at your institution?

11. How satisfied are you with opportunities for professional development at your school?

12. What does it take to get into a position of power or leadership in your school? Do you feel part of the decision-making process?

13. What would you say is the best thing about your law school? If you could change one thing, what would it be?

14. Similarly, can you tell me about the best day or event or period of time you experienced as a law professor? What about the worst?

I also have some questions specifically about diversity.

15. How does the diversity on your law school campus measure up to your expectations?

16. What are the advantages and disadvantages to having a diverse faculty at your law school? Do you experience any of those? [Probe for race/gender.]

17. What are the advantages and disadvantages to having a diverse student body at your law school? Do you experience any of those? [Probe for race/gender.]

18. Can you share some examples of classroom discussions regarding race, ethnicity, gender, sexual orientation, or socioeconomic status? Can you think of any missed opportunities for these types of discussions in class? Why were they missed? [Relevant cases may be *People v. Goetz, Roe v. Wade, Plessy v. Ferguson, Loving v. Virginia, Brown v. Board of Education, Grutter v. Bollinger,* and *Lawrence v. Texas.*]

Finally, I have a few questions about your overall professional experience.

19. Who or what do you rely on for support? Support may include financial, emotional, spiritual, intellectual, and other kinds of support.

20. Please tell me about your work/life balance—including family life, child care, elder care, and any other personal responsibilities.

21. How do your personal values align or conflict with your professional experiences?

22. In which ways has law teaching been as you expected it to be and how has it been different?

23. Can you identify any particular benefits you experience in legal academia that are based on your race and gender?

24. Can you identify any particular challenges you experience in legal academia that are based on your race and gender?

25. If you could pass along some of your wisdom to a woman of color entering legal academia today, what would you tell her? [In other words, what are some of the most important lessons you've learned in legal academia?]

26. Finally, why do you think there are relatively few women of color in legal academia? What suggestions would you have for administrators or others to improve your experience, or the experience of other female law faculty of color?

Diversity in Legal Academia

This is the end of my formal set of questions for this meeting. Is there anything else you would like to add about your experience in legal academia? Either something about diversity that we did not cover or something you want to elaborate on?

Probes

- Can you give an example?
- Did you talk about it with colleagues at or outside of your institution? Others?
- Would you explain further?
- Would you say more?
- Is there anything else?
- Please describe what you mean.
- I don't understand.
- Look through survey answers for particular follow up questions as well

Notes

Introduction

1. Race is a fluid concept that often defies easy characterization or categorization. *See, e.g.,* Ian F. Haney-Lopez, *The Social Construction of Race: Some Observations on Illusion, Fabrication, and Choice* 29 HARV. C.R.-C.L. L. REV. 1 (1994). While *race* deals more generally with the social construct of one's phenotypical or morphological presentation, and *ethnicity* refers more to individual or ancestral national or regional origin, the term *race* is sometimes used in the book for ease of reading to signify both race and ethnicity. For more on the differentiation between race and ethnicity and their interplay with the law, see Camille Gear Rich, *Performing Racial and Ethnic Identity: Discrimination by Proxy and the Future of Title VII*, 79 N.Y.U. L. REV. 1134, 1145 (2004). Similarly, gender scholars relate the term *sex* to the biological features differentiating men and women, whereas *gender* refers to the exhibition or presentation of oneself as either male or female. *See, e.g.,* Leslie Bender, *Sex Discrimination or Gender Inequality?*, 57 FORDHAM L. REV. 941, 946 (1989) (explaining how *sex* generally refers to "certain physical attributes, in particular our primary and secondary sexual characteristics and life-giving capacities," whereas *gender* is the "cultural/social construction and attribution of qualities to different biological sexes"). Terms and usage are explained further in the Appendix.

2. Because AALS data include many non-tenure-track positions, they are overinclusive when considering the tenured or tenure-track faculty participants in the DLA study presented in this book, who are not involved in clinical, legal writing, or library roles. AALS data is no longer available online, but AALS tables and analyses can be found in previously published DLA articles, including Meera E. Deo, *The Ugly Truth about Legal Academia*, 80 BROOK. L. REV. 943, 962 (2015).

3. The data presented here are from 2013, the year that data were collected for the empirical study guiding this book. ABA statistics are available online at https://www .americanbar.org/groups/legal_education/resources/statistics.html.

4. *See* Andrea Guerrero, Silence at Boalt Hall: The Dismantling of Affirmative Action 105 (2002) (discussing the significant decrease in minority student admittance under a "race-blind" admissions process); Meera E. Deo, *The Promise of* Grutter: *Diverse Interactions at the University of Michigan Law School*, 17 Mich. J. Race & L. 63 (2011) (indicating that "diversity discussions" bring the law to life); Celestial S. D. Cassman & Lisa R. Pruitt, *A Kinder, Gentler Law School? Race, Ethnicity, Gender, and Legal Education at King Hall*, 38 U.C. Davis L. Rev. 1209, 1217 (2005) (discussing diversity at UC Davis School of Law); Carole J. Buckner, *Realizing* Grutter v. Bollinger*'s "Compelling Educational Benefits of Diversity"—Transforming Aspirational Rhetoric Into Experience*, 72 UMKC L. Rev. 877, 877 (2004) (discussing the broad importance of diversity in education through *Grutter v. Bollinger*); Daniel Solórzano, Walter R. Allen & Grace Carroll, *Keeping Race in Place: Racial Microaggressions and Campus Racial Climate at the University of California, Berkeley*, 23 Chicano-Latino L. Rev. 15, 17 (2002) (discussing microaggressions on Berkeley's campus); Patricia Gurin et al., *Diversity and Higher Education: Theory and Impact on Educational Outcomes*, 72 Harv. Educ. Rev. 330, 333 (2002) (discussing different forms of diversity experiences on college campuses).

5. Meera E. Deo, *Looking Forward to Diversity in Legal Academia*, 29 Berkeley J. Gender L. & Just. 352, 369–70 (2014) (citing Richard Delgado & Derrick Bell, *Minority Law Professors' Lives: The Bell-Delgado Survey*, 24 Harv. C.R.-C.L. L. Rev. 349 (1989)).

6. Gabriella Gutierrez y Muhs, Yolanda Flores-Niemann, Carmen G. Gonzalez & Angela P. Harris (eds.), Presumed Incompetent: The Intersections of Race and Class for Women in Academia (2012).

7. For more discussion on these themes from *Presumed Incompetent* and on the relevant literature generally, see Meera E. Deo, *Looking Forward to Diversity in Legal Academia*, 29 Berkeley J. Gender L. & Just. 352, 371–75 (2014). See also Meera E. Deo, *Securing Support in an Unequal Profession*, in 2 Presumed Incompetent (2019).

8. Multiple events, workshops, and conferences on the topic of women of color in academia have taken place since that book's publication (see, e.g., Berkeley Journal of Gender, Law, and Justice Symposium honoring *Presumed Incompetent: The Intersections of Race and Class for Women in Academia,* at https://genderlawjustice.berkeley .edu/wp-content/uploads/2013/03/Presumed-Incompetent1.pdf; Stanford University Office of the Vice Provost for Faculty Development and Diversity Conference on Women of Color in the Academy: Staying Fit, Mind, Body, and Soul, at https:// facultydevelopment.stanford.edu/programs/women-color-academy-staying-fit-mind -body-and-soul; Faculty Women of Color in the Academy National Conference at http://www.cpe.vt.edu/fwca/).

9. Katherine Barnes & Elizabeth Mertz, *Is It Fair? Law Professors' Perceptions of Tenure*, 61 J. Legal Educ. 511, 517 (2012).

10. Katherine Barnes & Elizabeth Mertz, *Is It Fair? Law Professors' Perceptions of Tenure*, 61 J. Legal Educ. 511, 522–23 (2012).

11. News articles have reported on the significant decline in law school applications and accompanying challenges in legal education for over five years. *See, e.g.,*

Ashby Jones & Jennifer Smith, *Amid Falling Enrollment, Law Schools Are Cutting Faculty*, WALL STREET J. (July 15, 2013), available at http://www.wsj.com/articles/SB10001424127887323664204578607810292433272.

12. Robert Post, *Leadership in Educational Institutions: Reflections of a Law School Dean*, 69 STAN. L. REV. 1817, 1823 (2017) ("Law school deans who have had to downsize in the recent crisis have no doubt had to face zero-sum choices in deciding how to proceed."). The ongoing legal education crisis has been chronicled in both the media and academia. *See, e.g.*, Debra Cassens Weiss, *LSAT Test-Takers Continue to Decline; October Number Is at Lowest Point Since 1998*, A.B.A. J. (Nov. 4, 2013), available at http://www.abajournal.com/news/article/lsat_test_takers_continue_to_decline_october_number_is_at_lowest_point_sinc; *See* BRIAN Z. TAMANAHA, FAILING LAW SCHOOLS (2012); Luz E. Herrera, *Educating Main Street Lawyers*, 63 J. LEGAL EDUC. 189 (2013); Philip G. Shrag, *Failing Law Schools—Tamanaha's Misguided Missile*, 26 GEO. J. LEGAL ETHICS 387 (2013).

13. Robert Post, *Leadership in Educational Institutions: Reflections of a Law School Dean*, 69 STAN. L. REV. 1817, 1822 (2017).

14. Post writes that there are increasingly "insistent demands for more cost-effective legal education that would produce better-trained and accomplished lawyers" (Robert Post, *Leadership in Educational Institutions: Reflections of a Law School Dean*, 69 STAN. L. REV. 1817, 1820 (2017)).

15. TASK FORCE ON THE FUTURE OF LEGAL EDUC., AM. BAR ASS'N, REPORT AND RECOMMENDATIONS 14, available at http://www.americanbar.org/content/dam/aba/administrative/professional_responsibility/report_and_recommendations_of_aba_task_force.authcheckdam.pdf.

16. SECTION OF LEGAL EDUC. & ADMISSIONS TO THE BAR, AM. BAR ASS'N, ABA STANDARDS AND RULES OF PROCEDURE FOR APPROVAL OF LAW SCHOOLS, 2016–2017 STANDARD 301, at 15 (2016), available at http://www.americanbar.org/content/dam/aba/publications/misc/legal_education/Standards/2016_2017_aba_standards_and_rules_of_procedure.auth checkdam.pdf.

17. Robert Post, *Leadership in Educational Institutions: Reflections of a Law School Dean*, 69 STAN. L. REV. 1817, 1820 (2017).

18. Specifically, "faculty of color and female faculty are generally more proactive [than white male faculty] in discussing issues of race and gender in the classroom." Meera E. Deo, Rican Vue & Maria Woodruff, *Paint by Number? How the Race & Gender of Law School Faculty Affect the First Year Curriculum*, 29 CHICANO-LATINO L. REV. 1, 26 (2010).

19. Students appreciate opportunities to draw from their own and classmates' personal experiences to enliven what can be otherwise abstract and dry legal concepts. See, e.g., Meera E. Deo, *The Promise of* Grutter: *Diverse Interactions at the University of Michigan Law School*, 17 MICH. J. RACE & L. 63, 95 (2011). Additionally, law faculty members agree that deeper and more personal student engagement with substantive law improves learning outcomes. See Meera E. Deo, *Faculty Insights on Educational Diversity*, 83 FORDHAM L. REV. 3115, at III.B (2015).

20. Derek Black, *The Intricate Associations Between Diversity and Law Student Engagement by Deirdre Brown and Aaron Taylor*, EDUC. LAW PROF. BLOG, Mar. 11, 2015, available at http://lawprofessors.typepad.com/education_law/2015/03/the-intricate -associations-between-diversity-and-law-student-engagement-by-deirdre-bowen -and-aaron-t.html.

21. See Meera E. Deo, Rican Vue & Maria Woodruff, *Paint by Number? How the Race & Gender of Law School Faculty Affect the First Year Curriculum*, 29 CHICANO-LATINO L. REV. 1, 36–38 (2010) (finding that diverse faculty may be more interested and able to effectively facilitate diversity discussions); and Meera E. Deo, *The Promise of* Grutter: *Diverse Interactions at the University of Michigan Law School*, 17 MICH. J. RACE & L. 63, 110–11 (2011) ("the inclusion of diversity discussions creates conditions for improved student learning").

22. Aaron N. Taylor, LSSSE ANNUAL REPORT (2014), available at http://lssse .indiana.edu/wp-content/uploads/2016/01/LSSSE_2014_AnnualReport.pdf.

23. Robert Post, *Leadership in Educational Institutions: Reflections of a Law School Dean*, 69 STAN. L. REV. 1817, 1823 (2017).

24. Robert Post, *Leadership in Educational Institutions: Reflections of a Law School Dean*, 69 STAN. L. REV. 1817, 1822 (2017).

25. See, e.g., DERRICK BELL, FACES AT THE BOTTOM OF THE WELL: THE PERMANENCE OF RACISM (1992).

26. Kimberlé Crenshaw, *Mapping the Margins: Intersectionality, Identity Politics, and Violence Against Women of Color*, 43 STAN. L. REV. 1241, 1242 (1990–1991). See also Angela Harris, *Race and Essentialism in Feminist Legal Theory*, 42 STAN. L. REV. 581 (1990).

27. RICHARD DELGADO & JEAN STEFANCIC, CRITICAL RACE THEORY: AN INTRODUCTION 51–55 (2001). For more on critical race theory and intersectionality specifically, see PATRICIA HILL COLLINS, BLACK FEMINIST THOUGHT: KNOWLEDGE, CONSCIOUSNESS, AND THE POLITICS OF EMPOWERMENT (2d. ed., 2000); EVELYN NAKANO GLENN, UNEQUAL FREEDOM: HOW RACE AND GENDER SHAPED AMERICAN CITIZENSHIP AND LABOR (2002); Kimberlé Crenshaw, *Demarginalizing the Intersection of Race and Sex: A Black Feminist Critique of Antidiscrimination Doctrine, Feminist Theory and Antiracist Politics*, 1989 U. CHI. LEGAL F. 139 (1989); Kimberlé Crenshaw, *Mapping the Margins: Intersectionality, Identity Politics, and Violence Against Women of Color*, 43 STAN. L. REV. 1241 (1990–1991).

28. While most scholarship drawing on a framework of intersectionality focuses on the challenges or oppression facing groups that are marginalized across multiple dimensions, there could be opportunities for benefits based on these identity characteristics as well. *See, e.g.,* Nancy Leong, *Racial Capitalism*, 126 HARV. L. REV. 2151, 2152 (2013) (discussing instances in which whites have capitalized on the racial identity of people of color for the social and economic benefit of whites themselves).

29. While socioeconomic status, sexual orientation, and other characteristics are also critical components of an individual's intersectional identity, they are not covered as deeply as race and gender in this book for many reasons. First and foremost,

race and gender remain the primarily associations individuals themselves retain and that others ascribe to them. When DLA participants were asked to share characteristics at the core of their identity, the vast majority invoked race and gender identities (i.e., "Black woman"), though a few also included sexual orientation (i.e., "white lesbian"). Others alluded to class or sexual orientation identity during the course of the interview. This brings up the second point. Because the sample draws from a relatively small and vulnerable pool, especially when considering the faculty of color participants, particular details about individual faculty members are not shared to preserve anonymity. Similarly, faculty with disabilities are included in the study but not singled out in the text.

30. Although they refer to the same system, *institutional discrimination* refers to bias within particular institutions embedded in society, whereas *structural discrimination* refers to the collection of these various institutions and the broader structure that encompasses them. *See* Fred L. Pincus, *Discrimination Comes in Many Forms: Individual, Institutional, and Structural, in* READINGS FOR DIVERSITY AND SOCIAL JUSTICE 31 (Adams et al. eds., 2000).

31. Meera E. Deo, *Two Sides of a Coin: Safe Space & Segregation in Race/Ethnic-Specific Law Student Organizations*, 42 WASH. U. J.L. & POL'Y 83, 116–20 (2013) (quoting William M. Wiecek, *Structural Racism and The Law in America Today: An Introduction*, 100 KY. L.J. 1, 5 (2011–2012)). For more social science literature on structural racism, see EDUARDO BONILLA-SILVA, WHITE SUPREMACY & RACISM IN THE POST-CIVIL RIGHTS ERA 11 (2001); MICHAEL OMI & HOWARD WINANT, RACIAL FORMATION IN THE UNITED STATES 79 (2d. ed., 1994) (asserting that "the major institutions and social relationships of U.S. society—law, political organization, economic relationships, religion, cultural life, residential patterns etc.—have been structured from the beginning by the racial order"); Eduardo Bonilla-Silva, *Rethinking Racism: Toward a Structural Interpretation*, 62 AM. SOC. REV. 465, 469 (1997). Legal scholar Ian Haney-López has also argued similar sentiments using the term *institutional racism*. *See, e.g.,* Ian F. Haney-López, *Institutional Racism: Judicial Conduct and a New Theory of Racial Discrimination*, 109 YALE L.J. 1717 (2000).

32. *See generally* DARIA ROITHMAYR, REPRODUCING RACISM: HOW EVERYDAY CHOICES LOCK IN WHITE ADVANTAGE (2014).

33. The terms *intersectional bias* and *complex bias* are in many ways similar. *See, e.g.,* Minna J. Kotkin, *Diversity and Discrimination: A Look at Complex Bias*, 50 WM. & MARY L. REV. 1439 (2009).

34. Devah Pager & Hana Shepherd, *The Sociology of Discrimination: Racial Discrimination in Employment, Housing, Credit, and Consumer Markets*, 34 ANN. REV. SOC. 181, 182 (2008).

35. Devah Pager & Hana Shepherd, *The Sociology of Discrimination: Racial Discrimination in Employment, Housing, Credit, and Consumer Markets*, 34 ANN. REV. SOC. 181, 182 (2008).

36. Daniel Solórzano, Walter R. Allen & Grace Carroll, *Keeping Race in Place: Racial Microaggressions and Campus Racial Climate at the University of California, Berkeley*, 23 CHICANO-LATINO L. REV. 15, 17 (2002).

37. Much of the past scholarship on intersectionality has focused on who is excluded: "When African American women claim race discrimination, their experience is measured against that of sex-privileged (that is, male) African Americans; when African American women claim gender discrimination, their experience is measured against that of race-privileged (that is, white) women." Minna J. Kotkin, *Diversity and Discrimination: A Look at Complex Bias*, 50 WM. & MARY L. REV. 1439, 1482 (2009) (citing Kimberlé Crenshaw, *Demarginalizing the Intersection of Race and Sex: A Black Feminist Critique of Antidiscrimination Doctrine, Feminist Theory and Antiracist Politics*, 1989 U. CHI. LEGAL F. 139, 140 (1989)).

38. STEPHANIE M. WILDMAN, PRIVILEGE REVEALED: HOW INVISIBLE PREFERENCE UNDERMINES AMERICA (1996).

39. STEPHANIE M. WILDMAN, PRIVILEGE REVEALED: HOW INVISIBLE PREFERENCE UNDERMINES AMERICA, 29 (1996).

40. Stephanie M. Wildman & Adrienne D. Davis, *Making Systems of Privilege Visible, in* PRIVILEGE REVEALED: HOW INVISIBLE PREFERENCE UNDERMINES AMERICA, 7–24 (1996). See also Peggy McIntosh, *White Privilege: Unpacking the Invisible Knapsack*, PEACE AND FREEDOM MAGAZINE July–Aug. 1989.

41. Jerry Kang & Kristin Lane, *Seeing Through Colorblindness: Implicit Bias and the Law*, 58 UCLA L. REV. 465, 467 (2010).

42. Jerry Kang & Kristin Lane, *Seeing Through Colorblindness: Implicit Bias and the Law*, 58 UCLA L. REV. 465, 469 (2010).

43. Gregory S. Parks and Jeffrey J. Rachlinski, *Implicit Bias, Election '08 and the Myth of a Post-Racial America*, 37, FLA. ST. L. REV. 659, 683 (2010).

44. Jerry Kang & Kristin Lane, *Seeing Through Colorblindness: Implicit Bias and the Law*, 58 UCLA L. REV. 465, 467–68 (2010).

45. For more on implicit bias in courts, see Jerry Kang et al., *Implicit Bias in the Courtroom*, 59 UCLA L. REV. 1124 (2012).

Chapter 1

1. *See* Meera E. Deo, *Looking Forward to Diversity in Legal Academia*, 29 BERKELEY J. GENDER L. & JUST. 352, 359–64 (2014) (explaining why disparities based on race and gender "cannot be explained away by suggesting that the pool of applicants seeking positions in legal academia is non-diverse").

2. A recent posting for an open tenure-track position notes that for a successful candidate, a "JD or JD/PhD [is] required"—signaling increasing expectations among institutions that new hires will have multiple advanced degrees. Columbia Law School posted this tenure-track position (on file with the author) at http://law.academickeys.com/seeker_job_display.php?dothis=pdf&job%5BIDX%5D=86790.

3. Professor Lawrence B. Solum's Legal Theory Blog, *Details hiring trends at 18 top American Law Schools*, available at http://lsolum.blogspot.com/archives/2004_07_01_lsolum_archive.html#108912594144211701.

4. Columbia Law School posting "What Makes a Good Teaching Job Candidate," available at http://www.law.columbia.edu/law-teaching/what-you-need-know-about -law-school-teaching/what-makes-good-teaching-job-candidate.

5. Only 38% of Black women, 47% of Asian American women, 42% of Latinas, and 20% of Native American female women law faculty participants in the DLA study clerked before entering the legal academy. While these percentages are high compared to those of law school graduates overall, 100% of white male law professors and 82% of white female law professors in the DLA study also clerked. This indicates that law schools are willing to hire women of color without this particular elite marker, although Table 2 explains why doing so presents little risk.

6. AALS explains that the FAR "is a collection of information about registrants interested in teaching at law schools." (see https://www.aals.org/services/faculty -recruitment-services/far/.) In fact, some schools require participation in the formal process to even apply. See, e.g., a recent job posting for a tenure-track position at Brooklyn Law School: "Candidates for an entry-level position must participate in the AALS Faculty Appointments Register" (on file with the author; available at http:// www.law.columbia.edu/law-teaching/services-current-candidates/job-opportunities (last visited Mar. 13, 2017)). While requiring participation decreases the likelihood of simply hiring from among an existing (often "old boys") network, it also decreases the likelihood of utilizing "out of the box" recruiting strategies that are often more successful in recruiting diverse candidates as discussed in the Conclusion.

7. Columbia Law School posting on how to apply for a law faculty position, available at http://www.law.columbia.edu/law-teaching/what-you-need-know-about-law -school-teaching/how-do-i-apply-teaching-job.

8. The full form is available on the AALS website at https://www.aals.org/ services/faculty-recruitment-services/far/.

9. Denise C. Morgan, *Advice for Law Professor Wannabees*, in Gabriel J. Chin & Denise C. Morgan (eds.), *Breaking into the Academy: The 2002–2004* Michigan Journal of Race & Law *Guide for Aspiring Law Professors*, 7 MICH. J. RACE & L. 461 (2002).

10. Denise C. Morgan, *Advice for Law Professor Wannabees*, in Gabriel J. Chin & Denise C. Morgan (eds.), *Breaking into the Academy: The 2002–2004* Michigan Journal of Race & Law *Guide for Aspiring Law Professors*, 7 MICH. J. RACE & L. 457, 460 (2002).

11. Columbia Law School posting on how to apply for a law faculty position, available at https://web.law.columbia.edu/law-teaching/what-you-need-know-about -law-school-teaching/how-do-i-apply-teaching-job.

12. Denise C. Morgan, *Advice for Law Professor Wannabees*, in Gabriel J. Chin & Denise C. Morgan (eds.), *Breaking into the Academy: The 2002–2004* Michigan Journal of Race & Law *Guide for Aspiring Law Professors*, 7 MICH. J. RACE & L. 461 (2002).

13. For instance, one guide advises, "When you are asked what questions you have for your interviewers, do not ask about salary and benefits." Available at http://www .law.columbia.edu/law-teaching/what-you-need-know-about-law-school-teaching/ how-do-i-prepare-interviews.

14. In 2018, the fee for inclusion in the FAR distribution was $475. There is a fee waiver available for candidates, although it is unclear how answers on the five-page form determine eligibility. No criteria are listed or explained. See https://www.aals .org/wp-content/uploads/2016/08/2016-FAR-Fee-Waiver-Form1.pdf.

15. Columbia Law School posting on how to apply for a law faculty position, available at http://www.law.columbia.edu/law-teaching/what-you-need-know-about -law-school-teaching/how-do-i-prepare-interviews.

16. See, e.g., "Moot Fest," which exists "to furnish Stanford [Law] grads and fellows with the opportunity to have faculty members moot their mock job talks and screening interviews" (https://law.stanford.edu/careers/career-possibilities/ academia/get-hired), Duke Law School's "initiative to help our alumni interested in teaching" by hosting (https://law.duke.edu/events/mock-job-talk-blake-hudson), and University of Chicago Law School's annual "special one-day set of mock job talks and interviews for Chicago [Law] grads, during which time we will also answer questions and help you prepare for the AALS hiring convention" (https://www.law.uchicago .edu/careerservices/pathstolawteaching).

17. See Chavella Pittman, *Moving from Attitudes to Behavior: Using Social Influence to Understand Interpersonal Racial Oppression*, 143, 157, in CRISIS, POLITICS, AND CRITICAL SOCIOLOGY (Graham Cassano & Richard Dello Buono eds., 2010) (suggesting that "social psychological theories and concepts" guide "explanations for racial behavior" rather than "the current reliance on an assumed attitude-behavior relationship").

18. For instance, "whom we befriend, whose work we value, and whom we favor," are all shaped by implicit bias, even if we believe ourselves to be egalitarian. Jerry Kang & Kristin Lane, *Seeing Through Colorblindness: Implicit Bias and the Law*, 58 UCLA L. REV. 465, 467–68 (2010).

19. Paul Campos, *A Failure of the Elites*, LAWYERS, GUNS & MONEY (July 23, 2013), available at http://www.lawyersgunsmoneyblog.com/2013/07/a-failure-of-the-elites #more-46121 ("[A] study of entry-level tenure-track hires between 2003 and 2007 found that, out of 466 hires, 40.1% came from just two schools: Harvard and Yale (85.6% came from a total of 12 schools).").

20. For instance, in the late 1980s, when the Bell-Delgado study was conducted, there were approximately three hundred law faculty of color compared to more than one thousand today. See Richard Delgado & Derrick Bell, *Minority Law Professors' Lives: The Bell-Delgado Survey*, 24 HARV. C.R.-C.L. L. REV. 349, n. 17 (1989); Meera E. Deo, *The Ugly Truth about Legal Academia*, 80 BROOK. L. REV. 943, 962 (2015) (citing AALS statistics); ABA statistics, available at https://www.americanbar.org/groups/ legal_education/resources/statistics.html.

21. Meera E. Deo, *The Ugly Truth about Legal Academia*, 80 BROOK. L. REV. 943, 962 (2015) (citing AALS statistics).

22. Few women of color role models exist according to the statistics of current and former law faculty members. See Meera E. Deo, *The Ugly Truth About Legal Academia*, 80 BROOK. L. REV. 943, 962 (2015) (citing AALS statistics).

23. YALE LAW SCHOOL, http://www.law.yale.edu/academics/candidates_aals.htm (last visited Aug. 26, 2013) ("The vast majority of new law teachers, both academic

and clinical, are hired through the annual Faculty Recruitment Conference sponsored by the Association of American Law Schools (AALS)).”

24. Meera E. Deo, Rican Vue, & Maria Woodruff, *Paint by Number? How the Race & Gender of Law School Faculty Affect the First Year Curriculum*, 29 CHICANO-LATINO L. REV. 1, 8 (2010) (discussing the “overrepresentation of white males in legal academia,” accounting for roughly 66% of all full professors).

25. Habitus may be considered a “structuring structure, which organises practices and the perception of practices.” PIERRE BOURDIEU, DISTINCTION: A SOCIAL CRITIQUE OF THE JUDGMENT OF TASTE 170 (1984). Habitus helps identify preferences, options, and opportunities that particular individuals or communities believe are available to them, whether or not these encompass the actual full range. Thus, believing the role of legal academic to be “out of range” for oneself, as many women of color do, will naturally limit the number who go on to pursue legal academia.

26. Persistent wealth inequality by race places additional financial obligations toward extended family on people of color, regardless of their individual educational or professional position. See, e.g., MELVIN T. OLIVER & THOMAS M. SHAPIRO, WHITE WEALTH/BLACK WEALTH (1997).

27. Mentorship is key for women of color seeking to enter legal academia, with the vast majority of study participants identifying mentors as one of the main reasons they entered and remain in legal academia. Mentorship is covered in more detail in the Conclusion.

28. Those same “mentors” discouraged Jennifer from pursuing options at other schools, actually limiting her professional options and opportunities so they and their own school could benefit. Chapter 2 also covers ways in which some white faculty colleagues pose as mentors offering advice to junior women of color faculty that is actually not in the best professional interest of the women of color.

29. A discussion of the importance of redefining merit is beyond the scope of this book, though other scholars have addressed the topic extensively. *See, e.g.,* Richard O. Lempert et al., *Michigan’s Minority Graduates in Practice: The River Runs Through Law School*, 25 LAW & SOC. INQUIRY 395 (2000); *see also* Robert M. Hendrickson, *Rethinking Affirmative Action: Redefining Compelling State Interest and Merit in Admission*, 76 PEABODY J. EDUC. 117 (2001).

30. Stephanie K. Johnson, David R. Hekman, & Elsa T. Chan, *If There’s Only One Woman in Your Candidate Pool, There’s Statistically No Chance She’ll Be Hired*, HARVARD BUSINESS REVIEW, Apr. 26, 2016, available at https://hbr.org/2016/04/if-theres-only-one-woman-in-your-candidate-pool-theres-statistically-no-chance-shell-be-hired.

31. The numerous challenges that women of color endure from colleagues—from mansplaining to silencing—are discussed in Chapter 2. Those presented here are directly related to hiring.

32. This reflects a “surface” interest in diversity, rather than a commitment to diversity as a “core” goal. For more on this distinction, *see* Rebecca K. Lee, *Core Diversity*, 19 TEMP. POL. & CIV. RTS. L. REV. 477, 479–80 (2010) (discussing “surface” versus “core” diversity ideals in the workplace).

33. *See* Madeline E. Heilman, *The Affirmative Action Stigma of Incompetence: Effects of Performance Information Ambiguity*, 40 ACAD. OF MGMT. J. 3 (1997), available at http://www.jstor.org/discover/10.2307/257055?sid=21105345808961&uid=2&uid=3739256&uid=70&uid=3739560&uid=4&uid=2129.

34. See Jerry Kang & Kristin Lane, *Seeing Through Colorblindness: Implicit Bias and the Law*, 58 UCLA L. REV. 465, 467 (2010).

35. Victor Quintanilla, *Critical Race Empiricism: A New Means to Measure Civil Procedure*, 3 U.C. IRVINE L. REV. 187, 198 (2013).

36. Gregory S. Parks and Jeffrey J. Rachlinski, *Implicit Bias, Election '08 and the Myth of a Post-Racial America*, 37, FLA. ST. L. REV. 659, 683 (2010).

37. Even the ways that television represents various racial/ethnic groups can further harmful stereotypes. *See, e.g.*, Christina B. Chin, Meera E. Deo, Faustina M. Du-Cros, Jenny Jong-Hwa Lee, Noriko Milman, & Nancy Wang Yuen, *Tokens on the Small Screen: Asian Americans and Pacific Islanders in Prime Time and Streaming Television* (2017), available at http://www.aapisontv.com/uploads/3/8/1/3/38136681/aapisontv.2017.pdf

38. Stephanie K. Johnson, David R. Hekman, & Elsa T. Chan, *If There's Only One Woman in Your Candidate Pool, There's Statistically No Chance She'll Be Hired*, HARVARD BUSINESS REVIEW, Apr. 26, 2016, available at https://hbr.org/2016/04/if-theres-only-one-woman-in-your-candidate-pool-theres-statistically-no-chance-shell-be-hired.

39. Rebecca Lee, *Core Diversity*, 19(2) TEMP. POL. & CIV. RTS. L. REV. 477, 480 (2010).

40. Robert Post, *Leadership in Educational Institutions: Reflections of a Law School Dean*, 69 STAN. L. REV. 1817, 1823 (2017).

41. For more on South Asian American racial realities, *see* Vinay Harpalani, *Desicrit: Theorizing the Racial Ambiguity of South Asian Americans*, NYU ANN. SURV. OF AM. L. 77 (2013).

42. See LISA WOLF-WENDEL, SUSAN B. TWOMBLY, & SUZANNE RICE, THE TWO-BODY PROBLEM: DUAL-CAREER-COUPLE HIRING PRACTICES IN HIGHER EDUCATION (2004).

43. Destiny also received an offer from the school where her husband was visiting, though the terms they offered were subpar: "It wasn't really clear to me that they really wanted me. They really wanted [my husband]. They were much more interested in him and had been courting him for a couple of years. They were far less interested in me, so they were making some sort of accommodation, but it wasn't clear to me how that accommodation was going to play out [laughing]." Today, she laughs it off. But at the time, she never even bothered getting the full details of the position "because I felt their resistance" to her appointment and knew that her husband was their primary focus.

44. Stacey recalls that those schools "called me really, really late and they offered me one time slot"—though when schools are truly excited to meet a candidate they call early in the process and are flexible with timing. One school called immediately

before their meeting with Stacey to ask, "'Oh, can I give you another time slot?' And I was like, 'No.' I had already canceled with somebody else" to fill the one slot they initially offered. When Stacey had interviews with disinterested schools, that also "wouldn't ask you questions," even though questions and answers normally are the heart of these initial interviews.

45. Again, this is just one of many ways in one socioeconomic status affects outcomes for faculty, and illustrates an additional challenge for low-income women of color who feel the effects of class privilege.

46. In her article, *U.C.'s Women Law Faculty*, 36 U.C. DAVIS L. REV. 331 (2003), the late professor and former Berkeley dean Herma Hill Kay writes: "My definition of a 'professor' includes only tenure or tenure-track assistant, associate, and full professors. It excludes librarians, clinicians, adjunct professors, and legal writing teachers, even though some of the women who were law librarians during this period held professorial appointments. . . . Others have drawn similar distinctions. *See* Marina Angel, *Women in Legal Education: What It's Like to be Part of a Perpetual First Wave Or the Case of the Disappearing Women*, 61 TEMP. L. REV. 799, 803 (1988) (including "only those teachers with visibility and power within their school; namely, tenured or tenure-track regular assistant professors, associate professors, or professors"); Deborah Jones Merritt & Barbara F. Reskin, *Sex, Race, and Credentials: The Truth About Affirmative Action in Law Faculty Hiring*, 97 COLUM. L. REV. 199, 206 (1997) (stating that "we chose tenure-track law professors as the subject of our study because those faculty members hold influential posts, shaping both the next generation of lawyers and the development of legal doctrine"); Elyce H. Zenoff & Kathryn V. Lorio, *What We Know, What We Think We Know, and What We Don't Know About Women Law Professors*, 25 ARIZ. L. REV. 869, 871–72 (1984) (counting only tenure-track faculty, defined as "professor, associate professor, or assistant professor, unmodified by any other term such as adjunct, clinical, visiting, or emeritus" and noting that "librarians, although usually tenure track, were excluded because they constitute a distinct career line.")." Certainly, a separate study focusing on these populations would add a layer of understanding to our conceptions of legal education, especially one focused on how legal writing and clinical faculty are more diverse and have less job security and voting rights than other faculty. The DLA data bear out this two-track system. Carla notes, "We have faculty diversity in the clinic; we don't have it in the [non-clinical] faculty, [also known as] 'the podium professors.'"

47. In fact, many white women and women of color alike juggle personal and professional responsibilities in exactly this way, by picking up children in the early evening and working late into the night after bedtime. Yet academia is not necessarily more conducive than practice to meaningful work/life balance. This issue is covered in detail in Chapter 6.

48. Meera E. Deo, *The Ugly Truth About Legal Academia*, 80 BROOK. L. REV. 943, 962 (2015) (citing AALS statistics).

49. Social capital conceives of relationships "as resources that individuals can draw on in times of need." (Meera E. Deo & Kimberly A. Griffin, *The Social Capital*

Benefits of Peer Mentoring in Law School, 38 OHIO N.U. L. REV. 305, 309 (2011) (citing James S. Coleman, *Social Capital in the Creation of Human Capital*, 94 AM. J. SOC. 95, 98 (Supp. 1998); Larissa Larsen et al., *Bonding and Bridging: Understanding the Relationship between Social Capital and Civic Action*, 24 J. PLANNING EDUC. & RES. 64, 65 (2004); Francis Fukuyama, *Social Capital, Civil Society and Development*, 22 THIRD WORD Q. 7, 7 (2001). See also ROBERT PUTNAM, BOWLING ALONE: THE COLLAPSE AND REVIVAL OF AMERICAN COMMUNITY 288-89 (2000)). White male aspiring law professors seem best positioned among all racial and gender groups to draw from social networks to their own professional benefit.

Chapter 2

1. For a full table on the frequency of interaction with white faculty by race, see Meera E. Deo, *The Ugly Truth about Legal Academia*, 80 BROOK. L. REV. 943, 962, Table 4 (2015) (citing AALS statistics).

2. Technically, respondents were likely at different schools, though generalizing to all faculty, it is interesting that white faculty and faculty of color characterize interracial faculty interactions differently.

3. Though not presented analytically, it is highly unlikely that this difference in perception is due to Black male faculty being especially friendly with white faculty. Of the four Black men in the DLA sample, one reports "very friendly" interactions with white colleagues and the other three characterize them as "sociable." This is not a statistically reliable sample size but is offered here merely as an example.

4. Research on women in legal academia includes the following: Judith Resnik, *A Continuous Body: Ongoing Conversations About Women and Legal Education*, 53 J. LEGAL EDUC. 564 (2003); Marina Angel, *The Glass Ceiling for Women in Legal Education: Contract Positions and the Death of Tenure*, 50 J. LEGAL EDUC. 1 (2000); Deborah Merritt & Barbara Reskin, *Sex, Race, and Credentials: The Truth About Affirmative Action in Law Faculty Hiring*, 9 COLUM. L. REV. 199, 230–35 (1991); Deborah Merritt & Barbara Reskin, *The Double Minority: Empirical Evidence of a Double Standard in Law School Hiring of Minority Women*, 65 S. CAL. L. REV. 2299, 2315–20 (1992); Deborah Merritt, Barbara Reskin & Michelle Fondell, *Family, Place and Career: The Gender Paradox in Law School Hiring*, 1993 WIS. L. REV. 395. However, most of these studies do not focus on race in addition to gender, and all could certainly be updated to reflect current trends and patterns from the past decade or more.

5. *See, e.g.*, Marina Angel, *The Glass Ceiling for Women in Legal Education: Contract Positions and the Death of Tenure*, 50 J. LEGAL EDUC. 1 (2000).

6. To create meaningful change, diversity in numbers is a necessary first step. See, e.g., Meera E. Deo, *The Promise of Grutter: Diverse Interactions at the University of Michigan Law School*, 17 MICH. J. RACE & L. 63, 65 (2011). "Without inclusion, however, the crucial connections that attract diverse talent, encourage their participation, foster innovation, and lead to . . . growth won't happen." Laura Sherbin and Ripa

Rashid, *Diversity Doesn't Stick Without Inclusion*, HARVARD BUS. REV. (Feb. 1, 2017), available at https://hbr.org/2017/02/diversity-doesnt-stick-without-inclusion.

7. This manuscript does not discuss the viability of individual sexual harassment claims that female faculty could file. Nevertheless, characterizations of their work environments and descriptions of the incidents women have endured seem to rise to the level of sexual harassment, as defined by the law and in the literature. *See, e.g.*, Vicki Schultz, *The Sanitized Workplace*, 112 YALE L.J. 2061, 2084–90 (2003) (providing a primer on workplace sexual harassment jurisprudence).

8. In response to these tensions, Laura suggests that new law faculty "just avoid anybody who has negative karma [because] it's not worth the time or effort to engage in a pointless discussion."

9. The Conclusion offers more details on the benefits of community building within institutions as well as externally.

10. One contributor to *Presumed Incompetent* writes of a common feature of most law schools today: the lobby wall with numerous portraits of "dead white males and some living ones" memorializing famous and respected former faculty members, alumni, and donors to the school; she feared these sentries noted her entry as a faculty member when she first began law teaching and she could virtually hear them silently "screaming—intruder alert." Adrien Katherine Wing, *Lessons from a Portrait: Keep Calm and Carry On*, 356, 359–60 in PRESUMED INCOMPETENT: THE INTERSECTIONS OF RACE AND CLASS FOR WOMEN IN ACADEMIA (Gabriella Gutierrez y Muhs, Yolanda Flores Neimann, Carmen G. Gonzalez, & Angela P. Harris eds., 2012).

11. When April asked for course guidance as a first-year faculty member, she was told only, "'It's up to you what you cover.'" At a meeting with a senior white male scholar teaching the same subject, she shared course materials but received nothing in return, save a comment that his materials were "very similar" to her own. On the basis of her colleagues' reticence, and knowing how teaching can derail tenure and promotion, April worried, "This looks to me like a setup," where faculty were purposefully vague about requirements in order to later assert that her teaching was substandard. In fact, teaching challenges are frequently cited as rationales for tenure or promotion denials, as discussed in Chapter 4.

12. Student interactions are covered in depth in the following chapter, although these data are included here to show how unwelcome faculty intervention can complicate already-challenging situations between women of color faculty and their students.

13. Alicia ultimately decided to talk with her colleague about how his interference undermined her authority in the classroom and worsened her classroom situation. She used scholarship to connect with him: "I said, 'We need to talk about what happens in the classroom to women of color and I need you to read this article [about women of color professors.]'" To his credit, he did, and a productive discussion followed. Other individual strategies to combat raceXgender bias in legal academia are discussed in the Conclusion.

14. In fact, the importance of relationships forged with those similarly situated— especially friendships between female faculty of color and participation in groups or

meetings targeting people of color—parallel the ways in which law students of color rely on their peers and the broad supportive structures within student organizations that provide them with social, cultural, and emotional support to sustain them. For more on peer mentorship and organizational mentorship for law students of color, see Meera E. Deo, *Two Sides of a Coin: Safe Space & Segregation in Race/Ethnic-Specific Law Student Organizations*, 42 Wash. U.J.L. & Pol'y 83 (2013); Meera E. Deo & Kimberly Griffin, *The Social Capital Benefits of Peer Mentoring Relationships in Law School*, 38 Ohio N.U.L. Rev. 305, 311 (2011) ("[M]entorship is also positively associated with the mentee's likelihood of retention"); Yung-Yi Diana Pan, Incidental Racialization: Performative Assimilation in Law School (2017). Organizational support for women of color faculty is also discussed in the Conclusion.

15. Erin's appreciation for her current position is especially significant given the horrific sex-based experiences she endured as a female faculty of color in her first tenure-track position at a different law school, covered elsewhere in this chapter.

16. This expectation that women of color faculty carry an overload of the service burden is revisited in Chapter 4.

17. Meera E. Deo, *The Promise of* Grutter*: Diverse Interactions at the University of Michigan Law School*, 17 Mich. J. Race & L. 63 (2011) (quoting Nancy E. Dowd et al., *Diversity Matters: Race, Gender, and Ethnicity in Legal Education*, 15 U. Fla. J.L. & Pub. Pol'y 11 (2003)).

18. Judith Resnick, *A Continuous Body: Ongoing Conversations About Women and Legal Education*, 53 J. Legal Educ. 564, 570 (2003) (citing Catherine Weiss & Louise Melling, *The Legal Education of Twenty Women*, 40 Stan. L. Rev. 1299, 1299–1300 (1988)).

19. Judith Resnick, *A Continuous Body: Ongoing Conversations About Women and Legal Education*, 53 J. Legal Educ. 564, 564 (2003).

20. Katherine Barnes & Elizabeth Mertz, *Is It Fair? Law Professors' Perceptions of Tenure*, 61 J. Legal Educ. 511, 512 (2012).

21. Katherine Barnes & Elizabeth Mertz, *Is It Fair? Law Professors' Perceptions of Tenure*, 61 J. Legal Educ. 511, 512 (2012).

22. As stated earlier, this manuscript neither delineates the contours for a formal sexual harassment claim nor asserts that participants in the DLA study have formal legal grounds for a suit. The term is used broadly to refer to extreme gender-based exclusion and work conditions that provide challenges for women to succeed.

23. Ruth Gordon, *On Community in the Midst of Hierarchy (and Hierarchy in the Midst of Community)*, 313, 327, in Presumed Incompetent: The Intersections of Race and Class for Women in Academia (Gabriella Gutierrez y Muhs, Yolanda Flores Neimann, Carmen G. Gonzalez, & Angela P. Harris eds., 2012).

24. The invisibility of Native Americans is especially troubling given their virtual erasure from society and popular consciousness, aside from problematic stereotypes or historical mythology. *See, e.g.*, Angela Riley, 130 Harv. L. Rev. 173, 173 (2017) ("American Indians are—metaphorically and literally—outside the standard frame of American law," while individuals and tribes currently push back against a demonstrated past of problematic policies with "historical and continued resistance to integration and assimilation").

25. Rebecca Solnit, *Tomgram: Rebecca Solnit, The Archipelago of Arrogance*, TOM-DISPATCH.COM (Apr. 13, 2008, 6:14 AM), available at http://www.tomdispatch.com/post/174918. *See also* Jessica Valenti, *Mansplaining, Explained: "Just Ask an Expert. Who Is Not a Lady,"* GUARDIAN (June 6, 2014, 7:18 AM), available at http://www.theguardian.com/commentisfree/2014/jun/06/mansplaining-explained-expert-women.

26. Helen Lewis, *The Essay That Launched the Term "Mansplaining,"* NEW REPUBLIC (July 4, 2014), available at http://www.newrepublic.com/article/118555/rebecca-solnits-men-explain-things-me-scourge-mansplaining.

27. Rebecca Solnit, *Why Mansplaining Is Still a Problem*, ALTERNET.COM (Aug. 12, 2012), available at http://www.alternet.org/why-mansplaining still-problem.

28. Rebecca Solnit, *Tomgram: Rebecca Solnit, The Archipelago of Arrogance*, TOM-DISPATCH.COM (Apr. 13, 2008, 6:14 AM), available at http://www.tomdispatch.com/post/174918.

29. Lindsay Dodgson, *Men Are Getting the Credit for Women's Work through Something Called 'Hepeating,'* BUS. INSIDER (Sept. 26, 2017), available at http://www.businessinsider.com/what-is-hepeating-2017-9.

30. Rebecca Solnit, *Tomgram: Rebecca Solnit, The Archipelago of Arrogance*, TOM-DISPATCH.COM (Apr. 13, 2008, 6:14 AM), available at http://www.tomdispatch.com/post/174918.

31. Rebecca Solnit, *Tomgram: Rebecca Solnit, The Archipelago of Arrogance*, TOM-DISPATCH.COM (Apr. 13, 2008, 6:14 AM), available at http://www.tomdispatch.com/post/174918.

32. Mansplaining is so prevalent throughout academia generally that there is a website dedicated solely to academic mansplaining, *Academic Men Explain Things to Me, Where Women Recount Their Experiences of Being Mansplained, in Academia and Elsewhere*, available at http://mansplained.tumblr.com (last visited Feb. 2, 2015).

33. Judith Resnick, *A Continuous Body: Ongoing Conversations About Women and Legal Education*, 53 J. LEGAL EDUC. 564, 570–71 (2003).

34. For more on how intersectionality creates not only additive but cumulative effects, see RICHARD DELGADO & JEAN STEFANCIC, CRITICAL RACE THEORY: AN INTRODUCTION 51–55 (2001).

35. In terms of numeric representation, diversity in law firms at the associate level is slightly better than in legal academia, with roughly 11% women of color, 10% men of color, and 33% white women. Yet representation at the partnership level is even worse than at the tenure level in academia, with only 2% women of color, 5% men of color, and 18% white women at corporate firms. *Perspectives on Diversity*, NALP BULL. (June 2014), available at http://www.nalp.org/0614research.

36. The corporate law firm realm has its own serious issues with raceXgender representation and bias at the partnership level, including only 2% women of color, 5% men of color, and 18% white women partners—compared to a full 75% white male partners—at the time of data collection for the DLA study (see National Association for Law Placement Women and Minorities at Law Firms 2009-2013, Table 1 available at www.nalp.org/lawfirmdiversity_2013#table1). Some DLA participants reflected on those issues as well. For instance, Abigail noted, "I worked for the largest law firm in

the city at the time and was one of just a few females. One of the litigation partners downtown told me that 'litigation is like war, honey, and you just don't send women into combat.'" *See also* Lisa van der Pool, *Big Law Firms Wrestle with Gender Discrimination Suits*, BOS. BUS. J. (Feb. 15, 2013, 6:00 AM), available at http://www.bizjournals .com/boston/print-edition/2013/02/15/big-law-firms-wrestle-with-gender.html?page =all. This section points out that some women participants in DLA recognize that gender discrimination may be even more pronounced in legal academia than in the corporate world, though it does not seek to minimize the concerns and gender-based negative realities of women working in corporate law firms.

37. In addition to an earnings differential between corporate practice and academia, there may be widespread gender disadvantage with regard to pay even within legal academia. Multiple female professors have filed complaints alleging a gender wage gap, resulting in one recent $2.66 million settlement. Colleen Flaherty, *Closing the Pay Gap*, INSIDE HIGHER ED, May 18, 2018, available at https://www.insidehighered .com/news/2018/05/18/u-denver-settles-eeoc-agreeing-pay-266-million-seven -female-law-professors-who.

38. Rebecca K. Lee, *Core Diversity*, 19 TEMP. POL. & CIV. RTS. L. REV. 477, 479–80 (2010) (discussing "surface" versus "core" diversity ideals in the workplace).

39. ARLIE RUSSELL HOCHSCHILD, THE MANAGED HEART: COMMERCIALIZATION OF HUMAN FEELING, 7(1983); Yeong-Gyeong Choi & Kyoung-Seok Kim, *A Literature Review of Emotional Labor and Emotional Labor Strategies*, 3(7) UNIVERSAL J. MGMT. 283, 285 (2015).

40. Yeong-Gyeong Choi & Kyoung-Seok Kim, *A Literature Review of Emotional Labor and Emotional Labor Strategies*, 3(7) UNIVERSAL J. MGMT. 283, 285 (2015) (citing ARLIE RUSSELL HOCHSCHILD, THE MANAGED HEART: COMMERCIALIZATION OF HUMAN FEELING (1983). *See also* Pamela K. Adelmann & R.B. Zajonc, *Facial Efference and the Experience of Emotion*, 40 ANN. REV. PSYCHOL. 249 (1989); Devon Carbado and Mitu Gulati, *Working Identity*, 85 CORNELL L. REV. 1259 (2000)(women and people of color suffer "significant opportunity costs" and a "high level of risk" when they engage in the performative identity work necessary to survive in the workplace).

41. *See, e.g.*, Roy L. Brooks, *Life After Tenure: Can Minority Law Professors Avoid the Clyde Ferguson Syndrome?*, 20 U.S.F. L. REV. 419 (1986).

42. Patrice's challenges with colleagues are explored more fully in Chapter 4 while discussing her tenure process.

43. Angela Onwuachi-Willig, *Silence of the Lambs*, 142, 148 in PRESUMED INCOMPETENT: THE INTERSECTIONS OF RACE AND CLASS FOR WOMEN IN ACADEMIA (Gabriella Gutierrez y Muhs, Yolanda Flores Neimann, Carmen G. Gonzalez, & Angela P. Harris eds., 2012).

44. Not all coping mechanisms are problematic. Some healthy ones, involving time with family, practicing yoga and meditation, or physical exercise are explored more fully in Chapter 6 and the Conclusion.

45. Women of color in legal academia sometimes feel they are simply going through the motions, playing a part as an academic but remaining disinvested from the job because they cannot be themselves. Instead, they endure "feel[ing] like a

clown. You smile when you do not feel like smiling. You bite your tongue and make no sound when you want to speak." Angela Mae Kupenda, *Facing Down the Spooks*, 20, 23 in PRESUMED INCOMPETENT: THE INTERSECTIONS OF RACE AND CLASS FOR WOMEN IN ACADEMIA (Gabriella Gutierrez y Muhs, Yolanda Flores Neimann, Carmen G. Gonzalez, & Angela P. Harris eds., 2012).

46. Colleen Flaherty, *Study Finds Female Professors Outperform Men in Service—To Their Possible Professional Detriment*, INSIDE HIGHER ED (Apr. 12, 2017), available at https://www.insidehighered.com/news/2017/04/12/study-finds-female-professors-outperform-men-service-their-possible-professional (quoting sociology professor Joya Misra).

47. Again, this book does not seek to outline strategies for filing formal sexual harassment claims against institutions based on a hostile workplace, although further research should be done to determine whether these common experiences are actionable.

48. This parallels affirmative action misconceptions discussed in Chapter 1.

49. *See, e.g.,* Marina Angel, *Women in Legal Education: What It's Like to be Part of a Perpetual First Wave or the Case of the Disappearing Women,* 61 TEMP. L. REV. 799, 803 (1988).

Chapter 3

1. The Law School Admission Council (LSAC) reports that, in 2017, 69% of applicants admitted to law school were white (Admitted Applicants by Race/Ethnicity & Sex, available at https://www.lsac.org/lsacresources/data/ethnicity-sex-admits).

2. A full table reporting statistics on the frequency of interactions between faculty and white students is available at Meera E. Deo, *The Ugly Truth about Legal Academia*, 80 BROOK. L. REV. 943, 987 (2015) (see Table 6). Data on student reliance on faculty of color and female faculty is available at Meera E. Deo, Walter R. Allen, A.T. Panter, Charles Daye, and Linda Wightman, *Struggles & Support: Diversity in U.S. Law Schools*, 23 NAT'L BLACK L.J. 71, 87 (2010).

3. Jakki Petzold, Law Student Perceptions of Faculty, LSSSE Blog, Sept. 6, 2018, available at http://lssse.indiana.edu/uncategorized/law-student-perceptions-of-faculty.

4. Imani began her law teaching career at a historically Black institution. The experiences for both students and faculty at historically Black institutions differ greatly from those at predominantly white institutions, including diverse schools that were not founded on a mission of educating traditionally underrepresented students. *See, e.g.,* Douglas A. Guiffrida, *Othermothering as a Framework for Understanding African American Students Definitions of Student-Centered Faculty,* 76 J. HIGHER EDUC. 701, 701–03 (2005). In part for these reasons, historically Black law schools are not included in the DLA sample, though some experiences working within them come through from faculty who taught at those institutions before current positions at predominantly white law schools.

5. In this sense, Imani's experience at her previous institution with diverse colleagues and a diverse student body is more similar to those of the white male DLA participants discussed later in this chapter.

6. For more on faculty-student interactions from the student perspective, see Meera E. Deo et al., *Paint by Number? How the Race and Gender of Law School Faculty Affect the First-Year Curriculum*, 29 CHICANA-LATINA L. REV. 1, 17 (2010). Students from all backgrounds flock to white women and especially women of color for support with personal and professional matters.

7. It is a common occurrence for faculty diversity to lag behind student diversity, even or especially at schools with little student diversity. *See, e.g.*, Anupam Chander et al., *Why Don't Law Faculties Look Like Their Students? Some Conjectures*, Paper Presentation at Law & Society Annual Meeting (June 2012) (presentation slides on file with the author).

8. Cassandra M. Guarino and Victor M. H. Borden, *Faculty Service Loads and Gender: Are Women Taking Care of the Academic Family?* 58 RES. IN HIGHER ED. 672 (2017). This research shows that women's extra service work is not unique to law schools, as a survey of roughly 1,400 faculty from various disciplines determined that women contribute significantly more hours of service annually than their male counterparts ("women reported 0.6 hours more service per week than men, controlling for rank, race and discipline").

9. Colleen Flaherty, *Study Finds Female Professors Outperform Men in Service—To Their Possible Professional Detriment*, INSIDE HIGHER ED, Apr. 12, 2017, available at https://www.insidehighered.com/news/2017/04/12/study-finds-female-professors-outperform-men-service-their-possible-professional.

10. Meera E. Deo, Walter R. Allen, A. T. Panter, Charles Daye, and Linda Wightman, *Struggles & Support: Diversity in U.S. Law Schools*, 23 NAT'L BLACK L.J. 71, 87 (2010).

11. Lauren K. Robel, LSSSE ANNUAL REPORT (2006).

12. While uncommon, a few male participants in the DLA study also note a few close student interactions, including a white male named Joe who "had a number of students come and break down in my office, crying," and an Asian American named Vijay who has "an open-door policy," so lots of students come "asking for guidance" with regard to "career paths or thinking about doing things outside of the law," and even "personal problems [or] problems they are having with other faculty."

13. Diversity discussions are classroom conversations regarding sensitive and personal topics including race/ethnicity, gender, and sexual orientation. Meera E. Deo, *The Promise of* Grutter: *Diverse Interactions at the University of Michigan Law School*, 17 MICH. J. RACE & L. 63, 95 (2011).

14. Deeper and more personal student engagement with substantive law improves their learning outcomes. See Meera E. Deo, *Faculty Insights on Educational Diversity*, 83 FORDHAM L. REV. 3115, at III.B. (2015).

15. Douglas A. Guiffrida, *Othermothering as a Framework for Understanding African American Students Definitions of Student-Centered Faculty*, 76 J. HIGHER EDUC. 701, 701–03 (2005).

16. Manya Whitaker, *The Color of Teaching: Expectations of Mammy in the Classroom*, FEMINIST WIRE, Nov. 6, 2013, available at http://www.theblackinstitute.org/the_color_of_teaching_expectations_of_mammy_in_the_classroom.

17. Djanna A. Hill-Brisbane, *Black Women Teacher Educators, Race Uplift, and the Academic Other-Mother Identity*, 19 ADVANCING WOMEN IN LEADERSHIP (2005), available at http://www.advancingwomen.com/awl/fall2005/19_5.html.

18. Roy L. Brooks, *Life After Tenure: Can Minority Law Professors Avoid the Clyde Ferguson Syndrome?*, 20 USF L. REV. 419, 420 (1986).

19. In this sense, students may be burdening female faculty and faculty of color "out of necessity." Roy L. Brooks, *Life After Tenure: Can Minority Law Professors Avoid the Clyde Ferguson Syndrome?*, 20 USF L. REV. 419, 421 (1986).

20. Legal scholar Roy Brooks suggests law faculty of color be given "some relief from committee assignments" to compensate for the extra time they spend on law students. Roy L. Brooks, *Life After Tenure: Can Minority Law Professors Avoid the Clyde Ferguson Syndrome?*, 20 USF L. REV. 419, 425 (1986). For more on how service work affects tenure and promotion, see Chapter 4.

21. Richard Delgado and Derrick Bell, *Minority Law Professors' Lives: The Bell-Delgado Survey*, 24 HARV. C.R.-C.L. L. REV. 349, 369–70 (1989); Meera E. Deo, *A Better Tenure Battle: Fighting Bias in Teaching Evaluations,* 31 COLUM. J. GENDER & L. 7 (2015).

22. Sylvia Lazos, *Are Student Teaching Evaluations Holding Back Women and Minorities? The Perils of "Doing" Gender and Race in the Classroom*, 164, 177 in PRESUMED INCOMPETENT: THE INTERSECTIONS OF RACE AND CLASS FOR WOMEN IN ACADEMIA (Gabriella Gutierrez y Muhs, Yolanda Flores Neimann, Carmen G. Gonzalez & Angela P. Harris eds., 2012).

23. Ruth Gordon, *On Community in the Midst of Hierarchy (and Hierarchy in the Midst of Community)*, 313, 320, in PRESUMED INCOMPETENT: THE INTERSECTIONS OF RACE AND CLASS FOR WOMEN IN ACADEMIA (Gabriella Gutierrez y Muhs, Yolanda Flores Neimann, Carmen G. Gonzalez & Angela P. Harris eds., 2012) (quoting Linda Greene, *Tokens, Role Models, and Pedagogical Politics: Lamentations of an African American Female Law Professor*, 6 BERKELEY WOMEN'S L.J. 81, 83 (1990–1991)).

24. The numbers have increased significantly from the slightly more than three hundred faculty members in the legal academy whom Bell and Delgado attempted to include in their study, although the qualitative experience remains troublingly similar. Richard Delgado and Derrick Bell, *Minority Law Professors' Lives: The Bell-Delgado Survey*, 24 HARV. C.R.-C.L. L. REV. 349 n.17 (1989). Yet recent upheavals in legal education may signal perhaps the first decrease in numbers of faculty of color.

25. *See* Meera E. Deo, *The Promise of* Grutter: *Diverse Interactions at the University of Michigan Law School*, 17 MICH. J. RACE & L. 63, 84 (2011).

26. *See, e.g.*, Gregory M. Herek, *Myths About Sexual Orientation: A Lawyer's Guide to Social Science Research*, 1 L. & SEXUALITY REV. 133, 171 (1991) ("Empirical research with other minority groups has shown that inter-group contact often reduces prejudice in the majority group when the contact meets several conditions: When it is encouraged by the institution in which it occurs, makes shared goals salient, and fosters inter-group cooperation; when the contact is ongoing and intimate rather than brief and superficial; and when members of the two groups are of equal status and share important values.").

27. A. H. Wingfield and J. H. Wingfield, *When Visibility Hurts and Helps: How Intersections of Race and Gender Shape Black Professional Men's Experiences with Tokenization*, 20 CULTURAL DIVERSITY & ETHNIC MINORITY PSYCHOL. 483 (2014).

28. Linda Greene, *Tokens, Role Models, and Pedagogical Politics: Lamentations of an African American Female Law Professor*, 6 BERKELEY WOMEN'S L.J. 81, 82 (1990–1991).

29. *See* PRESUMED INCOMPETENT: THE INTERSECTIONS OF RACE AND CLASS FOR WOMEN IN ACADEMIA (Gabriella Gutierrez y Muhs, Yolanda Flores-Niemann, Carmen G. Gonzalez & Angela P. Harris eds., 2012).

30. See the Introduction to this book for detailed statistics on law faculty by race and gender. See also Meera E. Deo, *The Ugly Truth about Legal Academia*, 80 BROOK. L. REV. 943, 962 (2015) (citing AALS statistics in Table 4).

31. Some white male colleagues have a hard time believing these are anything other than legitimate questions. Yet many women of color in the DLA sample articulate Destiny's experience of the context coupled with the question, which indicates that these questions are meant as more of a challenge to authority than an innocent inquiry.

32. Many women of color in the DLA sample noted that students formally complained about them to administrators at their law schools.

33. For more on administrative opportunities to support faculty or further exacerbate challenges, see the Conclusion. See also, Meera E. Deo, *Securing Support in an Unequal Profession*, in PRESUMED INCOMPETENT, VOLUME 2 (forthcoming 2019).

34. ARLIE RUSSELL HOCHSCHILD, THE MANAGED HEART: COMMERCIALIZATION OF HUMAN FEELING (1983) (coining the term and discussing *emotional labor*).

35. Individual strategies for overcoming the structural challenge of being presumed incompetent, as well as structural solutions, are discussed in the Conclusion of this book.

36. Again, Latinas account for just 1.3% of American law professors—including not only tenured and tenure-track faculty but also visitors, contract, legal writing, library, and other faculty members. With just 138 Latinas out of 10,965 law faculty members total, this particular student would likely never encounter a professor who looked like Bianca again. Meera E. Deo, *The Ugly Truth about Legal Academia*, 80 BROOK. L. REV. 943, 962 (2015) (citing AALS statistics in Table 4).

37. For a more detailed discussion challenging the usefulness of teaching evaluations, see Sylvia Lazos, *Are Student Teaching Evaluations Holding Back Women and Minorities? The Perils of "Doing" Gender and Race in the Classroom*, 164, in PRESUMED INCOMPETENT: THE INTERSECTIONS OF RACE AND CLASS FOR WOMEN IN ACADEMIA (Gabriella Gutierrez y Muhs, Yolanda Flores Neimann, Carmen G. Gonzalez, & Angela P. Harris eds., 2012).

38. This parallels how many women of color are portrayed in the media and popular culture, with many being stereotyped as sexy or submissive. See, e.g., Christina B. Chin, Meera E. Deo, Faustina M. DuCros, Jenny Jong-Hwa Lee, Noriko Milman, and Nancy Wang Yuen, *Tokens on the Small Screen: Asian Americans and Pacific Island-*

ers in Prime Time and Streaming Television (2017), available at http://www.aapisontv .com/uploads/3/8/1/3/38136681/aapisontv.2017.pdf.

39. Of course, even "objective" measures of beauty are heavily influenced by the white male norm in the United States. "The mainstream beauty ideal is almost exclusively white, making it all the more unattainable for women of color," leaving female faculty of color in a paradox of sorts because they are judged even more harshly than white female faculty on their appearance. *See Beauty Whitewashed: How White Ideals Exclude Women of Color*, Beauty Redefined Blog (Feb. 1, 2015), available at http:// www.beautyredefined.net/beauty-whitewashed-how-white-ideals-exclude-women-of -color.

40. Daniel S. Hamermesh & Amy M. Parker, *Beauty in the Classroom: Instructors' Pulchritude and Putative Pedagogical Productivity*, 24 Econ. Educ. Rev. 369 (2005).

41. For more on how women of color navigate personal style in the workplace, see D. Wendy Greene, *A Multidimensional Analysis of What Not to Wear in the Workplace: Hijabs and Natural Hair*, 87 FIU L. Rev. 333 (2013).

42. *See* Sylvia Lazos, *Are Student Teaching Evaluations Holding Back Women and Minorities? The Perils of "Doing" Gender and Race in the Classroom*, 164, 167, in Presumed Incompetent: The Intersections of Race and Class for Women in Academia (Gabriella Gutierrez y Muhs, Yolanda Flores Neimann, Carmen G. Gonzalez & Angela P. Harris eds., 2012) (noting the "avalanche" of existing scholarship on evaluations); Linda Greene, *Tokens, Role Models, and Pedagogical Politics: Lamentations of an African American Female Law Professor*, 6 Berkeley Women's L.J. 81, 83 (1990–1991).

43. William Arthur Wines & Terence J. Lau, *Observations on the Folly of Using Student Evaluations of College Teaching for Faculty Evaluation, Pay, and Retention Decisions and Its Implications for Academic Freedom*, 13 Wm. & Mary J. Women & L. 167, 175 (2006) ("Minority faculty members receive lower teaching evaluations than do majority professors, and non-native English speakers receive substantially lower ratings than do natives."). Bias against people who speak non-standard English or speak English with an accent is beyond the scope of this study, but documented elsewhere.

44. William Arthur Wines & Terence J. Lau, *Observations on the Folly of Using Student Evaluations of College Teaching for Faculty Evaluation, Pay, and Retention Decisions and its Implications for Academic Freedom*, 13 Wm. & Mary J. Women & L. 167, 177 (2006).

45. Meera E. Deo, *A Better Tenure Battle: Fighting Bias in Teaching Evaluations*, 31 Colum. J. Gender & L. 7 (2015) (citing Sylvia Lazos, *Are Student Teaching Evaluations Holding Back Women and Minorities? The Perils of "Doing" Gender and Race in the Classroom*, 164, 168–69, in Presumed Incompetent: The Intersections of Race and Class for Women in Academia (Gabriella Gutierrez y Muhs, Yolanda Flores Neimann, Carmen G. Gonzalez & Angela P. Harris eds., 2012).

46. Meera E. Deo, *A Better Tenure Battle: Fighting Bias in Teaching Evaluations*, 31 Colum. J. Gender & L. 7 (2015) (citing Sylvia Lazos, *Are Student Teaching Evaluations Holding Back Women and Minorities? The Perils of "Doing" Gender and Race in the Classroom*, 164, 170, in Presumed Incompetent: The Intersections of Race

AND CLASS FOR WOMEN IN ACADEMIA (Gabriella Gutierrez y Muhs, Yolanda Flores Neimann, Carmen G. Gonzalez & Angela P. Harris eds., 2012).

47. Evaluations also reveal intersectional discrimination across other devalued identity characteristics, including sexual orientation, class, and age.

48. The intimate connection between tenure and evaluation bias is discussed in detail in Chapter 4.

49. Recall that microaggressions are the "subtle verbal and non-verbal insults directed toward non-Whites, often done automatically or unconsciously." They tend to be "layered insults based on one's race, gender, class, sexuality, language, immigration status, phenotype, accent, or surname." Daniel Solórzano et al., *Keeping Race in Place: Racial Microaggressions and Campus Racial Climate at the University of California, Berkeley*, 23 CHICANO-LATINO L. REV. 15, 17 (2002).

50. For more on how student evaluations affect tenure and promotion, see Chapter 4.

51. Diversity discussions are conversations about race, gender, sexual orientation, class, and other sensitive subjects that students appreciate discussing, but faculty often shy away from for fear of saying the wrong thing and appearing politically incorrect. Meera E. Deo et al., *Paint by Number? How the Race and Gender of Law School Faculty Affect the First-Year Curriculum*, 29 CHICANO-LATINO L. REV. 1, 2–3 (2010).

52. A standard response to racial microaggressions is "to 'prove wrong' the ideas, statistics, statements and attitudes that say People of Color are less intelligent or less capable than others." *See, e.g.,* Daniel Solórzano et al., *Keeping Race in Place: Racial Microaggressions and Campus Racial Climate at the University of California, Berkeley*, 23 CHICANO-LATINO L. REV. 15, 42 (2002).

53. As most evaluations do not track the student's race, gender, grade performance, or any other student information, there is little reliable information about which students leave which comments. The inclusion of some context—the racial background of the student, expected course grade, or gender—could be helpful in determining how useful evaluations are. Additional proposals to overcome student bias in evaluations are included in the Conclusion of this book.

54. Roy L. Brooks, *Life After Tenure: Can Minority Law Professors Avoid the Clyde Ferguson Syndrome?*, 20 USF L. REV. 419, 421 (1986).

55. Jack, an Asian American male, is especially sensitive to how some faculty fail to take him seriously or even mistake him for a student. Still, this has never been a hindrance in the classroom; he even won a teaching award soon after he started teaching law.

56. Mary Ann Mason, *In the Ivory Tower, Men Only*, SLATE (June 17, 2013), available at http://www.slate.com/articles/double_x/doublex/2013/06/female_academics _pay_a_heavy_baby_penalty.html.

57. Chapter 4 covers the tenure and promotion process in detail, including ways student evaluations are used to bar women of color from professional success.

Chapter 4

1. Katherine Barnes & Elizabeth Mertz, *Is It Fair? Law Professors' Perceptions of Tenure*, 61 J. LEGAL EDUC. 511 (2012).

2. See THE RACIAL GAP IN THE PROMOTION TO TENURE OF LAW PROFESSORS: REPORT OF THE COMMITTEE ON THE RECRUITMENT AND RETENTION OF MINORITY LAW TEACHERS, COMMITTEE COMMENTARY (2005) 13 (on file with the author) (showing after seven years on the tenure track, 63.2% of women of color remained untenured, compared to 54.5% of men of color and 28.9% of white men and white women).

3. See THE RACIAL GAP IN THE PROMOTION TO TENURE OF LAW PROFESSORS: REPORT OF THE COMMITTEE ON THE RECRUITMENT AND RETENTION OF MINORITY LAW TEACHERS, COMMITTEE COMMENTARY (2005) 13 (on file with the author) (showing after seven years on the tenure track, 63.2% of women of color remained untenured, compared to 54.5% of men of color and 28.9% of white men and white women).

4. In addition to problematic tenure disparities, the table also reveals both that white women were hired at more than twice the rate of women of color (forty-five compared to nineteen), and that the eighty-three white men hired account for almost half of all new law faculty hires, as white women, women of color, and men of color combined total only eighty-six people.

5. Katherine Barnes & Elizabeth Mertz, *Is It Fair? Law Professors' Perceptions of Tenure*, 61 J. LEGAL EDUC. 511 (2012).

6. Katherine Barnes & Elizabeth Mertz, *Is It Fair? Law Professors' Perceptions of Tenure*, 61 J. LEGAL EDUC. 511, 517, 519 (2012).

7. Employment discrimination law covers this topic directly, targeting ambiguity as a primary reason for having clearly written policies and guidelines governing workplace issues. See Christopher K. Marshburn, Nicole T. Harrington & Enrica N. Ruggs, *Taking the Ambiguity Out of Subtle and Interpersonal Workplace Discrimination*, 10 INDUS. & ORGANIZATIONAL PSYCHOL. 87 (2017).

8. Katherine Barnes & Elizabeth Mertz, *Is It Fair? Law Professors' Perceptions of Tenure*, 61 J. LEGAL EDUC. 511, 522–23 (2012).

9. A full table on satisfaction with the tenure process is produced in Meera E. Deo, *Intersectional Barriers to Tenure*, 51 U.C. DAVIS L. REV. 997 (2018).

10. Katherine Barnes & Elizabeth Mertz, *Is It Fair? Law Professors' Perceptions of Tenure*, 61 J. LEGAL EDUC. 511, 522–23 (2012).

11. The importance of allies and sponsors cannot be overstated. Mentors are instrumental in the professional lives of women of color law faculty. They are discussed in greater detail in the Conclusion of this book.

12. Identity networks and academic communities of color are critical to the success of women of color in legal academia. These are discussed in detail in the Conclusion of this book.

13. ARLIE RUSSELL HOCHSCHILD, THE MANAGED HEART: COMMERCIALIZATION OF HUMAN FEELING (1983) (coining the term *emotional labor* and discussing it as

performing emotion for a wage). Emotional labor is discussed in greater detail in Chapter 2 of this book.

14. Service burdens are discussed at length in Chapters 3 and 4.

15. Cassandra M. Guarino & Victor M. H. Borden, *Faculty Service Loads and Gender: Are Women Taking Care of the Academic Family?* 58 Res. in Higher Educ. 672, 690 (2017).

16. Cassandra M. Guarino & Victor M. H. Borden, *Faculty Service Loads and Gender: Are Women Taking Care of the Academic Family?* 58 Res. in Higher Educ. 672, 682 (2017).

17. Cassandra M. Guarino & Victor M. H. Borden, *Faculty Service Loads and Gender: Are Women Taking Care of the Academic Family?* 58 Res. in Higher Educ. 672, 684–689 (2017).

18. Manya Whitaker, *The Color of Teaching: Expectations of Mammy in the Classroom*, Feminist Wire, Nov. 6, 2013, available at http://www.theblackinstitute.org/the_color_of_teaching_expectations_of_mammy_in_the_classroom; Cassandra M. Guarino & Victor M. H. Borden, *Faculty Service Loads and Gender: Are Women Taking Care of the Academic Family?* 58 Res. in Higher Educ. 672 (2017).

19. One exception to scholarship being the linchpin of tenure is faculty hired expressly to teach, without publication expectations. For instance, "legal writing has not been a tenure-track faculty position for various reasons" in the past, though this tradition has been changing recently. Catherine Martin Christopher, *Putting Legal Writing on the Tenure Track: One School's Experience* 31 Colum. J. Gender & L. 65, 69 (2015).

20. Colleen Flaherty, *Study Finds Female Professors Outperform Men in Service—To Their Possible Professional Detriment*, Inside Higher Ed, Apr. 12, 2017, available at https://www.insidehighered.com/news/2017/04/12/study-finds-female-professors-outperform-men-service-their-possible-professional.

21. *See, e.g.,* Tara J. Yosso, *Whose Culture Has Capital? A Critical Race Theory Discussion of Community Cultural Wealth*, 8 Race Ethnicity & Educ. 69 (2005).

22. Recent op-eds by women of color law faculty include those on racial identity as a social construct (Angela Onwuachi-Willig, *Race and Racial Identity are Social Constructs*, N.Y. Times, Sept. 6, 2016, available at https://www.nytimes.com/roomfordebate/2015/06/16/how-fluid-is-racial-identity/race-and-racial-identity-are-social-constructs), Dreamers' options under Trump (Rose Cuison Villazor, *What Do Dreamers Do Now?*, N.Y. Times, Sept. 4, 2017, available at https://www.nytimes.com/2017/09/04/opinion/trump-daca-repeal-security.html), and Muslim and LGBTQ unity in the wake of gun violence (Sahar Aziz, *Don't Let Terror Divide LGBTQ, Muslim Communities*, CNN, June 14, 2016, available at http://edition.cnn.com/2016/06/14/opinions/lgbtq-muslim-community-cooperation-aziz).

23. *See, e.g.,* Arlie Russell Hochschild, The Managed Heart: Commercialization of Human Feeling (1983) (discussing *emotional labor* as performing a professionally appropriate emotion for work).

24. This harkens back to the general distrust of colleagues discussed in Chapter 2.

25. When asked to provide advice for junior scholars, most senior scholars of color in the DLA study suggest that publishing prolifically from their very first year is a requirement especially for female faculty of color, fully expecting they may be judged with harsher standards and against higher expectations than white junior faculty.

26. Katherine Barnes & Elizabeth Mertz, *Is It Fair? Law Professors' Perceptions of Tenure*, 61 J. LEGAL EDUC. 511, 517 (2012).

27. Existing literature suggests that critical race theory, feminist legal scholarship, and other social justice–oriented research is often devalued by particular faculty, although many women and people of color gravitate toward that work as central to and validating of their own experiences. *See, e.g.,* Tara J. Yosso, *Whose Culture Has Capital? A Critical Race Theory Discussion of Community Cultural Wealth*, 8 RACE ETHNICITY & EDUC. 69 (2005).

28. Daniel Solórzano, Walter R. Allen & Grace Carroll, *Keeping Race in Place: Racial Microaggressions and Campus Racial Climate at the University of California, Berkeley*, 23 CHICANO-LATINO L. REV. 15, 17, 42 (2002). Other responses to microaggressions include giving up, fighting back, or disengaging.

29. In Aisha's case, there was what she calls "a smoking gun" involving racial comments made during the faculty vote on her application. The details of this smoking gun are not discussed here to preserve her anonymity.

30. See, e.g., Cassandra M. Guarino & Victor M. H. Borden, *Faculty Service Loads and Gender: Are Women Taking Care of the Academic Family?* 58 RES. IN HIGHER EDUC. 672 (2017).

Chapter 5

1. *See, e.g.,* DEBORAH RHODE, LAWYERS AS LEADERS (2013).

2. ABA statistics are available online at https://www.americanbar.org/groups/legal_education/resources/statistics.html. These disparities are not unique to legal education but pervade leadership in most fields. A lack of diversity in legal academia is unsurprising given that there are more CEOs named John (5.3%) and David (4.5%) than there are women CEOs (4.1%). Stephanie K. Johnson, David R. Hekman & Elsa T. Chan, *If There's Only One Woman in Your Candidate Pool, There's Statistically No Chance She'll Be Hired*, HARV. BUS. REV., Apr. 26, 2016, available at https://hbr.org/2016/04/if-theres-only-one-woman-in-your-candidate-pool-theres-statistically-no-chance-shell-be-hired.

3. Margot Slade, *Women, Minorities Land Majority of New Law Dean Appointments* LawDragon Campus, June 25, 2014, available at http://campus-search.lawdragon.com/2014/06/25/women-minorities-land-majority-of-new-dean-appointments/ (noting, "Fourteen law schools have lost their deans in the last six months" and "[o]f the 15 new deans at law schools accredited by the American Bar Association, eight are women and almost half are minorities."). See also Tracy Thomas, *New Women Law*

School Deans, GENDER AND THE LAW PROF BLOG, June 8, 2017, available at http://lawprofessors.typepad.com/gender_law/2017/06/new-women-law-school-deans.html (stating that 50% of new deanships (14 of 28) in 2017 went to women, including two women of color, compared to 46% of new deans being women in 2015; increasing numbers have brought the overall percentage of female deans from 21% in 2014 to roughly 30% in 2017).

4. Tomas Chamorro-Premuzic, *Why Do So Many Incompetent Men Become Leaders?*, HARV. BUS. REV., Aug. 22, 2013, available at https://hbr.org/2013/08/why-do-so-many-incompetent-men.

5. Tomas Chamorro-Premuzic, *Why Do So Many Incompetent Men Become Leaders?*, HARV. BUS. REV., Aug. 22, 2013, available at https://hbr.org/2013/08/why-do-so-many-incompetent-men.

6. Tomas Chamorro-Premuzic, *Why Do So Many Incompetent Men Become Leaders?*, HARV. BUS. REV., Aug. 22, 2013, available at https://hbr.org/2013/08/why-do-so-many-incompetent-men.

7. Bourree Lam, *How Office Culture Can Crush Women's Ambitions*, THE ATLANTIC, Apr. 19, 2017, available at https://www.theatlantic.com/business/archive/2017/04/ambition-office-women/523443.

8. Work/life balance is addressed directly and in more detail in Chapter 6 of this book.

9. Bourree Lam, *How Office Culture Can Crush Women's Ambitions*, THE ATLANTIC, Apr. 19, 2017, available at https://www.theatlantic.com/business/archive/2017/04/ambition-office-women/523443 (citing Boston Consulting Group).

10. Bourree Lam, *How Office Culture Can Crush Women's Ambitions*, THE ATLANTIC, Apr. 19, 2017, available at https://www.theatlantic.com/business/archive/2017/04/ambition-office-women/523443 (citing Boston Consulting Group).

11. The ABA notes that 83% of deans and 79% of associate deans are white, leaving very few possible role models who share the racial background of women of color. ABA statistics are available online at https://www.americanbar.org/groups/legal_education/resources/statistics.html.

12. For more on how a lack of role models is a barrier to entry for aspiring women of color legal academics, see Chapter 1.

13. Robert Post, *Leadership in Educational Institutions: Reflections of a Law School Dean*, 69 STAN. L. REV. 1817, 1817–18 (2017). See Chapter 2 for more on challenging intersectional (raceXgender) relationships among faculty.

14. *See, e.g.*, Robert Post, *Leadership in Educational Institutions: Reflections of a Law School Dean*, 69 STAN. L. REV. 1817, 1826 (2017) ("One moment I was a colleague, and the next I was an authority figure subject to all the projections that ordinary people cast onto [leaders].").

15. Colleen Flaherty, *Study Finds Female Professors Outperform Men in Service— To Their Possible Professional Detriment*, INSIDE HIGHER ED, Apr. 12, 2017, available at https://www.insidehighered.com/news/2017/04/12/study-finds-female-professors-outperform-men-service-their-possible-professional.

16. One DLA participant referenced the highly publicized lawsuit filed by a white male faculty member at Widener Law School against the school's Black female dean Linda Ammons (which was filed after the white male faculty member used hypotheticals in class about him shooting Dean Ammons and naming her as a drug dealer). *Widener Law Professor Settles Lawsuit with School*, NAT'L JURIST, Feb. 8, 2012, available at http://www.nationaljurist.com/content/widener-law-professor-settles-lawsuit -school). After settling the lawsuit, Dean Ammons, who was "both the first female and first African American dean of the law school," took a sabbatical and then retired from law teaching. Robin Brown, *Ammons Steps Down as Widener Law Dean*, DELA-WAREONLINE, Apr. 29, 2014, available at http://www.delawareonline.com/story/news/ education/2014/04/29/ammons-steps-widener-law-dean/8495405/.

17. See Chapter 3 of this book for more on faculty-student interactions and teaching evaluations.

18. See Angela Onwuachi-Willig, *Silence of the Lambs*, 142–51, 142, 143 in PRE-SUMED INCOMPETENT: THE INTERSECTIONS OF RACE AND CLASS FOR WOMEN IN ACADEMIA (Gabriella Gutierrez y Muhs, Yolanda Flores Neimann, Carmen G. Gonzalez & Angela P. Harris eds., 2012).

19. While the negative health effects of performing emotional labor affect many women of color faculty, the costs are likely even higher for women of color administrators who are frequently in positions where they must hide their true feelings, "perform" the role expected of them, or adjust their behavior to conform to traditional norms of institutional leadership. See Devon Carbado and Mitu Gulati, *Working Identity*, 85 CORNELL L. REV. 1259, 1262 (2000)(detailing the "extra" identity work that women and people of color engage in to counter negative stereotypes about them on the job, as well as the "significant opportunity costs" and "high level of risk" inherent in doing so).

20. Bourree Lam, *How Office Culture Can Crush Women's Ambitions*, THE ATLAN-TIC, Apr. 19, 2017, available at https://www.theatlantic.com/business/archive/2017/ 04/ambition-office-women/523443. As stated earlier, "implicit bias [often] coexists with egalitarian beliefs and the denial of personal prejudice" (Victor Quintanilla, *Critical Race Empiricism: A New Means to Measure Civil Procedure*, 3 U.C. IRVINE L. REV. 187, 198 (2013)).

21. Tomas Chamorro-Premuzic, *Why Do So Many Incompetent Men Become Leaders?*, HARV. BUS. REV., Aug. 22, 2013, available at https://hbr.org/2013/08/why-do -so-many-incompetent-men.

22. Tomas Chamorro-Premuzic, *Why Do So Many Incompetent Men Become Leaders?*, HARV. BUS. REV., Aug. 22, 2013, available at https://hbr.org/2013/08/why-do -so-many-incompetent-men.

23. Stephanie K. Johnson, David R. Hekman & Elsa T. Chan, *If There's Only One Woman in Your Candidate Pool, There's Statistically No Chance She'll Be Hired*, HAR-VARD BUSINESS REVIEW, Apr. 26, 2016, available at https://hbr.org/2016/04/if-theres -only-one-woman-in-your-candidate-pool-theres-statistically-no-chance-shell-be -hired.

24. Tomas Chamorro-Premuzic, *Why Do So Many Incompetent Men Become Leaders?*, HARV. BUS. REV., Aug. 22, 2013, available at https://hbr.org/2013/08/why-do -so-many-incompetent-men.

25. Melissa Murray, *Thoughts on Whispered Conversations Amplified*, Presentation at AALS Annual Meeting (Jan. 2018).

26. External networks and communities of support provide significant encouragement and support to women of color faculty, which is discussed in detail in Chapter 6 of this book. The distrust marking many relationships between women of color and their white faculty colleagues is discussed at length in Chapter 2 of this book.

27. DERRICK BELL, FACES AT THE BOTTOM OF THE WELL: THE PERMANENCE OF RACISM, 19 (1992).

28. Asaf Levanon, Paula England, and Paul Allison, *Occupational Feminization and Pay: Assessing Causal Dynamics Using 1950-2000 U.S. Census Data*, 88 SOCIAL FORCES 865 (2009)(finding that as women move into previously male-dominated careers the value and pay of those positions decrease).

29. Robert Post, *Leadership in Educational Institutions: Reflections of a Law School Dean*, 69 STAN. L. REV. 1817, 1818 (2017).

30. Carla put forth significant emotional labor by not pushing back to insist on her leave, at great cost to herself given the personal and professional plans she had made for the time away. ARLIE RUSSELL HOCHSCHILD, THE MANAGED HEART: COMMERCIALIZATION OF HUMAN FEELING (1983).

31. Cassandra M. Guarino & Victor M. H. Borden, *Faculty Service Loads and Gender: Are Women Taking Care of the Academic Family?* 58 RES. IN HIGHER EDUC. 672 (2017).

32. Cassandra M. Guarino & Victor M. H. Borden, *Faculty Service Loads and Gender: Are Women Taking Care of the Academic Family?* 58 RES. IN HIGHER EDUC. 672 (2017); Manya Whitaker, *The Color of Teaching: Expectations of Mammy in the Classroom*, FEMINIST WIRE, Nov. 6, 2013, available at http://www.theblackinstitute.org/the _color_of_teaching_expectations_of_mammy_in_the_classroom.

33. The following chapter reaches similar conclusions regarding the intersectional raceXgender realities of work/life balance, with women from all backgrounds taking on more and thereby juggling more on average than their male counterparts.

34. Although the quantitative data indicate that white men are no more likely to be interested in leadership as their ultimate career goal than white women, individual white men do discuss their interests and experiences as leaders in the qualitative data. Data from these interviews support the conclusion that white men do pursue formal leadership roles at greater rates.

35. Tomas Chamorro-Premuzic, *Why Do So Many Incompetent Men Become Leaders?*, HARV. BUS. REV., Aug. 22, 2013, available at https://hbr.org/2013/08/why-do -so-many-incompetent-men.

36. Lisa Wade, *The Invisible Workload That Drags Women Down*, MONEY.COM, Dec. 28, 2016, available at http://time.com/money/4561314/women-work-home -gender-gap. As a whole, white men and men of color enjoy greater work/life balance

than women, as discussed in Chapter 6 of this book. Those who have less to balance personally are more interested in taking on more professionally, including administrative duties.

37. In addition to tenure and leadership, advancement includes the opportunity to move laterally to more prestigious institutions. The DLA study did not ask directly about lateral moves, though some participants discussed relevant experiences. Surya expected when she had two law review articles published in top law reviews in her first few years of law teaching that she would have opportunities to move. She says: "I thought that because other people who did that called me to congratulate me when I got an article [published in a top journal] and said, 'Oh [snap!] When I published at *Stanford* [*Law Review*] for my first article that was my ticket out to [teach at] Columbia Law school. That was my ticket to places.' And they did go to those places. And I didn't." She worries that "people of my race and gender have published really well, but they didn't move. They didn't go beyond whatever institution they were in." Although there are "so few Asian Americans at top law schools," there are nevertheless "Asian Americans publishing well and getting good reviews on their work and teaching well and winning the teaching awards and yet they're not getting ahead." Surya's observations about how excellent publication records yielded lateral movement for whites but not for Asian Americans parallels Trisha's observation that what had been a secure path for white women to administrative leadership was not sufficient for her as a Black woman.

38. Pierre Bourdieu, Distinction: A Social Critique of the Judgment of Taste 170 (1984).

39. Tomas Chamorro-Premuzic, *Why Do So Many Incompetent Men Become Leaders?*, Harv. Bus. Rev., Aug. 22, 2013, available at https://hbr.org/2013/08/why-do -so-many-incompetent-men.

Chapter 6

1. Business Dictionary, definition of work/life balance, available at http://www .businessdictionary.com/definition/work-life-balance.html.

2. *How to Really Measure Work-Life Balance*, Forbes, June 26, 2017, available at https://www.forbes.com/sites/forbescoachescouncil/2017/06/26/how-to-really -measure-work-life-balance/#1cad9eae19d4

3. See Trina Jones, *Single and Childfree! Reassessing Parental and Marital Status Discrimination*, 46 Arizona St. L. J. 1253 (2014).

4. Research on work/life balance has nearly unanimous agreement that "the most consistent family characteristic predicting imbalance is being a parent," indicating that those raising children do not have better work/lifework-life balance than those without children. Mary Tausig & Rudy Fenwick, *Unbinding Time: Alternate Work Schedules and Work-Life Balance*, 22 J. Fam. & Ec. Issues 101 (2001).

5. For more on intersectional (raceXgender) experiences with tenure, see Chapter 4 of this book.

6. *See, e.g.,* Flex by Fenwick, providing flexible and job opportunities for attorneys (many of whom are women who left full-time corporate practice after the birth of a child) who can set their own hours and work remotely, available at http://www.flexbyfenwick.com/attorneys.

7. Bright Horizons is a popular backup care option for working mothers with sick children, often paid for or supplemented by law firms (see Cathy Benton & Nicole Brown, *Taking Care of Lawyers Taking Care of Children*, 17 ABA Business Law Section, BUS. LAW TODAY, Jan.–Feb. 2008, available at http://apps.americanbar.org/buslaw/blt/2008-01-02/brown.shtml) (discussing Alston and Bird's decision to offer childcare and backup care). Latham & Watkins as well as other corporate firms also pay to ship breast milk home so working mothers can more easily opt in to business travel (Claire Zillman, *This Law Firm Is the Latest Employer to Pay for Working Moms to Ship Their Breast Milk*, FORTUNE, Sept. 16, 2016, available at http://fortune.com/2016/09/16/ship-breast-milk-law-firm-latham).

8. ARLIE RUSSELL HOCHSCHILD, THE SECOND SHIFT: WORKING PARENTS AND THE REVOLUTION AT HOME (1989).

9. SUSAN WALZER, THINKING ABOUT THE BABY, GENDER AND TRANSITIONS INTO PARENTHOOD (1998) (discussing the invisible and uncompensated work that mothers engage in at home); see also Lisa Wade, *The Invisible Workload That Drags Women Down*, MONEY.COM, Dec. 28, 2016, available at http://time.com/money/4561314/women-work-home-gender-gap/.

10. This term was popularized on one site (M. Blazoned, *The Default Parent*, HUFFINGTON POST, Oct. 28, 2014, available at http://www.huffingtonpost.com/m-blazoned/the-default-parent_b_6031128.html), and soon gained a following among a number of others, including Lindsey, *A Letter from the Backup Parent to the Default Parent*, THE MOTHERCHIC, Nov. 5, 2014, available at https://themotherchic.com/2014/11/05/letter-default-parent-back-parent/, Christa, *Here's A Short List of Some of What Default Parents Do*, HELLO MAMAS, Nov. 12, 2014, available at http://dish.hellomamas.com/index.php/heres-what-default-parents-do/, and M. Blazoned, *The Default Parent Resume*, Feb. 15, 2016, available at http://www.mblazoned.com/the-default-parent-resume. Note also that in two-parent male-female households, both parents frequently contribute to the children's welfare, yet even when a father does a lot, if he is not managing the home life, then "in terms of logistics and administrative duties, he's the backup parent." M. Blazoned, *The Default Parent*, HUFFINGTON POST, Oct. 28, 2014, available at http://www.huffingtonpost.com/m-blazoned/the-default-parent_b_6031128.html

11. The primary caregiver is not synonymous with the default parent. The default parent is not necessarily the one who spends the most time with the children, but rather the one who keeps track of the daily requirements, plans weekly logistics, and organizes the lives of the children. For more on the default parent, see M. Blazoned, *The Default Parent*, HUFFINGTON POST, Oct. 28, 2014, available at http://www.huffingtonpost.com/m-blazoned/the-default-parent_b_6031128.html.

12. Christa, *Here's a Short List of Some of What Default Parents Actually Do*, HELLO MAMAS, Nov. 12, 2014, available at http://dish.hellomamas.com/index.php/heres-what-default-parents-do/

13. Christa, *Here's a Short List of Some of What Default Parents Actually Do*, Hello Mamas, Nov. 12, 2014, available at http://dish.hellomamas.com/index.php/heres -what-default-parents-do/.

14. M. Blazoned, *The Default Parent*, Huffington Post, Oct. 28, 2014, available at http://www.huffingtonpost.com/m-blazoned/the-default-parent_b_6031128.html.

15. *See, e.g.*, Susan Walzer, Thinking About the Baby: Gender and Transitions into Parenthood (1998) and Lisa Wade, *The Invisible Workload that Drags Women Down*, Money.com, Dec. 28, 2016, available at http://time.com/money/4561314/ women-work-home-gender-gap/.

16. Lisa Wade, *The Invisible Workload That Drags Women Down*, Money.com, Dec. 28, 2016, available at http://time.com/money/4561314/women-work-home -gender-gap.

17. Lisa Wade, *The Invisible Workload That Drags Women Down*, Money.com, Dec. 28, 2016, available at http://time.com/money/4561314/women-work-home -gender-gap.

18. Numerous single parents participated in the DLA sample. They are occasionally identified as such in the data, though their background details are left purposefully vague in order to preserve anonymity. Same-sex parents also participated and are sometimes not identified to preserve anonymity, though many issues are similar.

19. Only three women of color in the DLA sample mention partners (all men) who have been primary caregivers, even temporarily. Carla's partner "took time out to be the primary caregiver for our son," from birth through middle school. Aarti's husband left his job to be a "full-time stay-at-home dad." Though the transition was stressful, Aarti admits that his decision "really helped *my* work/life balance." Lori, an Asian American professor, also appreciates that her husband "does most of the day-to-day care, and I do homework and some cooking—not very much. And then I do the clothes shopping and he does the grocery shopping." While they have managed the division of labor, "managing expectations" has been "quite difficult" because culturally Lori feels she is "supposed to be the stay-at-home Mommy, and he's supposed to go out and be the breadwinner." Carla, Aarti, and Lori are clear outliers in the DLA sample, as most women of color who are parents are the default parents.

20. Sofia is not truly single parenting, where one parent carries the full physical and emotional load of parenting children, during the day-to-day as well as in emergencies. Her husband is not physically nearby for much of the time, but still contributes to their household and would certainly be available emotionally and likely in person for any emergencies.

21. See Chapter 3 in this book for more on student interactions and Chapter 4 in this book for more on how women of color are overburdened by service demands.

22. Lisa Wade, *The Invisible Workload That Drags Women Down*, Money.com, Dec. 28, 2016, available at http://time.com/money/4561314/women-work-home -gender-gap.

23. While single individuals who are not parents clearly deserve to balance their personal and professional lives as much as any others, DLA data do not support the theoretical suggestion of discrimination based on *singlism*, which posits that single

people are asked to carry additional burdens to ease obligations on mothers, fathers, other caretakers, or those in other familial or romantic relationships. For more on singlism, see Trina Jones, *Single and Childfree! Reassessing Parental and Marital Status Discrimination*, 46 Arizona St. L. J. 1253 (2014).

24. Arlie Russell Hochschild, The Second Shift: Working Parents and the Revolution at Home (1989).

25. Communities of color often depend on this aid. See Michelle Anderson, *Legal Education Reform, Diversity, and Access to Justice*, 61 Rutgers L. Rev. 1011 (2009) (providing a historical perspective on the lack of access to justice for people of color).

26. Those who provide care simultaneously to young children and aging parents are sometimes referred to as the *sandwich generation*. See Carol Bradley Bursack, *A Story from the Sandwich Generation: Caring for Kids and Parents*, AGINGCARE.COM, June 19, 2017, available at https://www.agingcare.com/articles/the-sandwich-generation -caring-for-children-and-elderly-parents-123286.htm.

27. *See, e.g.*, Daniel Solórzano et al., *Keeping Race in Place: Racial Microaggressions and Campus Racial Climate at the University of California, Berkeley*, 23 Chicano-Latino L. Rev. 15, 42 (2002).

28. See Michelle Anderson, *Legal Education Reform, Diversity, and Access to Justice*, 61 Rutgers L. Rev. 1011 (2009) (providing a historical perspective on the lack of access to justice for people of color).

29. Lisa Wade, *The Invisible Workload That Drags Women Down*, Money.com, Dec. 28, 2016, available at http://time.com/money/4561314/women-work-home -gender-gap.

30. Adam's experience of providing extra service to students parallels research done with law students, indicating that not only women of color and white women, but also white men with a nontraditional background for legal academics, including those who identify as gay—are seen as more approachable and accessible. Meera E. Deo, Rican Vue & Maria Woodruff, *Paint by Number? How the Race & Gender of Law School Faculty Affect the First Year Curriculum*, 29 Chicano-Latino L. Rev. 1, 25 (2010).

31. Men not taking advantage of parental leave may encourage colleagues to continue thinking of it as "maternity" leave, a gender issue, or something relevant only to women—as was the case at Ken's school when he was denied.

Conclusion

1. Work/life balance—including shared responsibilities with partners and other family members—is the focus of Chapter 6 of this book.

2. As discussed in Chapter 2, traditional outsiders in legal academia often hold their tongues on campus, investing in the emotional labor of hiding their true feelings rather than opening up to colleagues they distrust. Angela Onwuachi-Willig, *Silence of the Lambs*, 142–51, 142, 143, in *Presumed Incompetent: The Intersections of Race and Class for Women in Academia* (Gabriella Gutierrez y Muhs, Yolanda Flores Neimann, Carmen G. Gonzalez & Angela P. Harris eds., 2012). *See also* Arlie Russell Hochs-

CHILD, The Managed Heart: Commercialization of Human Feeling (1983) (discussing emotional labor).

3. For near and peer mentors in the student context, see Meera E. Deo & Kimberly Griffin, *The Social Capital Benefits of Peer Mentoring Relationships in Law School*, 38 Ohio N.U. L. Rev. 305 (2011).

4. LatCrit grew out of a meeting of like-minded scholars focused on "Latina/o Communities and Critical Race Theory," who "aim to center Latinas/os multiple internal diversities and to situate Latinas/os in larger inter-group frameworks, both domestically and globally, to promote social justice awareness and activism." For more about LatCrit, see http://www.latcrit.org/content/about/. CAPALF seeks to provide "Asian Pacific American law faculty with scholarship support and various networking and professional development opportunities." More at https://www.capalf.org.

5. In the higher education context, the Supreme Court has defined *critical mass* as referring to "'meaningful numbers' or 'meaningful representation' . . . that encourages underrepresented minority students to participate in the classroom and not feel isolated," and also "numbers such that underrepresented minority students do not feel isolated or like spokespersons for their race." Grutter v. Bollinger, 539 U.S. 306, 318, 319 (2003) (quotations omitted). That definition can be adopted to apply to faculty of color in the employment context.

6. The Society of American Law Teachers (SALT) provides a network for progressive law faculty, including many people of color. SALT is a "Community of Progressive Law Teachers Working For Justice, Diversity and Academic Excellence." More at https://www.saltlaw.org. The Lutie summer workshop focuses primarily on scholarship, but also emphasizes "professional and personal skill-building" for aspiring and current Black women faculty. See https://law.uiowa.edu/sites/law.uiowa.edu/files/wysiwyg_uploads/boyd_memo_on_lutie_a._lytle_history.pdf.

7. Although parental leave is not solely a women's issue—since men and women can both be involved parents—it is often viewed that way. Chapter 6 of this book includes a perspective from Jack, who refused his school's offer of parental leave; if senior scholars had explained to Jack that taking leave would pave the way for future faculty, to do so, not just women but also men, perhaps he would have taken it too.

8. *See, e.g.,* Daniel Solórzano et al., *Keeping Race in Place: Racial Microaggressions and Campus Racial Climate at the University of California, Berkeley*, 23 Chicano-Latino L. Rev. 15, 42 (2002) (indicating one standard response to microaggressions is to work harder to prove wrong the naysayers).

9. Research confirms Emma's fears. Heather Antecol, Kelly Bedard, & Jenna Stearns, *Equal but Inequitable: Who Benefits from Gender-Neutral Tenure Clock Stopping Policies?*, discussion paper available at http://ftp.iza.org/dp9904.pdf; *see also* Justin Wolfers, *A Family Friendly Policy That's Friendliest to Male Professors*, N.Y. Times, June 24, 2016, available at https://www.nytimes.com/2016/06/26/business/tenure-extension-policies-that-put-women-at-a-disadvantage.html?mcubz=0.

10. This book does not suggest that most white male law professors are not innovative or excellent teachers; the inclusion of Brianna's quote is simply to highlight a pattern in the data identifying the opportunity for older white male professors to

rest on their laurels (even if they are not doing so), while women of color rarely have laurels available.

11. Tomas Chamorro-Premuzic, *Why Do So Many Incompetent Men Become Leaders?*, HARV. BUS. REV., Aug. 22, 2013, available at https://hbr.org/2013/08/why-do -so-many-incompetent-men.

12. For a more detailed discussion of Eliana's approach as a utilization of gender judo, see Meera E. Deo, *The Ugly Truth about Legal Academia*, 80 BROOK. L. REV. 943, 1007 (2015); *see also* Joan C. Williams, *Women, Work and the Art of Gender Judo*, WASH. POST, Jan. 24, 2014, available at http://www.washingtonpost.com/opinions/ women-work-and-the-art-of-gender-judo/2014/01/24/29e209b2-82b2-11e3-8099 -9181471f7aaf_story.html.

13. Rather than individual faculty educating colleagues, organizing diversity-focused workshops or trainings should be a structural solution. Thus, it is discussed later in this chapter.

14. One recent article similarly highlights female staffers of President Obama *amplifying* one another's perspectives to claim them for the original female speaker (Keli Goff, *How the Women of the Obama White House Fought Gender Inequality—and We Can Too*, DAILY BEAST, Sept. 23, 2016, available at https://www.thedailybeast.com/how -the-women-of-the-obama-white-house-fought-gender-inequalityand-we-can-too).

15. DLA data indicate that only 5% of Black women, 13% of Asian American women, and 27% of white women provide more than ten hours a month of mentorship to faculty at their institution. Even fewer hours are spent mentoring faculty at other institutions, with only 10% of Black women faculty and 18% of men of color spending more than ten hours per month doing so.

16. Similarly, students of color rely on other students as mentors to support them through law school. See Meera E. Deo & Kimberly Griffin, *The Social Capital Benefits of Peer Mentoring Relationships in Law School*, 38 OHIO N.U. L. REV. 305 (2011).

17. There is often an overlap between female faculty who are the default parent (M. Blazoned, *The Default Parent*, HUFFINGTON POST, Oct. 28, 2014, available at http://www.huffingtonpost.com/m-blazoned/the-default-parent_b_6031128.html), carrying the mental load (SUSAN WALZER, THINKING ABOUT THE BABY: GENDER AND TRANSITIONS INTO PARENTHOOD (1998)), and contributing extra service work on campus (Colleen Flaherty, *Study Finds Female Professors Outperform Men in Service—To Their Possible Professional Detriment*, INSIDE HIGHER ED, Apr. 12, 2017, available at https://www.insidehighered.com/news/2017/04/12/study-finds-female-professors -outperform-men-service-their-possible-professional). Extra burdens at work and at home contribute to the challenging work/life balance most women of color faculty bemoan.

18. For a detailed overview of "key theorists and their models, relevant research findings, and interventions that create changes in the cognitive, behavioral, and physical well-being of individuals" based on self-care, see V. D. Lachman, *Stress and Self-Care Revisited: A Literature Review*, 10 HOLISTIC NURSING PRACTICE 1 (1996).

19. Women taking care of the home life frees their partners to pursue greater professional success. *See, e.g.,* Lisa Wade, *The Invisible Workload That Drags Women Down,* MONEY.COM, Dec. 28, 2016, available at http://time.com/money/4561314/ women-work-home-gender-gap.

20. SUSAN WALZER, THINKING ABOUT THE BABY, GENDER AND TRANSITIONS INTO PARENTHOOD (1998); M. Blazoned, *The Default Parent,* HUFFINGTON POST, Oct. 28, 2014, available at http://www.huffingtonpost.com/m-blazoned/the-default-parent_b _6031128.html.

21. Laura's prediction is confirmed by research revealing that "working mothers have an overwhelmingly positive influence on their children." Girls of working mothers grow into women who earn more at better jobs than those whose mothers did not work outside the home; boys of working mothers contribute more to the household as adults than boys with stay-at-home mothers. Kristen Bahler, *Girls with Working Moms Get Better Jobs and Higher Pay, According to Research,* MONEY.COM, May 10, 2018, available at https://amp-timeinc-net.cdn.ampproject.org/c/amp.timeinc.net/time/money/ 5272659/working-moms-better-kids

22. Robert Post, *Leadership in Educational Institutions: Reflections of a Law School Dean,* 69 STAN. L. REV. 1817 (2017).

23. In one positive example, Madison "ended up having one student who is notoriously difficult[, which] made the day-to-day class more challenging" during her first semester teaching. However, "the full support of the faculty" made it "easier to manage," especially because "the associate dean did end up intervening and having a chat" with the problem student to get him in line. This basic level of support should be the norm, rather than an outlier.

24. *See, e.g.,* Jodi Kantor and Meghan Twohey, *Harvey Weinstein Paid Off Sexual Harrassment Accusers for Decades,* N.Y. TIMES, Oct. 5, 2017; *Misconduct,* L.A. TIMES, Dec. 18, 2017, available at http://www.latimes.com/politics/la-pol-ca-judge-alex -kozinski-20171218-story.html; and Susan Svrluga, *Berkeley Law School Dean Resigns After Sexual Harassment Complaint,* WASHINGTON POST, Mar. 10, 2016, available at https://www.washingtonpost.com/news/grade-point/wp/2016/03/10/berkeley-law -school-dean-resigns-after-sexual-harassment-complaint.

25. For instance, "55 colleges and universities nationwide [are] under scrutiny by the U.S. Department of Education for [their] handling of reported sex crimes on campus." Jack Flynn, *Amherst College, Responding to Federal Title IX Probe, Cites Major Improvements in its Handling of Sexual Assault Complaints,* MASSLIVE, May 1, 2014, available at http://www.masslive.com/news/index.ssf/2014/05/amherst_college_responding _to.html.

26. This book does not seek to expound on the requirements of Title IX or suggest that particular law schools are out of compliance, though there is a real possibility that federal authorities could intervene or investigate concerns.

27. Lest these women stand accused of working less than a full time day or somehow shirking their professional duties, most likely resume their workday for many

hours starting at 8 or 9 p.m. after their children are in bed, as discussed in Chapter 6 of this book.

28. Colleen Flaherty, *Study Finds Female Professors Outperform Men in Service—To Their Possible Professional Detriment*, INSIDE HIGHER ED, Apr. 12, 2017, available at https://www.insidehighered.com/news/2017/04/12/study-finds-female-professors -outperform-men-service-their-possible-professional (citing Cassandra M. Guarino & Victor M. H. Borden, *Faculty Service Loads and Gender: Are Women Taking Care of the Academic Family?* 58 RES. IN HIGHER ED 672 (2017)).

29. Cassandra M. Guarino & Victor M. H. Borden, *Faculty Service Loads and Gender: Are Women Taking Care of the Academic Family?* 58 RES. IN HIGHER EDUC. 672 (2017).

30. Colleen Flaherty, *Study Finds Female Professors Outperform Men in Service—To Their Possible Professional Detriment*, INSIDE HIGHER ED, Apr. 12, 2017, available at https://www.insidehighered.com/news/2017/04/12/study-finds-female-professors -outperform-men-service-their-possible-professional.

31. Stephanie K. Johnson, David R. Hekman & Elsa T. Chan, *If There's Only One Woman in Your Candidate Pool, There's Statistically No Chance She'll Be Hired*, HARV. BUS. REV., Apr. 26, 2016, available at https://hbr.org/2016/04/if-theres-only-one -woman-in-your-candidate-pool-theres-statistically-no-chance-shell-be-hired.

32. Bourree Lam, *How Office Culture Can Crush Women's Ambitions*, THE ATLAN-TIC, Apr. 19, 2017, available at https://www.theatlantic.com/business/archive/2017/ 04/ambition-office-women/523443.

33. Bourree Lam, *How Office Culture Can Crush Women's Ambitions*, THE ATLAN-TIC, Apr. 19, 2017, available at https://www.theatlantic.com/business/archive/2017/ 04/ambition-office-women/523443.

34. Although a lack of diversity in legal academia cannot be attributed to simply a pipeline problem, this solution is included for two reasons. First, this solution, like all of those presented in this part, is one that DLA participants suggested directly during data collection. Second, to the extent that the pipeline can be fully stocked with overwhelming numbers of qualified women of color candidates, it truly would become harder for even stalwart naysayers to ignore their presence or refuse to hire them. For a thorough discussion of why a lack of qualified applicants cannot explain the current lack of diversity in legal academia, see Meera E. Deo, *Looking Forward to Diversity in Legal Academia*, 29 BERKELEY J. GENDER L. & JUST. 352, 359–64 (2014).

35. As noted earlier, 40.1% of recent faculty hires graduated from Harvard or Yale, with 85.6% of new hires graduating from just twelve elite law schools. Paul Campos, *A Failure of the Elites*, LAWYERS, GUNS & MONEY, July 23, 2013, available at http:// www.lawyersgunsmoneyblog.com/2013/07/a-failure-of-the-elites#more-46121.

36. Scholars have long suggested better outreach to legal practitioners to improve faculty diversity. *See, e.g.*, Rennard Strickland, *Scholarship in the Academic Circus or the Balancing Act of the Minority Side Show*, 20 USF L. REV. 491 (1986).

37. Tables and analysis on current law faculty statistics are available in previously published DLA articles including Meera E. Deo, *The Ugly Truth about Legal Academia*, 80 BROOK. L. REV. 943, 962 (2015) (see Table 4).

38. Sylvia Lazos, *Are Student Teaching Evaluations Holding Back Women and Minorities? The Perils of "Doing" Gender and Race in the Classroom*, 164, 167, in PRESUMED INCOMPETENT: THE INTERSECTIONS OF RACE AND CLASS FOR WOMEN IN ACADEMIA (Gabriella Gutierrez y Muhs, Yolanda Flores Neimann, Carmen G. Gonzalez & Angela P. Harris eds., 2012).

39. Administrators would have to ensure that certain faculty did not use peer evaluations as an opportunity to sabotage women of color. Administrators could also circulate class recordings or invite nearby scholars onto campus for "outside review" of teaching, as is done with scholarship.

40. Faculty salary differentials are not discussed in this book, though others have taken on the controversial topic of ongoing gender inequality, resulting in at least one recent $2.66 million settlement. Colleen Flaherty, *Closing the Pay Gap*, INSIDE HIGHER ED (May 18, 2018), available at https://www.insidehighered.com/news/2018/05/18/u-denver-settles-eeoc-agreeing-pay-266-million-seven-female-law-professors-who; *see also* Karen Sloan, *Three More Female Law Profs Sue U of Denver Over Pay Gap*, LAW.COM, June 19, 2017, available at http://www.law.com/sites/almstaff/2017/06/19/three-more-female-law-profs-sue-u-of-denver-over-pay-gap; Tyler Kingdale, *Male Faculty Are Making a Lot More Than Female Faculty at Some of the Best Colleges*, HUFFINGTON POST, June 23, 2014, available at http://www.huffingtonpost.com/2014/06/23/male-female-faculty-salaries_n_5521422.html.

41. Vivian's observations are borne out in the research, which confirms that implicit bias infects "everyday behaviors such as whom we befriend, whose work we value, and whom we favor." Jerry Kang & Kristin Lane, *Seeing Through Colorblindness: Implicit Bias and the Law*, 58 UCLA L. REV. 465, 467–468 (2010).

42. Tomas Chamorro-Premuzic, *Why Do So Many Incompetent Men Become Leaders?*, HARV. BUS. REV., Aug. 22, 2013, available at https://hbr.org/2013/08/why-do-so-many-incompetent-men.

43. Fisher v. Texas, 133 S. Ct. 2411, 2421 (*"Fisher I"*) (quoting Adarand Constructors, Inc. v. Pena, 515 U.S. 200, 237 (1995)).

44. Professor Michael Olivas has circulated a list of Latinx applicants on the law teaching market to interested law schools for many years. His commitment has contributed greatly to the increase in Latinx law professors and broad diversity in legal academia. Yet institutions that seek meaningful progress should do more than simply peruse names on a list that others compile.

45. Dafina-Lazarus Stewart, *Colleges Need a Language Shift, but Not the One You Think*, INSIDE HIGHER ED, Mar. 30, 2017, available at https://www.insidehighered.com/views/2017/03/30/colleges-need-language-shift-not-one-you-think-essay.

46. Dafina-Lazarus Stewart, *Colleges Need a Language Shift, but Not the One You Think*, INSIDE HIGHER ED, Mar. 30, 2017, available at https://www.insidehighered.com/views/2017/03/30/colleges-need-language-shift-not-one-you-think-essay.

47. *Deadline for Diversity Issued by Top MetLife Lawyer*, BIG LAW BUS., Apr. 3, 2017, available at https://biglawbusiness.com/deadline-for-diversity-issued-by-top-metlife-lawyer.

48. *Deadline for Diversity Issued by Top MetLife Lawyer*, BIG LAW BUS., Apr. 3, 2017, available at https://biglawbusiness.com/deadline-for-diversity-issued-by-top-metlife -lawyer.

49. Ellen Rosen, *Facebook Pushes Outside Law Firms to Become More Diverse*, N.Y. TIMES, Apr. 2, 2017, available at https://www.nytimes.com/2017/04/02/business/dealbook/facebook-pushes-outside-law-firms-to-become-more-diverse.html?mcubz=0.

50. Note that even this white male defender and educator referred to his female colleagues as "girls," not "women."

Appendix

1. The terms *African American* and *Black* are used interchangeably throughout the book to refer to those who self-identified using those terms. Participants who identified as "API," "Asian," "Asian American," or within one of the pan-ethnic Asian-American identities are identified as *Asian American*, while those who self-identified as "Latina" or "Hispanic" are referred to as *Latina*. Those who identified only as "white" are identified as such in the book. *Multiracial* participants are those who self-identified as having two or more racial/ethnic backgrounds. A multiracial identity is complex, specifically because people with different blends of multiracial background may have vastly different experiences from one another (see, e.g., Lauren Sudeall Lucas, *Undoing Race? Reconciling Multiracial Identity with Equal Protection*, 102 CALIF. L. REV. 1243 (2014)). It is also true that pan-ethnicity in the Asian American and Latino communities encompass diverse and even contrasting experiences between different ethnic groups (YEN LE ESPIRITU, ASIAN AMERICAN PANETHNICITY: BRIDGING INSTITUTIONS AND IDENTITIES (1992)). Similarly, the African American community includes both recent immigrants and others with deep roots in America as well as Puerto Ricans and others who identify as "Afro-Latino." (MARY C. WATERS, BLACK IDENTITIES (1999)). These complex theories and themes have been explored elsewhere; the terms used here are adapted from those utilized in AALS and ABA statistics.

2. Leo A. Goodman, *Snowball Sampling*, 32(1) ANN. MATH. STATIST. 148 (1961).

3. Leo A. Goodman, *Snowball Sampling*, 32(1) ANN. MATH. STATIST. 148 (1961).

4. Katherine Browne, *Snowball Sampling: Using Social Networks to Research Non-heterosexual Women*, 8(1) INTERNATIONAL JOURNAL OF SOCIAL RESEARCH METHODOLOGY 47 (2005).

5. Katherine Browne, *Snowball Sampling: Using Social Networks to Research Non-heterosexual Women*, 8(1) INTERNATIONAL JOURNAL OF SOCIAL RESEARCH METHODOLOGY 47 (2005).

6. D. D. Heckathorn, *Respondent-Driven Sampling: A New Approach to the Study of Hidden Populations*, 44(2) SOCIAL PROBLEMS 174, 175 (1997).

7. Dr. Linda Pololi, principal investigator of the C-Change study of academic medicine, reports her methodology as "snowball sampling," although she too followed more of a target sampling approach, with periodic checks to ensure all domains were

represented throughout data collection in order to generalize final results (*See* LINDA POLOLI, CHANGING THE CULTURE OF ACADEMIC MEDICINE: PERSPECTIVES OF WOMEN FACULTY (2010); *see also* private correspondence with Dr. Pololi on file with the author).

8. J. K. Watters and P. Biernacki, *Targeted Sampling: Options and Considerations for the Study of Hidden Populations*, 36 SOCIAL PROBLEMS 416 (1989).

9. J. K. Watters and P. Biernacki, *Targeted Sampling: Options and Considerations for the Study of Hidden Populations*, 36 SOCIAL PROBLEMS 416 (1989).

10. A list of conferences at which DLA interviews took place is included in Meera E. Deo, *Looking Forward to Diversity in Legal Academia*, 29 BERKELEY J. GENDER L. & JUST. 352 n.182 (2014).

11. Methodologically, face-to-face interviewing is considered "the best form of data collection when one wants to minimize nonresponse and maximize the quality of the data collected" (Isaac Dialsingh, *Face-to-Face Interviewing* in *Encyclopedia of Survey Research Methods* (Paul J. Lavrakas ed., 2008)), although phone interviews generate a more inclusive sample overall.

12. BARNEY G. GLASER & ANSELM L. STRAUSS, DISCOVERY OF GROUNDED THEORY: STRATEGIES FOR QUALITATIVE RESEARCH 1 (1967).

13. IRB certification is on file with the author.

Index

and tenure and promotion, 5, 80–81, 83, 86, 89–94, 94–95, 211n2, 213n25; and work/life balance, 103–104, 131–134

Wildman, Stephanie, 8–9, 194n38, 194n39, 194n40

workaholics, 119, 120–124, 132, 134, 136, 137–138, 217n4

work/life balance: about, 119–120; default parents, 124–129, 218n11; defined, 120; extended family, 129–131; men of color, 134–135; workaholics, 119, 120–124, 132, 134, 136, 137–138, 217n4. *See also* workaholics, family, childcare, motherhood

CPSIA information can be obtained
at www.ICGtesting.com
Printed in the USA
LVHW031720210220
647794LV00003B/586

9 781503 607842